THE AERONAUTS

A History of Ballooning 1783–1903

The Aeronauts

A History of Ballooning
1783–1903

L. T. C. ROLT

LONGMANS

LONGMANS, GREEN AND CO LTD
48 Grosvenor Street, London W1
Associated companies, branches and representatives
throughout the world

© *L. T. C. Rolt* 1966
First published 1966

Printed in Great Britain by Ebenezer Baylis and Son Ltd.
The Trinity Press, Worcester, and London

Dedicated
With respect and affection to
Charles Dollfus,
Aeronaut

The calm Philosopher in Ether sails,
Views broader stars and breathes in purer gales;
Sees like a map in many a waving line,
Round earth's blue plains her lucid waters shine;
Sees at his feet the forky lightnings glow
And hears inocuous Thunders roar below.

Erasmus Darwin, *The Loves of the Plants*

I would . . . make it death for a man to be convicted of flying, the moment he could be caught. . . . Historians would load my memory with reproaches of phlegm, and stupidity, and oppression; but in the mean time the world would go on quietly, and if it enjoyed less liberty, would at least be more secure.

William Cowper, Letter to the Rev. W. Unwin

Beautiful invention; mounting heavenward, so beautifully – so unguidably! Emblem of much and of our Age of Hope itself.

Thomas Carlyle, *The French Revolution*

CONTENTS

LIST OF ILLUSTRATIONS

protect the balloon from the wind, the carboys of acid and the generating barrel. Lunardi's elaborate car with its wings and oars stands ready for attachment. The balloon is not drawn full size.

Foreword

WE WERE WALKING up the Champs-Elysées, and had reached the corner of the Rue Washington when my friend suddenly halted and, to the mild surprise of passers-by, struck the pavement a sharp blow with his stick. 'Here,' he announced, 'Santos-Dumont landed in his balloon.'

My companion, Charles Dollfus, had known Santos-Dumont. As a youth he had stood in the vast Gallerie des Machines in the Champ de Mars gazing in awe and wonderment at the world's first practical navigable balloon, the Lebaudy airship. That was in November 1903. It kindled in him a passion for aeronautics, and for balloons particularly, which burns as brightly today as it did then. His knowledge, not only of aeronautics, but of engineering history generally, is encyclopaedic, yet he is no pedant because he is an enthusiast. Your pedant hoards knowledge just as a miser hoards gold and for precisely the same reason – it gives him a sense of power and so inflates his ego. Your enthusiast, on the other hand, is spendthrift of knowledge for, like all the best things in life, enthusiasm is of little value unless it can be shared – communicated.

Like all true enthusiasts, the knowledge of Charles Dollfus is founded on a wealth of practical experience, for knowledge which lacks that foundation is fit only for the miser's hoard. Today, with nearly six hundred balloon ascents to his credit he wears a mantle that only a very few have worn before him. It would be no empty flattery to call him the greatest living aeronaut. Still an active pilot, he is an inspiration to the younger balloonists of today, perpetuating as he does the traditions and the skill of a golden age of ballooning. It was his infectious enthusiasm that inspired his son, the astronomer Audouin Dollfus, to pursue the suggestion of Professor Piccard that astronomical observations might be made with great advantage from the nacelle of a high altitude balloon. With equipment specially made at the Meudon Observatory, Audouin Dollfus, watched by his father, made a remarkable and revolutionary ascent from Villacoublay on 22nd April, 1959, which proved that in the clarity of the upper air a comparatively small telescope could yield better results than a giant ground-based instrument. This lead has now been followed up in the United States by the *Stratoscope II*, a 36 in. telescope in an aerial observatory suspended at a height of 80,000 ft by two giant helium-filled balloons each 210 ft high.

It was the same enthusiasm that infected me with the desire to write this book – the story of the aeronauts. Its starting point, 1783, the birthday of the balloon, was obvious, but the question was where to stop. To attempt to cover the whole story of lighter-than-air craft down to the present day with any adequacy in one reasonably sized book would be impossible. In any case, the big rigid airship initiated by Count Zeppelin is very much a subject in itself which has been fairly well covered in recent years at the expense of the long earlier history. It was Charles Dollfus himself who suggested 1903 as a logical terminal date. It was not only the year of the Lebaudy airship; it was also the year of the Wright Brothers' historic first heavier-than-air flight at Kitty Hawk.

The point that this foreword is designed to stress is that although the following chapters are concerned wholly with a past that now seems remote to most of us, they should not be read as a nostalgic valedictory for something dead and gone. If the book gave the reader such an impression it would be grossly misleading and unfair to Charles Dollfus who has done more than he knows to inspire it and who is the living refutation of such a notion. The balloon is not a by-gone; nor is it just a quaint survival. Man's first aerial vehicle has proved extraordinarily tenacious of life. If the pun may be forgiven, it has had many ups and downs in its long history, but at the present time it is ascending rapidly, so rapidly that it seemed a propitious moment to recall something of the long history of balloons and of the men who flew in them – the aeronauts.

I am deeply indebted, not only to Charles Dollfus but to my friend Charles Gibbs-Smith. Without their help this book could not have been written. Because both have made this field so much their own, I confess I approached them in the first place in some trepidation, fearing I might encounter a sign saying 'Trespassers will be Prosecuted'. I should have known better. Because both are enthusiasts they could not have given me more help or greater encouragement. I would also acknowledge the help of many friends, particularly that of Frank Smith, Librarian of the Royal Aeronautical Society, whose patience under inquisition has been inexhaustible. I am indebted also to Mr St John C. Nixon for information concerning early Daimler aero engines and to the U.S. Library of Congress for supplying copies of material from their archives.

Finally, it is a happy coincidence that this book should appear in the year in which our Royal Aeronautical Society celebrates its centenary.

L.T.C.R.

CHAPTER ONE

Per Ardua ad Astra

'O I'LL LEAP UP to my God! Who pulls me down?' The anguished cry of Doctor Faustus echoes the aspiration of two thousand years. The journey from cradle to grave is hazardous and often painful, perilously poised between heaven and hell. Beneath the feet of medieval man lay the fiery domain of the Prince of Darkness and his damned legions, but above his head was a vast firmament of sweetness and light, the heavenly source of all good. Small wonder that he yearned always to leap upward when a-weary of the world. Frustrated by the inexorable force of gravity that held him down, he must needs give his dreams of flight divine form: Gods riding the winds in aerial chariots, angels with the wings of eagles soaring to the music of the spheres.

Some, not content with this heavenly mythology, conceived wondrous gravity-defying vessels. They drew an analogy between the earth's atmosphere and the sea, believing that if their aerial ship could but rise through the envelope of air it would then float upon its upper surface. Others, more venturesome, studied the flight of birds and built themselves wings. Flapping in heroic but vain defiance against gravity, they would fling themselves from cliffs or from tall buildings only to fall like Lucifer and break their bones. When one of the latest of these optimistic bird-men, the Marquis de Bacqueville, leapt from the roof of his Paris house in 1742 he displayed more discretion than most by directing his flight across the Seine. Unfortunately he fell upon the deck of a washer-woman's barge that was moored in the river, a humiliating landing from which he was lucky to escape with no more than a broken leg.

It is not, however, the purpose of this book to record either the impractical schemes of the floaters or the painful but monotonous experiences of the tower-jumpers. One modern historian of flight believes that the aspirations of these two groups have a sexual

21

significance, the desire to float passively, upon the currents of the air representing the female principle while the urge to cleave through them upon aggressive wings typifies the male. Whether this entertaining theory be true or no, the fact is that the floaters were the first to win the skies and it is with their victory that we are here concerned. It could not be claimed as a victory for feminism. To be borne aloft for the first time by a frail envelope of paper or silk a man needed as much courage as a tower-jumper. No, the reasons why the balloon preceded winged heavier-than-air flying machines by so many years were technological, not psychological.

Nevertheless, there *is* something essentially feminine about a balloon. No other work of man so richly deserves to be called by the feminine gender and yet, strangely enough, it is less frequently applied to balloons than to such forceful machines as the steam locomotive or the motor-car. Just as the world will dote upon a lovely woman, captivated by her beauty and charm as by a work of art and scorning to ask whether she can bake a cake or stitch a seam, so also the world doted upon the first balloons. No other invention has ever excited so much popular wonderment, nor were any other pioneers so extravagantly acclaimed as the first aeronauts. On the earth beneath, that tireless black Vulcan the steam engine was already changing man's world, enabling him to plumb unheard of depths in quest of coal or prisoning him in dark satanic mills. Yet for every eye that looked in wonder at this labouring giant a hundred were turned aloft to gaze in rapturous astonishment at the balloon. Suspended in still summer air or drifting helplessly at the whim of every wind, it served no useful purpose whatever, yet it represented the conquest of a new element, the fulfilment of a dream as old as man. And how beautiful it was! A great globe of parti-coloured silks, it rose from the earth as soundlessly and as lightly as thistledown, bearing aloft on slender rigging the intrepid flag-waving aeronaut in his triumphal car to soar among the clouds.

The effect of this admiration was that within weeks of its conquest of the air the balloon became a pin-up whose popularity the most voluptuously upholstered film star has never rivalled. Not only did it become the subject of innumerable prints, good, bad and indifferent; its elegant curvilinear form featured in the designs of wall-papers and fabrics and influenced fashion designers. In jewels and enamel the balloon appeared on snuff and patch boxes, it was painted on china and porcelain, inlaid or carved on furniture; there were balloon chandeliers and balloon clocks. Its shape was seized upon no less enthusiastically by the cartoonists and those of the coarser sort were soon exploiting, more or less pornographically, a fancied resemblance between its burgeoning envelope and the rotundities of breasts or buttocks. Even today when the vast majority have never seen a free balloon, its popularity as a decorative motif persists.

It is not only an elegant shape and a gaudy silken dress that makes the balloon the most feminine of man's creations. It is feminine also in its wayward temperament and in the ephemeral quality of its beauty. It is only upon the aerial stage that this beauty is revealed as the balloon sails with a serenity that no storm can disturb. Once off that stage it becomes an unruly termagant in all but the lightest airs. Before an ascent a balloon can be as restive and as impatient as any prima donna awaiting her first call. As for the end of the performance – the return to earth – this is more than anticlimactic, it can be positively frightening. In an instant the calm beauty becomes a hideous virago, a wildly threshing monster with the strength of ten threatening death and destruction to herself and to those who seek to restrain her. For this ungovernable and self-destroying madness a speedy quietus is the only cure. The silken clothing is ripped up and, after a few weakening death throes, beauty is reduced to an unsightly and inert heap of crumpled cloth and tangled cordage.

There could be no more eloquent symbol of transience than this. Similarly, the story of the men who sailed in these frail and fickle craft – the Aeronauts as they so proudly styled themselves – epitomizes the human condition. For it is a tale of heroism and high endeavour, of bravura and folly, of tragedy, comedy and, occasionally, sheer knockabout farce. Shakespeare himself could not have interwoven so boldly the threads of the sublime and the ridiculous, for life is always larger than drama. One moment the aeronaut and his companions are lords of all they survey, poised God-like far above the world and its follies. In the next they may be reduced to a helpless tangle of arms, legs, ropes and flapping fabric, a spectacle as ludicrous to the beholder as Falstaff in the laundry basket.

Yet the pride was always well worth the fall. For the floaters there were rewards that no masterful heir to the tower-jumpers could ever earn. It is significant that whereas only the outstanding pioneer flights of powered aircraft have been recorded, for more than a century aeronauts and their passengers habitually set down in detail their flights in balloons. Inevitably these accounts make somewhat repetitive and therefore monotonous reading, the more so because literary ability and the desire to ride in a free balloon seldom seem to go together. Nevertheless the unique quality of the experience that inspired them does shine through. A sense of complete detachment was the outstanding feature of that experience. Suspended in air in silence and stillness, with no sense of motion, a fixed point beneath which the world seemed to spin, the balloon gave its crew the impression that they were not only stationary in space but in time also. In that unearthly stillness familiar sounds from far below, the bark of a dog, a voice calling, even a torrent of wind rushing through trees, though uncannily clear, had a poignantly remote quality.

When darkness fell, the sense of withdrawal from the world became the more profound. After his great flight of over a thousand miles from Paris to Korosticheff in Russia, Comte Henri de la Vaulx said: 'At night, when sailing far above a sparsely inhabited region you seem to be a part, not only of the wind, but of the darkness; you are without sensation, life, motion, noise, anything . . . a silent mite floating through a world of dark that is without shape, substance, contrast, form, sound . . . "And the earth was void." ' Few aeronauts could express themselves so eloquently as this and it is greatly to our loss that no great poet or philosopher ever mounted with them to share, and subsequently to communicate, an experience so salutary and inspiring. Every aeronaut was affected and in some degree *changed* by it as men are changed by the sea or the desert. For no pilot of a powered aircraft can ever hope to know the awesome loneliness of the upper air as they did who surrendered themselves utterly to its currents. In 1936, after he had interviewed Ernest Demuyter, greatest of latter-day Belgian aeronauts, a journalist wrote: 'He returns from his ascensions full of ecstasy. I believe all aeronauts are a little like him. All those who have tried ballooning return from it as from an artificial paradise . . .' True enough except that 'artificial' is scarcely the right word for intimations conveyed so directly through the agency of a vehicle so simple.

Both the utilitarian steam engine and the balloon stemmed from scientific inquiries into the nature and composition of the earth's atmosphere. The discoveries of Torricelli and Pascal that the atmosphere had a measurable weight that logically decreased with altitude, combined with the creation of a vacuum by Otto von Guericke to signpost a path that led to the 'atmospheric' engine of Thomas Newcomen. Newcomen created a vacuum in the lower part of his engine cylinder and so enabled the weight of the atmosphere to press the piston down. An Italian Jesuit priest named Francesco de Lana-Terzi reasoned in an opposite fashion that a vessel from which all air had been excluded should be capable of rising through the atmosphere as an air bubble rises through water. On the strength of this, de Lana postulated an aerial ship buoyed up by four exhausted copper globes. Unlike all earlier schemes for aerial ships, this one was based on sound theory, but in practice such a construction was impossible. Copper globes light enough to bear themselves aloft in this way, let alone lift any useful weight, would be instantly crushed by atmospheric pressure. The Jesuit did not seem disconcerted by this realization. He explained that his was only a theoretical exercise, arguing that since God had not intended man to fly, any serious practical attempt to flout His designs must be impious and fraught with peril for the human race. One suspects that the Jesuit Fathers may have had a serious talk with their scientifically minded son and that he made this disclaimer because he could smell faggots burning.

Before man could rise into the air, something lighter than de Lana's exhausted globes was required. It was the discovery by the English scientist Henry Cavendish in 1766 of what he called 'Phlogiston' or 'inflammable air' that supplied the answer, though it was some years before it was recognized as such, and it was not until 1790 that Lavoisier named this very light and dangerous gas hydrogen. In 1774, Dr Priestley of Birmingham discovered 'dephlogisticated air', or oxygen as Lavoisier later called it, and subsequently printed the results of his researches in his *Experiments and Observations on Different Kinds of Air*. In 1783 Henry Cavendish and James Watt simultaneously discovered the composition of water and showed how it might be decomposed to produce hydrogen. The Scientists of England had supplied the knowledge to enable men to invade the air. Yet it was not in England and it was not by the aid of hydrogen that the first balloons soared into the skies in 1783.

CHAPTER TWO

Hot Air or Hydrogen?

'MAN IS BORN to trouble as sparks fly upward.' In making this gloomy pronouncement the prophet Job made effective use of an occurrence of common observation. His analogy underlines the fact that this simple phenomenon was accepted without question. For centuries men watched the sparks of their camp fires soar into the air like fireflies without asking themselves why they should thus defy the law of gravity. The question had to be asked and an answer sought before this natural object lesson could be applied to the problem of flight. This may seem to us an absurdly simple mental exercise, but it was alien to the climate of thought in the Age of Faith. It required the speculative temper of the Age of Reason, typified in this case by the brothers Montgolfier, to ask the question, to venture an answer and to put that theory to the proof in a series of experiments that astonished the world.

The name Montgolfier means literally and not inappropriately Master of the Mountain and their ancient home stood upon a hill overlooking the town of Ambert in the Auvergne. They were an enterprising family. One of that name took part in the sixth and last crusade and discovered, while he was held captive in Damascus, the secret of paper making, at that time an eastern monopoly known as 'Carta Damascena'. On his return to Ambert in 1386, this Montgolfier established a paper mill there. Moreover, he very soon proved that paper could be made just as successfully and much more cheaply from rags as from the new cotton used exclusively in the east. This made the family's fortune and their association with paper making continued down to the time with which we are here concerned. Their adoption of the reformed religion brought about their only serious set-back. After the massacre of St Bartholomew in 1572, the Montgolfiers had to fly for their lives; their goods and estates were confiscated and their paper mills at Ambert destroyed. Nothing daunted, however, they began making paper once again in their mountain refuge near Lyons in the neighbourhood of St Didier.

In 1693, the brothers Michel and Raymond Montgolfier married the two daughters of Antoine Schelle of Vidalon, the wealthy owner of a number of mills in the neighbourhood of Annonay. As a result of this fortunate match, Schelle's mills were converted to paper manufacture and the fortunes of the family were not merely re-established but prospered as never before. Thanks to the patronage of the Kings of France, the family business boasted the title of Royal Manufactory by the time Pierre Montgolfier was in control, and his two sons, Joseph (1740–1810) and Etienne (1745–1799), began to speculate upon the problems of flight in 1782.

In the series of experiments that culminated so dramatically, Joseph Montgolfier is commonly said to have played the leading part. Certainly he began the experiments, but he soon infected his younger brother with his enthusiasm and Etienne thereafter associated himself so closely and actively with Joseph's efforts that credit for the results is justly awarded to both of them.

What was it that first turned Joseph's thoughts in this direction? As in the case of other famous discoveries, a considerable mythology has grown up around this question. Some say that Madame Montgolfier's chemise took off when placed before the fire to air, others that it was Joseph's own shirt which was levitated in this way. Another legend has it that Madame took the conical paper wrapping from a sugar-loaf and threw it in the fire, whereupon Joseph observed that it filled with hot air and flew up the chimney without igniting. The chemise, the shirt and the sugar-loaf wrapper were the equivalent of Newton's apple and Watt's kettle. What the originators of such myths habitually overlook is the inter-acting stimulus of other minds, in this case Cavendish and Priestley. We have it on Joseph Montgolfier's own authority that it was the appearance of Priestley's book *Experiments and Observations on Different Kinds of Air* in a French translation in 1776 which first gave him the urge to experiment.

The implications of the discovery by Cavendish of a gas which was but one-thirteenth of the weight of common air were not lost upon his fellow scientists in Britain. That good friend to James Watt, the celebrated Doctor Joseph Black, was said to have filled the bladder of a calf with this 'inflammable air' and allowed it to float up to the ceiling for the edification of his pupils and friends at Glasgow. But the Doctor himself stated that, although he contemplated making such an experiment he never, in fact, attempted it. Moreover, the subsequent experience of Cavallo, the first historian of flight, indicates that Black would not have succeeded.

Tiberius Cavallo was born in Naples in 1749, but spent most of his life in England where he became a Fellow of the Royal Society. In his *History and Practice of Aerostation*, published in 1785, he describes how he tried Black's experiment in 1782 but failed because he could not obtain a natural bladder which was light enough in proportion to its volume. Cavallo had to be content with an apparatus producing hydrogen-filled soap bubbles.

Joseph Montgolfier was inspired by Priestley's writings to make experiments of a similar kind. It seems likely that he learnt to produce hydrogen and used it to fill a small paper globe. But, like Cavallo, who made precisely the same experiment, he found that the gas passed through the paper as readily as water through a sieve. Silk proved equally pervious so Joseph abandoned this line of attack and turned his attention to what would soon become known as 'rarified air' as a lifting agent.

The explanation of the spark flying upward – or the levitation of Madame Montgolfier's chemise if it ever took place – is that air expands when it is heated with the effect that its weight per cubic foot is reduced as its volume increases. Odd though it may seem to us, Joseph Montgolfier did not grasp this. Instead he assumed that the process of combustion produced a special kind of gas which sometimes assumed the visible form of smoke. From this false premise he argued that different substances produced different qualities of gas in the burning, some lighter than others. By some mysterious route he reached the conclusion that the gas or smoke produced by burning a mixture of damp straw and chopped wool was the lightest and best for his purpose. Later, so far from perceiving this fallacy, Montgolfier's notions became even more eccentric. In a letter describing the famous experiment at Versailles on 19th September, 1783, Bachaumont wrote in his *Memoires Secrets*: 'They [the Montgolfier brothers] had caused all the old shoes that could be collected to be brought here, and threw them into the damp straw that was burning, together with pieces of decomposed meat; for these are the substances which supply their gas. The King and the Queen came up to examine the machine, but the noxious smell thus produced obliged them to retire at once.'[1]

In 1782, Britain's stubborn defence of Gibraltar against the combined strength of France and Spain was very galling to all patriotic Frenchmen, Joseph Montgolfier included. 'I possess,' he is reported to have said, 'a super-human means of introducing our soldiers into this impregnable fortress. They may enter through the air; the gas produced by the combustion of a little straw or a few rags should not pass, like the subtle inflammable air, through the pores of a paper bag. By making the bag large enough, it will be possible to introduce into Gibraltar an entire army, which, borne by the wind, will enter right above the heads of the English.'

Joseph was staying at Avignon at the time he made this pronouncement and it was there, in November 1782, that he made his first small-scale experiment with a hot-air balloon. He constructed an envelope of fine silk in the shape of a parallelepiped with an open aperture or 'neck' at the base. When he held burning paper beneath this aperture the envelope inflated and rose to the ceiling of his apartment in the most satisfying manner. According to Cavallo the inflated capacity of this first Montgolfier balloon was about 40 cubic feet, but others say it was much smaller than this.

Encouraged by this success, soon after his return to Annonay, Joseph repeated the experiment in the open air and in the presence of his brother. Etienne was obviously captivated by the sight of the little balloon as it rose in the air to a height of about 70 ft, and from this time forward he became an active and enthusiastic partner in Joseph's experiments.

The brothers then constructed successively two larger experimental balloons. The first of these had a capacity of about 650 cubic feet and rose successfully to a height of 600 ft. No details of this second balloon have been recorded, but it was probably made of paper and it is likely that it was of the more logical spherical or pear shape. The third and still larger balloon was certainly spherical for Cavallo tells us that it was 35 ft in diameter. It may have been made of that combination of cloth and paper which the brothers decided was the most satisfactory. It is said to have had a lifting power of

[1] Quoted by M. C. Flammarion, *Travels in the Air*, p. 159.

450 lb. An attempt to fly this balloon on 3rd April, 1783, was frustrated by a strong wind, but on the 25th of that month it made a perfect ascent to a height of 1,000 ft. Floating away on the wind, it fell gently to earth three-quarters of a mile away from the launching point.

The Montgolfiers thereupon resolved to build a much larger balloon for public demonstration at Annonay. Etienne has left us the following description of this: 'The aerostatic machine was constructed of cloth lined with paper, fastened together on a network of strings fixed to the cloth. It was spherical; its circumference was 110 ft, and a wooden frame sixteen feet square held it fixed at the bottom. Its contents were about 22,000 cubic feet, and it accordingly displaced a volume of air weighing 1,980 lb. The weight of gas was nearly half the weight of the air, for it weighed 990 lb, and the machine itself, with the frame, weighed 500; it was therefore impelled upward with the force of 490 lb. Two men sufficed to raise it and fill it with gas, but it took eight to hold it down till the signal was given. The different pieces of the covering were fastened together with buttons and button-holes.'

On Thursday, 5th June, 1783, officials, nobles and peasantry of the Vivarais district flocked to the square at Annonay to witness – with considerable scepticism – the experiment of the brothers Montgolfier. The inflation of this large balloon must have been a decidedly tricky operation for the classic method of doing so had not then been adopted. The two men detailed to handle the envelope and prevent it catching fire must have been mightily relieved when, to the surprise of all beholders, it rose out of harm's way and assumed its graceful, globular shape. This surprise was as nothing to the sensation caused when Joseph Montgolfier gave the 'hands off' signal to the eight men who now clung to the frame of the balloon. With incredulous wonderment the crowd watched it sail soundlessly upward to a height of about 6,000 ft. Carried by a light northerly wind, it landed lightly about a mile and a half away after a flight of ten minutes. So ended the first large scale balloon flight that the world had ever seen. It was of short duration because, as Etienne explained afterwards: 'the loss of gas by the button-holes and other imperfections did not permit it to continue longer.'

Prints of this historic balloon and of its famous flight do not tally with Etienne's description and are probably inaccurate. That produced from a drawing of the ascent by de Lorimier does, however, show the unsatisfactory arrangement of button-holes securing the sections of the envelope, although it depicts only a small neck instead of a large wooden frame.

The news of these goings-on at Annonay speedily spread to Paris where it caused a great sensation and much speculation among the learned members of the Academy of Sciences who were, indeed, somewhat piqued by it. The effect was similar to that earlier produced among the savants of London by the news that a provincial blacksmith had built a successful steam engine. Who were these brothers Montgolfier and what was this mysterious 'gas' they had discovered? So far as the Parisian scientists were concerned there was only one gas which could produce such a result and that was 'inflammable air' – hydrogen.

Later in the year, when George III wrote to Sir Joseph Banks, President of the Royal Society, offering to finance what he called 'air-globe' experiments, the Society replied that: 'no good whatever could result from them, as the properties by which such a globe acts are as well known as if twenty experiments were made.' The members of the Paris Academy, however, were not content to rest aloof upon an Olympian cloud of theory while a provincial paper manufacturer stole their thunder. The honour and reputation of the Academy were at stake; a practical experiment must be made and to this end they set to work with remarkable speed and efficiency.

The most promising of the younger physicists in the Academy at this time was Jacques Alexandre César Charles (b. Beaugency 1746, d. Paris 1823). Charles offered to produce a balloon in association with the brothers Aîné and Cadet Robert, two ingenious practical craftsmen who claimed to be able to make fine silk cloth impermeable by hydrogen by coating it with a solution of rubber. This would prove the answer to the problem which had defeated Joseph Montgolfier. The offer was eagerly accepted and in order to defray the cost of the balloon, Faujas de Saint-Fond, an influential friend of Charles and préparateur of the King's cabinet, opened a public subscription at the popular Café Caveau which was situated near the workshop of the brothers Robert in the Place des Victoires. A contribution of one crown entitled the donor and two friends to view the ascent of the balloon from a special enclosure and popular interest was such that the whole expense of the venture was soon covered.

By subsequent standards the balloon was a very small one, a perfect sphere 12 ft in diameter weighing 25 lb and having a capacity of 943 cubic feet. Even so, the job of generating enough hydrogen to fill it proved very difficult and tedious, the experimenters having to learn in the hardest possible way, by trial and many errors, how the job could be done.

The gas was generated by the action of sulphuric acid on iron filings and altogether 498 lb of acid and 1,000 lb of iron were consumed. Inflation was begun at 8 a.m. on the morning of 23rd August, 1783 in an enclosed yard adjacent to the workshop in the Place des Victoires. By means of a ring at its North Pole the balloon was suspended over the generating apparatus, a rope, stretched between two masts being threaded through the ring and carried down the masts to cleats. When the balloon was inflated and was secured from premature release from below, the suspension rope could be readily withdrawn from the top ring. This would become for many years the standard method of inflating both hydrogen and hot-air balloons.

The first generator resembled a chest of drawers, the iron and acid being fed into a series of lead-lined compartments each linked by a pipe to a main coupled to the neck of the balloon. The leakage of gas from this apparatus was so great, however, that it was very soon discarded and a large up-ended barrel was substituted. A filling orifice with closure was made in the end of this barrel and also an outlet pipe for the gas which was connected to the balloon by means of a rubberized leather pipe. This extemporized arrangement was completed by 2 p.m. on this first day of effort and for a while the results seemed much more promising. Then fresh difficulties arose. Charles had under-estimated the amount of heat which would be generated by the action of the acid on the iron; this heated the gas passing into the balloon to such a degree that, in order to preserve its fabric, water had to be poured over it repeatedly. This revealed another snag which was that a considerable quantity of water vapour was being carried into the balloon with the gas. When the balloon was cooled this vapour condensed and water began to accumulate above the neck. Charles and his companions struggled manfully against these

The man who began it all:
Joseph Montgolfière

First public balloon ascent from
Annonay, June, 1783

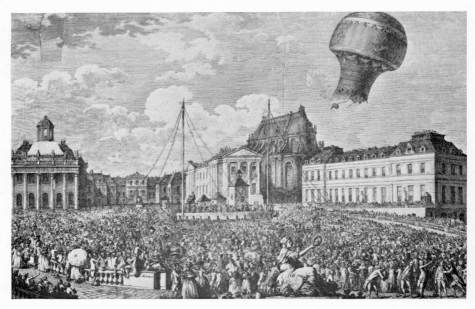

The sheep, the cock and the duck become airborne, Versailles, September, 1783

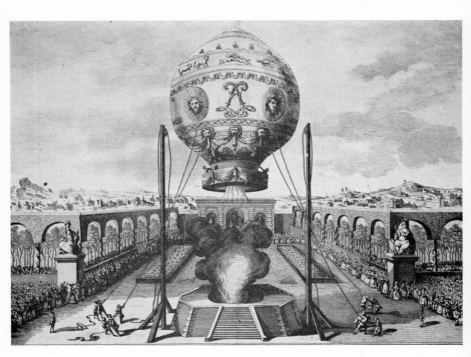

Tentative assay: Pilâtre de Rozier ascends captive at the Reveillon Gardens, October, 1783

difficulties, but at 9 p.m. that night, when they decided to call it a day, the balloon was still only one-third filled.

When they returned to the fray next morning they were surprised to find the balloon standing perfectly full. This was too good to be true and sure enough when Charles tested the balloon for lift he realized that the remaining two-thirds of the balloon had become filled with common air. Cavallo attempts to explain this away on the principle of nature abhorring a vacuum, but she has got to find a way in, and one suspects that after a long and exhausting day someone had omitted to shut the stop-cock that was fitted to the neck of the balloon so that it could be cut off from the generator while the latter was being re-charged.

Undeterred by this latest disappointment, Charles and the brothers Robert set to work with a will and to such purpose that by 7 p.m. that evening the balloon appeared full of gas and the tension of the restraining ropes made it obvious that it now had considerable lift. Next morning (25th August) a very early start was made. The balloon, which had stood well overnight, was topped up with gas and at 6 a.m. the ropes were slacked off, allowing the balloon to ascend captive so that Charles could test its lifting power with weights. He found that it would lift 21 lb, whereas theoretically the lift should have been 35 lb, and when he made another test at 9 p.m. that evening, the lift had fallen to 18 lb. There was evidently a considerable leakage of gas through the fabric and this would be due, not so much to inherent defects as to the treatment it had received in the filling. Apart from the heating, it was not then realized – though it soon would be – that damaging acid would be carried into the balloon with the gas.

Sated as we are with demonstrations of scientific expertise, it is scarcely possible for us to conceive the popular furore which this modest experiment created in eighteenth-century Paris. An amateur scientist could scarcely cause such a stir today if he announced his intention to launch himself forth in a space rocket from a suburban back yard. Bulletins of progress were frequently issued and avidly read. So long as the balloon had remained tethered to its masts in the seclusion of the walled yard, the three experimenters had been left in comparative peace, but when, on the 26th, they allowed it to rise to a height of 100 ft on the rope the effect of its appearance was magnetic.

3

Such huge crowds invaded the Place des Victoires that the situation became out of control and it was only with the greatest difficulty that the people could be kept from the yard. Had they forced an entry the destruction of the fragile balloon would have been certain.

This alarming experience forced a hurried change of plan. The date fixed for the public ascent of the balloon – 27th August – would stand, but the scene of the great experiment must be moved from the constricted Place des Victoires to the more spacious Champ de Mars where the Eiffel Tower now stands. Moreover, to avoid the unwelcome attentions of the people it was essential that the balloon be moved thither secretly at dead of night. So, in the silence of the small hours, the balloon, tied to a cart and stirring restlessly like a live thing, was borne for two miles under armed escort through the empty streets, through the Petits Champs and le Carrousel, over the Pont Royal, along the Rue de Bourbon and the Esplanade des Invalides until it reached the safety of a hastily erected enclosure in the centre of the Champ de Mars. This is how Faujas de Saint-Fond described this extraordinary procession:

'No more wonderful scene could be imagined than the Balloon being thus conveyed, preceded by lighted torches, surrounded by a "cortege" and escorted by a detachment of foot and horse guards; the nocturnal march, the form and capacity of the body, carried with so much precaution; the silence that reigned, the unseasonable hour, all tended to give a singularity and mystery truly imposing to all those who were acquainted with the cause. The cab-drivers on the road were so astonished that they were impelled to stop their carriages, and to kneel humbly, hat in hand, whilst the procession was passing.'

That the cart with its negative 'load' ever reached its destination intact must have been nothing short of miraculous, for anything more fraught with peril than the combination of flaring torches and a leaking hydrogen balloon would be difficult to conceive. Had the almost inevitable conflagration occurred the story of the birth of the balloon might have been very different, for it is unlikely that authority would have favoured further experiments of any kind.

It was as well that Charles took the precaution of bringing the hydrogen generator along to the Champ de Mars, for the balloon evidently needed a lot of topping up after its journey. Either because of leakage or more trouble with the generator it was not until 5 p.m. on the following day that the balloon was judged ready to ascend. Meanwhile the Champ de Mars was cordoned by troops who would allow only the few privileged ticket holders to pass to the enclosure that screened the *Globe*, as it was called. All day the crowds grew in avenues and streets, on roof tops and river quays, until every vantage point was packed with impatient spectators. On the towers of Notre-Dame, on the roof of l'Ecole Militaire and the marble terraces of Couronne, astronomers and other members of the Academy waited tensely with telescopes poised at the ready. At last a single cannon shot woke the echoes and immediately the balloon rose into the air from the rim of the enclosure as lightly as a bubble rises from a child's pipe. At the same moment a shower of rain fell, but no one, not even the ladies of fashion, appeared to notice it; every eye was riveted on the wonderful balloon. Soaring to a height of 3,000 ft, it disappeared in two minutes into the rain cloud. Then it sailed out again into a clear sky, its reappearance greeted by another cannon shot and an excited roar from the crowd. Raptly they watched this wonderful, gravity-defying *Globe* until it was lost to sight over the Paris skyline.

Three-quarters of an hour later the balloon fell to earth in a field near the village of Gonesse, fifteen miles from Paris. This was a very short flight, but the stop-cock on the neck of the balloon had been left in place and closed. Hence when the gas expanded under reduced atmospheric pressure the envelope must have burst. It has been said that Charles deduced this from an examination of the fallen balloon, but since we are also told that the terrified villagers of Gonesse tore the balloon to shreds, it is difficult to see how he could have done so. Nevertheless, Charles evidently realized what had happened for he did not make the same mistake again.

It is easy for us to mock those frightened French peasants of Gonesse who thought that some fearful monster had descended upon them and attacked it with muskets and pitchforks. A balloon just deflated does strangely resemble some prostrate beast in travail as pockets of hydrogen, stirring and struggling to escape, belly out the crumpled fabric. Translated to their situation in time and place we too might think that what we saw was some monstrous Thing from Outer Space.

In order to allay such fears and so safeguard future balloons, the French Government issued the following proclamation:

Avertissement au peuple on the ascent of balloons or globes in the air. The one in question has been raised in Paris this said day, 27th August, 1783, at 5 p.m., in the Champ de Mars.

A discovery has been made, which the Government deems it right to make known, so that alarm be not occasioned to the people.

On calculating the different weights of inflammable and common air, it has been found that a balloon filled with inflammable air will rise towards heaven till it is in equilibrium with the surrounding air; which may not happen till it has attained a great height.

The first experiment was made at Annonay, in Vivarais, by MM Montgolfier, the inventors; a globe formed of canvas and paper, 105 feet in circumference, filled with inflammable air, reached an uncalculated height.

The same experiment has just been renewed at Paris (27th August, 5 p.m.) in presence of a great crowd. A globe of taffetas, covered by elastic gum, 36 ft in circumference, has risen from the Champ de Mars, and been lost to view in the clouds, being borne in a north-easterly direction; one cannot foresee where it will descend.

It is proposed to repeat these experiments on a larger scale. Any one who shall see in the sky such a globe (which resembles 'la lune obscurcie'), should be aware that, far from being an alarming phenomenon, it is only a machine, made of taffetas, or light canvas covered with paper, that cannot possibly cause any harm, and which will some day prove serviceable to the wants of society.

Read and approved, 3rd September, 1783.   DE SAUVIGNY
Permission for printing   LENOIR

The most interesting point about this proclamation is its disclosure that at this date government officials in Paris still believed that Joseph Montgolfier's 'gas' was really hydrogen. This is the more surprising when we learn that his brother Etienne was actually in Paris at the time the proclamation was written. He had come to the capital with the object of demonstrating their invention before the King and the Academy of Science and he had arrived in time to witness the ascent of the *Globe*. Indeed, de Fonvielle, in his *Adventures in the Air*, declares that Montgolfier sought admission to the balloon enclosure on the Champ de Mars but was brusquely refused.

Here and elsewhere in his book de Fonvielle pictures Charles and the Montgolfier brothers as bitterly hostile to one another, but one suspects that this author was more concerned with dramatic effect than strict truth. There is no other evidence to suggest that there was anything more than friendly rivalry between the champions of the two systems.

The Montgolfiers established themselves with their friend and fellow tradesman Reveillon, owner of the royal manufactory of stained paper in the Rue de Montreuil, Faubourg St Antoine. There they proceeded to construct a balloon of strangely eccentric shape using as material two layers of paper with an intermediate layer of linen packing cloth as reinforcement. 'Its middle part was prismatic' Cavallo tells us, 'of about 25 ft height; its top was a pyramid, of 29 ft; and its lowest part consisted of a truncated cone, of near 20 ft, in height; so that the whole machine, from the upper to the lower extremity, measured about 74 ft, and its diameter was near 43.' It weighed, 1,000 lbs and was estimated to displace 4,500 lbs of air. Assuming the balloon could have been completely filled with hot air at half this weight, its useful lift would have been 1,250 lb. The balloon was most elaborately painted in blue decorated with gold, being presumably intended to represent a kind of aerial Royal pavilion.

This was by far the largest balloon so far attempted and because of its size the sections had to be stitched together in the open air in M. Reveillon's garden, a difficult and delicate task at the best of times and made more so in this case by bad weather. Twenty men were employed in manipulating the sections of the envelope with extreme care, for the heavy paper tended to crack if it became folded acutely. The ascent, in the presence of Louis XVI, Marie Antoinette and their Court, had been fixed for 19th September, but the Montgolfiers proposed to make a trial ascent from the garden in the presence of members of the Academy before transporting their balloon to Versailles for the great occasion. With infinite difficulty the balloon was completed and, encouraged by an improvement in the weather, the trial inflation was arranged for the 14th September. For this purpose the classic method of inflating and launching a large Montgolfier was used for the first time.

A raised stage was erected, this having a large circular orifice at its

centre over which the neck of the balloon could be placed. The
furnace was situated beneath the stage and directly under this orifice.
On either side of the stage were the masts with their pulleys and
suspension rope as used by Charles. By this means the balloon could
be raised as it filled and then released at will by withdrawing the
rope from the ring in the balloon's north pole.

What most impressed the witnesses of this experiment was the
speed of inflation compared with Charles's infinitely laborious and
tedious process of generating hydrogen. Under the wondering gaze
of the scientists from the Academy, the Montgolfiers fed their furnace with fifty pounds of straw and several pounds of wool. The
result was magical. Within ten minutes the shapeless mass of fabric
upon the stage had swollen and risen to tower high above their
heads in all its extravagant splendour of blue and gold. It was allowed
to rise captive for a short distance when it was found that it required
a force of 500 lb to restrain it. But alas, this glory was to be short-
lived. By a most cruel stroke of fortune, at this moment a violent
storm of wind and rain broke over the Faubourg St Antoine. In an
instant the frail balloon became a wild and self-destructive monster,
fighting against the ropes that held it. The Montgolfiers were faced
with the agonizing choice between setting it free or attempting to
haul it down in the teeth of the wind. They decided to retrieve it,
but as their men struggled with the ropes in the blinding rain the
sodden paper began to peel from the linen and great rents appeared.
It was an irreparable ruin, torn, crumpled and saturated, that finally
fell back upon the launching platform – and in less than a week the
Montgolfiers were due at Versailles by Royal command.

Undaunted and doggedly determined, the Montgolfier brothers,
helped by Reveillon and his men, set to work to build another balloon and by unsparing effort, day and night, they succeeded. This time
a much stronger cotton cloth was used with a paper backing on the
inside only. The fancy shape was abandoned in favour of an almost
spherical form, the balloon being 57 ft high and 41 ft in diameter.
Like its ill-fated predecessor, it was beautifully decorated in blue and
gold and bore the Royal insignia. It was somewhat smaller than the
former, its capacity being 37,500 cubic feet, representing a displace-
ment of 3,192 lb of air. It was completed in four days, successfully
flown captive in the Reveillon Gardens on 18th September and

conveyed to Versailles on the morning of the following day. Honour was saved.

A staging sixty feet square had been erected for the reception and launch of the balloon in the First or Ministers' Court in the Palace of Versailles. This was not only cordoned by troops but screened from prying eyes by decorated cloth hung from scaffolding. Here the Montgolfiers and their supporters were entertained to a well deserved banquet before the serious business of the day began at 1 p.m.

It had been widely rumoured that a man would ascend in the balloon, but in fact such a notion had been firmly vetoed by the King as far too perilous. As a compromise, a wicker cage containing a sheep, a cock and a duck would be attached to the balloon. A barometer was also to be taken aloft in a special case hung from the cage, while two eminent astronomers, Jeaurat and Le Gentil, had been summoned to the Palace Observatory to estimate the height attained by the balloon. The former took up his station on the terrace and the latter on the roof.

When the banquet was over and preparations for inflating the balloon had begun, King Louis and Marie Antoinette appeared to inspect the arrangements at close quarters but, as we have seen, the nauseating ingredients that the Montgolfiers had gathered to generate their 'gas' soon drove them to a more remote vantage point. By this time the crowd was immense and every road leading to Versailles was blocked with carriages. Happily for the Montgolfiers everything went smoothly and exactly an hour after they had begun their preparations the great blue and gold globe was straining at its ropes. The Balloon with its freight of livestock weighed 900 lb so that, in theory, it had a lift of 696 lb. On this occasion there was a dramatic 'count down' of three cannon shots and as the third explosion echoed round the Palace walls the balloon sailed into the air followed by a great shout of wonder and applause.

In the estimation of the astronomers the balloon reached a height of about 1,700 ft before it began gradually to descend as it drifted away on a light air. Only eight minutes later, two gamekeepers saw the balloon gently descend into the forest of Vaucresson scarcely two miles distant. Joseph Montgolfier had estimated that his balloon should rise to 12,000 ft and stay aloft for 20 minutes and he attributed its failure to fulfil his expectations to two tears in the fabric. Nevertheless, everybody, from the King downwards, appeared to be highly satisfied.

The course of the balloon was followed on foot by some of the more enthusiastic spectators. Well in the forefront were Faujas de Saint-Fond, the friend and patron of Charles, and the Chevalier de Lorimier, an artist whose paintings of early balloon ascents were reproduced as engravings and widely sold. But the first to reach the fallen balloon was a young scientist named Pilâtre de Rozier, soon to become famous. He found that the wicker cage had been broken open by a branch as the balloon sank slowly through the trees, and by the time he appeared on the scene the sheep was placidly grazing. The duck seemed to be in excellent heart also, but it was evident that the cock had slightly damaged one of its wings. This mishap seems to have caused a quite disproportionate amount of concern, being attributed to the perils of aerial travel until ten witnesses solemnly testified that they had seen the sheep kick the cock before the balloon took off. With confidence thus restored, the stage was set for the first aeronauts.

CHAPTER THREE

The First Aeronauts

IN 1783 THE UPPER AIR was believed to hold unknown perils for those foolhardy enough to venture into it. This awe of the air was akin to the twentieth century attitude towards outer space before man invaded that realm also. The sheep, the duck and the cock of Versailles played the same 'guinea pig' role as the dogs and monkeys that became the first space travellers. Yet when we recall the modest heights attained by the balloons described in the previous chapter this parallel between aeronaut and cosmonaut breaks down. For whereas the first cosmonaut ventured into a realm never penetrated, on mountains men had climbed to high altitudes long before balloons were thought of. Mt Aiguille was climbed by order of Charles VIII of France in 1492; Leonardo da Vinci climbed to the snowfields near the Val Sesia to make scientific observations and Titlis, the first true snow-mountain, was conquered in 1744. Although the historic first ascent of Mont Blanc by Dr Michel Paccard and Jacques Balmat was not made until 1786, high mountaineering by the aid of axes and ropes was already an established art in Switzerland when Joseph Montgolfier began his experiments.

History provides no explanation for this curious inconsistency. It can only be assumed that, notwithstanding the scientific evidence which already existed to the contrary, men harboured the belief that the atmosphere followed the contours of the earth with the effect that an aeronaut ascending to 10,000 ft in a balloon might encounter conditions very different from those experienced by a mountaineer at the same altitude. Whether this be true or not, it is a fact that the prejudice against a manned balloon ascent was not easily overcome.

No sooner had the Versailles demonstration passed off successfully than the Montgolfier brothers announced their intention to build a large man-carrying balloon. This proposal caused a great deal of head-shaking at the Court, but the King at length agreed on condition that the passengers should be two criminals. If they returned to earth alive, a contingency which Louis evidently considered pretty remote, they would be granted a free pardon. This proposal scandalized the spirited Pilâtre de Rozier. 'Eh quoi!' he is said to have exclaimed, 'de vils criminels auraient les premiers la gloire de s'élever dans les airs! Non, non, cela ne sera point.' He found an enthusiastic and influential ally in the Marquis d'Arlandes, a gentleman of Languedoc, who, provided he could accompany Pilâtre on the flight, offered to press this cogent argument upon the King. The Marquis found a friend at Court in the person of the Duchesse de Polignac, governess to the Royal children, who persuaded Marie Antoinette to exercise her wiles upon the King on behalf of the would-be aeronauts. Under this combined assault Louis gave way and consented to the flight.

Francis Pilâtre de Rozier was born at Metz in Lorraine on 30th March, 1757. At the age of eighteen he came to Paris to study under Sage where his brilliance soon made him a member of the Academy. He developed a breathing apparatus, forerunner of the gas mask, for use in sewers, and founded a Museum of Science where he lectured and gave demonstrations. He delighted in these performances, his most spectacular and popular feat being to inhale hydrogen and then ignite the gas as he breathed it out. His best known portrait depicts him doing this trick. Now he had committed himself with enthusiasm to carry out a much more dangerous and spectacular experiment.

Pilâtre himself worked on the new Montgolfier balloon which, like its two forerunners, was made and tested in the Reveillon gardens. Following their experience at Versailles, the Montgolfier brothers decided upon a stronger and somewhat heavier material for their new balloon and upon an ovoid form which would thereafter be the accepted shape for 'Montgolfières'. Practically every source quotes different figures for the dimensions of this first man-carrying balloon, but the most reliable is probably the inscription on a contemporary print in the Cuthbert Collection. This states that the height was 70 ft (Fr.) and the diameter 46 ft (Fr.), for which the English equivalents are 75 ft 6 in and 49 ft. The neck of the balloon was 16 ft diameter and around it was constructed a wickerwork gallery 3 ft broad having a cloth-covered balustrade 3 ft 6 in high. This gallery was secured to the balloon by a great number of small cords sewn into the fabric. A fire basket made of wrought-iron wire was slung from the bottom of the neck by chains and in each side of the neck ports were provided so that fuel could be fed to the fire from the gallery. The balloon was painted blue and decorated in gold with the Royal cipher and the signs of the Zodiac. When completed, it weighed 1,600 lb and with a capacity of approximately 79,000 cubic feet its estimated useful lift was 1,700 lb.

With human lives at stake in this experiment, the Montgolfiers determined to take their time over construction so that no detail should be scamped. They also tried to avoid unwelcome attention from the public and to restrict access to the gardens to members of a small committee of the Academy, but in this they were unsuccessful. The crowd in the Rue de Montreuil grew daily as the balloon neared completion, while amongst the influential a great deal of successful string-pulling went on to gain admission to the enclosure. An announcement in the *Journal de Paris* stating that the experiments were of a scientific kind of interest only to *savants* had little effect, for Paris was becoming balloon mad.

On Wednesday, 15th October, the fire was lit and the balloon inflated for the first time. Pilâtre de Rozier then stepped into the gallery to make the first trial captive ascent. Naturally, however, only a few feet of rope had been paid out before it was found that the weight of the aeronaut had thrown the balloon out of balance. 110 lb of ballast was placed on the opposite side of the gallery to correct this and de Rozier then ascended to the limit of the rope than available – 84 ft. By feeding straw onto the fire he kept the restraining rope taut for 4 minutes 25 seconds before allowing the balloon to descend very gently to the launching platform to the great relief of the watchers below. Understandably excited by the success of this first experiment, de Rozier broke one of the most important rules of ballooning by jumping from the gallery as soon as he touched down, whereupon the balloon in its unbalanced state immediately shot up again to the limit of its rope. However, no harm was done; the balloon was safely retrieved and the lesson was not forgotten.

Taking advantage of calm weather conditions, de Rozier made further ascents that day, learning to regulate the vertical movement of the balloon by controlled firing, the fuel used being straw and rags soaked in spirits of wine. The effect of this success was that a great crowd had collected in the Rue de Montreuil when the experiment was repeated on Friday, 17th October, but the patience of these eager watchers was poorly rewarded for a stiff breeze was blowing and on this account de Rozier wisely decided to call it a day after one ascent. He realized that under such weather conditions a captive ascent was far more dangerous than a free flight because of the stresses and strains to which the frail balloon was subjected as it fought against the wind. The world's first aeronaut was learning his lessons fast.

On Sunday, 19th October, weather conditions were more favourable and in the meantime enough rope had been obtained to allow the balloon to ascend more than 300 ft. The crowds in the streets and the more fortunate spectators on the surrounding roof tops saw de Rozier make four ascents. On the first of these 210 ft of rope was paid out and the balloon remained at this altitude for six minutes with no fire in the basket. On a second ascent to 262 ft de Rozier kept the balloon aloft for eight and a half minutes by feeding straw to the furnace and gave the crowd a striking demonstration of his ability to control it by this means. For as the balloon was descending a sudden puff of wind from the east carried it into the upper branches of a tall tree in a neighbouring garden. The watchers held their breath, expecting to see the gallery overset, but instead they saw the aeronaut coolly throw more straw on the fire whereupon the balloon sailed clear, descending gently and safely to the platform a few moments later. For the third ascent of the day a passenger, Girond de Villette, took the place of the ballast on the opposite side of the gallery and the two men remained aloft for nine minutes at 324 ft. Finally, de Rozier repeated this last experiment with the Marquis d'Arlandes as passenger. At this greater altitude the balloon was visible over a wide area of the city and its appearance generated intense excitement that would only be surpassed by the great occasion of the first free flight.

The site chosen for this historic ascent was in the gardens of the Château La Muette in the Bois de Boulogne and the date 20th

November. The château was the residence of the Dauphin who proposed to witness the event with his suite in attendance. Despite the fact that the ascent was not advertised, word of it had spread through Paris like wild fire and, according to Cavallo, 'a vast multitude' assembled. They were doomed to disappointment, for soon after preparations were begun a sudden storm of wind and rain broke and the attempt was abandoned.

Next morning the weather had improved somewhat and although the skies were threatening and the wind still blustery, preparations were renewed. Cautious almost to a fault, the Montgolfier brothers insisted that de Rozier should made a preliminary captive ascent to test the lifting power of the balloon yet once more. In the process a strong wind caught the balloon and by the time it had been retrieved with difficulty and brought back to the launching platform it had been badly damaged. Only prompt action aided by luck saved the balloon from being totally destroyed by fire and there were serious rents in the fabric. By this time the crowd were becoming threateningly impatient, but an ugly situation was saved by a hastily recruited team of volunteer seamstresses who worked with such a will that in two hours the balloon had been repaired and was again ready for inflation. By this time, too, the threatening clouds had dispersed and the wind had dropped. De Rozier and the Marquis d'Arlandes stepped into opposite sides of the gallery and a few moments later, at 1.54 p.m., the great blue and gold balloon rose lightly from its stage. When it had reached a height of about 280 ft, the two intrepid aeronauts removed their hats and saluted the sea of upturned faces below as a light north-westerly breeze wafted the balloon gently towards the Seine. Some accounts say that the balloon reached a height of 3,000 ft, but if this was the case, which seems unlikely, it was not sustained, for practically the whole flight was made at low altitude.

But let us not on this account under-estimate the historic significance of the occasion. For the slender navel string that till now had still linked man to his mother earth was severed and for the first time in the history of the world man rode freely and proud upon the limitless plain of air. In the minds of the breath-bated watchers below, the two heroes faced unimaginable perils upon this light and treacherous ocean. As we now know, these fears were groundless,

yet de Rozier and his companion were heroes none the less. Ironically, the last danger which the crowd considered was a mundane
one, though very great. This was that the suspended fire which the
balloon bore aloft would set light to the fragile fabric of painted
cloth and paper and consume it like tinder. By the two aeronauts
this danger was recognized and accepted, but their only counter to
a prospect of fearful disaster was to take aloft with them a pail of
water and a sponge apiece.

The Marquis d'Arlandes subsequently wrote an account of the
flight which merits quotation almost in full. It disappointed its
original readers who had evidently been expecting some kind of
heroic myth like the voyage of Ulysses. It invariably happens, however, that when they are making history men are far too busily
occupied to indulge in heroics. For this reason, first-hand accounts
of great events are never epical and often seem to be masterpieces
of understatement. The account of man's first free flight is no exception; it has, too, a comic element inseparable from the balloon. This
arises from the fact that throughout their great adventure the two
aeronauts were invisible to each other because they had to remain
on opposite sides of the balloon in order to maintain its equipoise.

'We went up,' writes the Marquis, 'on the 21st of November, 1783, at
near two o'clock, M. Rozier on the west side of the balloon, I on the east.
The wind was nearly north-west. The machine, say the public, rose with
majesty; but really the position of the balloon altered so that M. Rozier was
in the advance of our position, I in the rear.

'I was surprised at the silence and the absence of movement which our
departure caused among the spectators, and believing them to be astonished and perhaps awed at the strange spectacle; they might well have
reassured themselves. I was still gazing when M. Rozier cried to me –

' "You are doing nothing, and the balloon is scarcely rising a
fathom."

' "Pardon me," I answered, as I placed a bundle of straw upon the fire
and slightly stirred it. Then I turned quickly, but already we had passed
out of sight of La Muette. Astonished, I cast a glance towards the river. I
perceived the confluence of the Oise. And naming the principal bends of
the river by the places nearest them, I cried, "Passy, St. Germain, St. Denis,
Sèvres!" '

' "If you look at the river in that fashion you will be likely to bathe in it
soon,' cried Rozier. "Some fire, my dear friend, some fire!"

'We travelled on; but instead of crossing the river, as our direction seemed to indicate, we bore towards the Invalides, then returned upon the principal bed of the river, and travelled to above the barrier of La Conférence, thus dodging about the river but not crossing it.

'"That river is very difficult to cross," I remarked to my companion.

'"So it seems," he answered; "but you are doing nothing. I suppose it is because you are braver than I and don't fear a tumble."

'I stirred the fire, I seized a truss of straw with my fork; I raised it and threw it in the midst of the flames. An instant afterwards I felt myself lifted as it were into the heavens.

'"For once we move," said I.

'"Yes, we move," answered my companion.

'At the same instant I heard from the top of the balloon a sound which made me believe that it had burst. I watched, yet I saw nothing. My companion had gone into the interior no doubt to make some observations. As my eyes were fixed on the top of the machine I experienced a shock, and it was the only one I had yet felt. The direction of the movement was from above downwards. I then said –

'"What are you doing? Are you having a dance to yourself?"

'"I'm not moving."

'"So much the better. It is only a new current which I hope will carry us from the river," I answered.

'I turned to see where we were, and found we were between the Ecole Militaire and the Invalides.

'"We are getting on," said Rozier.

'"Yes, we are travelling."

'"Let us work, let us work." said he.

'I now heard another report in the machine, which I believed was produced by the cracking of a cord. This new intimation made me carefully examine the inside of our habitation. I saw that the part that was turned towards the south was full of holes, of which some were of considerable size.

'"It must descend," I then cried.

'"Why?"

'"Look!" I said. At the same time I took my sponge and quietly extinguished the little fire that was burning some of the holes within my reach; but at the same moment I perceived that the bottom of the cloth was coming away from the circle that surrounded it.

'"We must descend," I repeated to my companion.

'He looked below. "We are upon Paris," he said.

' "It does not matter," I answered, "only look! Is there no danger? Are you holding on well?"

' "Yes."

'I examined from my side, and saw that we had nothing to fear. I then tried with my sponge the ropes which were within my reach. All of them held firm. Only two of the cords had broken. I then said, "We can cross Paris."

'During this operation we were rapidly getting down to the roofs. We made more fire and rose again with the greatest ease. I looked down, and it seemed to me we were going towards the towers of St. Sulpice; but, on rising, a new current made us quit this direction and bear more to the south. I looked to the left, and beheld a wood, which I believed to be that of Luxembourg. We were traversing the boulevard, and I cried all at once – "Get to ground!"

'But the intrepid Rozier, who never lost his head, and who judged more surely than I, prevented me from attempting to descend. I then threw a bundle of straw on the fire. We rose again, and another current bore us to the left. We were now close to the ground, between two mills. As soon as we came near the earth I raised myself over the gallery, and leaning there with my two hands, I felt the balloon pressing softly against my head. I pushed it back, and leapt down to the ground. Looking round and expecting to see the balloon still distended, I was astonished to find it quite empty and flattened. On looking for Rozier I saw him in his shirt-sleeves creeping out from under the mass of canvas that had fallen over him.'

So ended the world's first flight. It had lasted twenty-five minutes and had brought the aeronauts to earth on the Butte-aux-Cailles, near the present Place d'Italie and 9,000 yards from their starting point. It is greatly to the credit of the Marquis that, unlike some future aeronauts, he told a plain unvarnished tale in which he did not attempt to present himself as a hero. Indeed de Rozier emerges from the account as by far the cooler and more level-headed of the two. But we should salute the courage of both these men who, on this first-ever flight, calmly extinguished with their sponges the 'little fires' that could so easily have sent them hurtling down like a flaming torch.

As they were walking towards the nearest house, the aeronauts were met by the Duc de Chartres who had followed the balloon on horseback. The balloon was folded up, loaded into a cart and taken back to the Reveillon gardens.

The First Aeronauts: Pilâtre de Rozier and the Marquis d'Arlandre ascend from La Muette, November, 1783

Pioneer of the hydrogen balloon:
J. A. C. Charles

F. Pilâtre de Rozier
"Premier Navigateur Aerien"

Destruction of Charles' first hydrogen balloon by the villagers of Gonesse, 1783

Meanwhile the champions of the hydrogen balloon, Charles and the brothers Aîné and Cadet Robert, had not been content to leave the field, or rather the air, to the Montgolfiers. Only two days before de Rozier's historic flight a subscription to cover the cost of building a man-carrying hydrogen balloon was launched in the Paris *Journal* for 19th November. The balloon must have been under construction before this because in less than a week from this date it was exhibited, filled with air, in the Tuileries Palace.

In designing and constructing this balloon, Charles and his collaborators achieved an extraordinary feat. To call it an advance upon its predecessor would be an understatement. At one inspired stroke they gave the hydrogen balloon its definitive form, a form which would subsequently be improved upon only in detail. It was a perfect sphere 27 ft 6 in in diameter consisting of alternating red and yellow gores of rubberized silk, correctly shaped to taper to the poles like the segments of an orange, and sewn together. Profiting by the experience gained in his previous experiment, the stop cock at the south pole of the balloon was now replaced by an open 'neck' or 'appendix'. Through this the balloon could be filled and from it gas could issue freely if it expanded owing either to reduced atmospheric pressure at high altitude or to the heat of the sun. The open neck therefore acted as a safety valve to prevent the balloon bursting. In addition, Charles provided a valve at the north pole of the balloon through which gas could be released by the aeronaut if he wished to descend. This was a flap valve set in a wooden ring attached to the fabric. Opening inwards, it was normally held in the closed position by an external spring, but it could be opened by pulling a cord (the valve line) that passed down through the centre of the balloon.

In order to distribute the weight of the car evenly over the envelope, the upper hemisphere of the balloon was covered by cord netting attached to a large wooden ring or hoop at the equator. To the lower part of this hoop the car lines were attached.[1] Although the principle of this method of suspension was sound and has been followed ever since, experience soon led to a modification of Charles's arrangement. Some prints of the balloon at rest show a slight clearance between the distended envelope and the hoop as

---

[1] According to Benjamin Franklin this arrangement was a modification of an original intention to suspend the car from the neck of the balloon. (see Chapter 3.)

4

Charles doubtless intended, whereas the most accurate of the prints depicting the balloon taking off on its historic first flight show that at this time the hoop was actually restricting the envelope. The balloon is distinctly 'waisted' at the equator and the hoop is somewhat askew. These pictures underline the fault of such an arrangement. The hoop and the car lines would inevitably chafe the delicate fabric, causing damage which, at the least, would soon result in a leakage of gas and at the worst might lead to a serious failure. Hence, as we shall see, on later balloons the netting was extended to what might be called the southern arctic circle of the envelope where 'crow's feet' and leading-lines connected it to a small diameter hoop well clear of the fabric and only a little distance above the car.

The car of Charles's balloon was made of wicker-work, 8 ft long, 4 ft wide and 3 ft 6 in deep, weighing 130 lb. It was so extravagantly shaped and so elaborately bedizened with painted cloth and decoration that it resembled some mythical chariot of the gods as conceived by a master of the baroque. A car of such a shape must have been difficult to suspend truly, nor could it have made life easy for its occupants. Nevertheless, symbolizing as it did the conquest of the air and the heroic stature of the aeronauts, the triumphal car concept died hard and some years would pass before it gave place to the more mundane but far more practical rectangular basket.

The ascent of Charles and Ainé, the elder of the brothers Robert, took place on 1st December, 1783 from the gardens of the Tuileries and despite the lateness of the season the weather was perfect. The interest and excitement the event provoked far surpassed anything previously known. It has been estimated that no less than 400,000 people – half the population of Paris at that time – assembled to see the ascent, probably the greatest crowd the world had ever seen. The large round pond directly in front of the Palace had been drained and a launching stage erected over it upon which the car was placed. Some prints of the scene show the hydrogen generating apparatus on this platform, but these are incorrect. In fact Charles decided to inflate the balloon in the comparative seclusion of the nearby Grande Avenue, using the sheltering trees as masts to support the envelope, and with the help and protection of soldiery. In this Charles showed his wisdom. Although the process was gradually improved, the inflation of a hydrogen balloon remained for many years such a slow and tedious proceeding that if it was carried out in full public view the crowd was all too apt to lose patience, with disastrous results as many less prudent aeronauts discovered to their cost.

When the balloon was fully inflated it was carried from the shelter of the trees to the platform where it was attached to the car. That the careful and orderly preparations which then followed would become accepted routine for all subsequent aeronauts is evidence of Charles's calibre, of the genius and forethought he had devoted to every detail of the enterprise. While the balloon was held down by many willing hands, equipment, warm clothing, and provisions were carefully stowed in the car. The equipment included a thermometer and a mercury barometer to enable the aeronauts to calculate their altitude. When all this gear was aboard, bags of sand were added as ballast until the balloon was securely weighted down. With the two aeronauts in the car, ballast was then removed until weight and lift were exactly balanced, a proceeding which would become known as 'weighing off'.

Charles set yet another precedent by equipping himself with a small trial balloon, a five-foot globe of hydrogen painted a bright emerald green that could be liberated just before the ascent to indicate the set of the wind currents in the upper air. Turning to Joseph Montgolfier who stood among the privileged spectators by the platform, Charles handed him the cord that restrained the little balloon with the words: 'It is for you, monsieur, to show us the way to the skies.' Seldom has one pioneer made to another so appropriate and generous an acknowledgement. Montgolfier released the balloon and together the two men watched it soar skywards and sail away to the north-east. Then Charles and his companion stepped into the car, threw out 19 lb of ballast to give them their initial lift and in a few moments at 1.45 p.m., the boom of a cannon signalled 'hands off'.

In contrast to the somewhat ponderous ascent of the big Montgolfières, slow, uncertain and fire-breathing, the little candy-striped balloon with its gilded car leapt easily and so eagerly into its element that it reached a height of 1,800 ft in a few moments. So swiftly, and above all so confidently was this feat accomplished that during those first few moments it held the whole vast crowd silent and spell-bound.

Then, as the aeronauts were seen to wave their flags as a signal that all was well, the tension was broken and with a great roar of voices a whole city saluted them. We may well imagine that reaction, for, like only the greatest art, such a superb combination of high courage and perfect expertise is always deeply moving. It makes the hair stand up and causes some to laugh or cheer and some to weep. In that mood of exaltation it seemed that in the future all miracles were possible to men who could soar into the air with such sublime confidence. Asked why she wept, one old woman answered: 'Alas! When they shall have discovered the means of escaping death, I shall not be able to take advantage of them.'

Meanwhile, what of the aeronauts? Said Charles afterwards: 'Nothing will ever equal that moment of joyous excitement which filled my whole being when I felt myself flying away from the earth. It was not mere pleasure; it was perfect bliss.' 'I care not what may be the condition of the earth,' he said to Robert, 'it is the sky that is for me now. What serenity! what a ravishing scene!' But instead of joining in these ecstasies, Robert the practical craftsman was checking over their stores and deciding that they could afford to jettison some of them and so conserve their sand ballast. Although the thermometer registered only 12 degrees above zero, the December sun shone warmly and Robert held up a blanket questioningly. 'Good,' said Charles, 'throw that out.' The blanket floated down, landing upon the dome of the church of l'Assomption. Other blankets and articles of heavy clothing followed, but what became of them and what consternation they caused on landing is not recorded. We are told that the stores included bottles of 'champagne and other wines' and from the light-hearted behaviour of the aeronauts it is safe to infer that these did not go overboard until they were empty.

Borne upon light south-westerly airs, they saw the panorama of Paris reel slowly away beneath them. They crossed the Seine twice, first between St Ouen and Asnières and again beyond Gennevilliers. Individual voices could now be heard calling to them from below: 'My good friends, have you no fear?' 'Are you not sick?' 'Heaven preserve you!' To these wellwishers the aeronauts replied by shouting 'Vive le Roi!' and vigorously waving their flags. After 56 minutes' flying the distant report of a cannon told them that they had passed out of sight of the crowds in the Tuileries gardens. Sanois, Franconville, Eaubonne, St Leu-Taverny and l'Isle-Adam all drifted by, for they seemed to hang motionless above a turning world. Finally, after two hours, they found themselves over the open plain of Nesle. 'Let us go down,' said Charles, and to set the seal on his extraordinary achievement he proceeded to make a classically perfect landing. Pulling the valve line to release gas, he put the balloon into a long, slanting descent until a tree appeared in their path. Instantly Charles threw out 2 lb of ballast. The balloon rose over the treetop, descended once more, skimmed low over the ground for a hundred feet or more and then came gently to rest, twenty-seven miles from their starting point. A group of peasants had been chasing the balloon across the plain 'like children pursuing a butterfly', as Charles put it, and they were soon recruited as a ground crew to hold the car of the balloon.

As people came flocking out from the small town of Nesles, the prudent Charles wrote a short report of the flight and got the local magistrates to sign it. Then three horsemen came in sight, galloping towards them over the plain. They turned out to be the Duc de Chartres, the Duc de Fitz-James and an Englishman named Farrer who had followed the balloon from the Tuileries. Strangely enough it was the Englishman who was the most excited. Flinging himself from his horse he rushed to Charles and seized him in his arms crying 'Monsieur Charles, I was first!'

The sun had just set, but Charles was so exhilarated and so confident that he determined to ascend again and alone. Promising his anxious friends that he would return to earth in half-an-hour, he climbed back into the car and told those who were holding it down to stand clear as soon as he gave the signal. In his account of the flight, Charles says that by this time the balloon was 'quite flabby and soft' through loss of gas. Maybe this fact and the excitement of the moment made him under-estimate the lift it would have when relieved of the weight of his companion. For the instant the car was released the balloon shot skywards like an arrow and in a few minutes had shrunk to a small speck, glittering like an evening star in the light of the lost sun. Charles boasted afterwards that he was the first man in the world to see the sun set twice in one day. 'I passed in ten minutes from the temperature of spring to that of winter,' he said, 'The cold was keen and dry, but not insupportable. I examined all my sensations calmly,' and then he added in a strange and graphic phrase, 'I could hear myself live, so to speak.' He saw that the envelope above him had become fully distended owing to the reduced atmospheric pressure and that the balloon was now in equilibrium. From his barometer he estimated his height as a little under 3,000 metres or nearly 10,000 ft. A sudden acute pain in his right ear and jaw made him decide to descend. He thought it was caused by the high altitude whereas it was doubtless an after effect of the rapid climb and the accompanying temperature drop. By opening the valve Charles set the balloon on a downward course and as it neared the ground he threw out three pounds of ballast to check its rate of descent and make, for the second time that day, a perfect landing. In the light of a rising moon the car came gently to rest in a ploughed field near the wood of Tour du Lay, three miles from Nesles and 35 minutes after take-off. Next day, the balloon was loaded onto a cart and brought back to Paris in triumph.

It is obvious that as an aeronaut, Charles was a 'natural' and yet, although his collaborators, the brothers Robert, made many subsequent ascents, this was his first and last flight. For this mystery there is no positive explanation, but it is believed by many that despite his calm and collected account of the episode, his meteoric solo ascent so alarmed him that he resolved never to fly again.

This was the last flight made in that historic year, 1783, and it represented an amazing advance upon the first tentative experiments made by Joseph Montgolfier only twelve months before. Paris could think and talk of nothing but balloons and all over the city that Christmas season her craftsmen were busy adapting the form of the balloon to every conceivable article of use and ornament from buttons to bird-cages and from fans to sword hilts. Significantly, it was the Charles balloon – the Charlière as it was now called – which almost invariably featured in these designs.

There was also a craze for flying miniature balloons. This is said to have originated in a suggestion made to the Baron de Beaumanoir by a Parisian painter named Deschamps that a successful balloon might be made by gluing together pieces of gold-beaters' skin. The artist made such a balloon for the baron and the material, made from the lining of the intestines of oxen, proved remarkably resistant to penetration by hydrogen. Later, large floating figures in many fantastic forms would be made of this material by shaping it over deflatable moulds. Miniature balloons, some filled with hydrogen and others using hot air, were also made from silk and other fabrics by enterprising umbrella makers, the hot air type being raised by a lighted cloth soaked in spirits of wine. For example, a Monsieur Guyot in the Faubourg St Martin published a price list ranging from a little nine ounce model in a gold-beaters' skin at 3 livres 10 francs up to a 12 ft diameter silk balloon at 800 livres. Eventually, so many of these small balloons were flying about over the city that they created a serious fire hazard and the authorities had to issue an order prohibiting them.

So far as Paris was concerned the amazing performance by Charles had completely eclipsed the Montgolfier star. The two brothers left the capital and returned to the south where they celebrated the New Year by planning a new balloon of truly heroic proportions. Constructed at Les Brotteaux, a suburb of Lyons, between 7th and 10th January from sections previously prepared, this monster was 131 ft high and 104 ft in diameter. It was financed by a subscription launched the previous autumn with the curious aim of lifting a horse or some other large animal into the air. However, arguments against this by Pilâtre de Rozier eventually prevailed and led to the provision of the usual circular wicker gallery for human freight. In honour of the Governor of Lyons, M. le Flesselle, who had actively sponsored the project, the balloon was named after him. Its great envelope was given the now usual elaborate decoration on a ground of white and grey.

With a capacity of more than 700,000 cubic feet, *le Flesselle* was by far the largest Montgolfière ever made. To attempt to launch so unwieldy a giant in the depths of winter was asking for trouble, and trouble there was sure enough, so much so that the ascent was repeatedly postponed. Damage occurred needing extensive repairs before it was ever inflated. Frost following rain caused further damage and during attempts to thaw out the frozen fabric it caught fire. Nevertheless, in the course of one trial inflation it is said to have risen three feet despite the fact that fifty men were holding it down.

Secured to the gallery by eight iron rods was a fire-basket five feet

in diameter, and in addition to the usual straw it was decided to feed
this with 6 lb bundles of alder wood. Between the stacks of fuel and
the clutter of fire-irons, pails of water, hand-pumps and sponges on
the gallery, spaces were arranged for six passengers and it was estimated that this would represent a total all up weight of approximately
7 tons 7 cwt – a prodigious load to lift into the air.

In charge of the operation was Pilâtre de Rozier and with him went
Joseph Montgolfier, making his first and only ascent. Amongst the
aristocracy of France competition for the remaining four places was
very keen, the lucky ones being Prince Charles de Ligne and the
Comtes de Laurencin, de Dampierre and de la Porte d'Anglefort.
The ascent on the 19th January from Les Brotteaux was watched by
100,000 people and was marked by extraordinary scenes. In view of
the damage the balloon had sustained in the earlier mishaps, de
Rozier decided that the number of passengers should be reduced to
three and the authorities, including M. le Flesselle, supported him.
But the four noblemen leapt into the gallery, drew their swords and
defied anyone to remove them.[1] De Rozier and Montgolfier were
equally determined not to be left behind so, while the furnace blazed
below and the towering mass of fabric strained against its ropes, there
was a very heated and undignified argument upon the platform.
Finally, the repeated commands of the four noblemen prevailed and
the ropes were cut, but at this moment not only did de Rozier and
Montgolfier fling themselves onto the gallery but also a young man
named Fontaine who had helped in the construction of the balloon
and who later became a celebrated architect.

The providence-tempting size of the balloon, the many mishaps
that had befallen it and the final sword-flashing fracas on the launching platform all combined to generate a sense of impending doom
and disaster as this huge, frail phoenix staggered into the unwelcom-
ing January sky with its seven occupants. They must have looked
like so many wizards round a magic cauldron as they flung their
faggots into the flames and smoke of the furnace. The fantastic sight
drew cries of terror from the crowd. Many fell to their knees and a
number of women fainted. Yet all was well; the balloon steadied
itself and continued to mount until it reached a height of 3,000 ft

---

[1] According to another account they held pistols to their heads and threatened to shoot
themselves if any attempt was made to remove them.

where it hung almost motionless for a while. But, unknown to those below, the fabric had failed at a point of previous damage and through this 4 ft rent the hot air was escaping so fast that the balloon soon defeated the efforts of the firemen to keep it aloft. After fifteen minutes it began to descend so rapidly that the crowd feared for the lives of the aeronauts. In fact with the rent rapidly lengthening to 14 ft, the balloon came down in under three minutes and within two seconds of landing the whole fabric had completely collapsed. Happily, however, none of its occupants was injured by this forceful home-coming. There were rapturous scenes in Lyons that night when the bold aeronauts attended a performance of *Iphigenia in Aulis* at the Opera House.

The next major event in the history of ballooning took place on 25th February, 1784, when the Chevalier Paul Andreani ascended in a Montgolfière from the grounds of his villa at Moncuco near Milan. This was the first manned ascent in Italy. Andreani was accompanied on his flight by the brothers Augustin and Charles Gerli who had built the balloon to his order. This differed from the French design in that, instead of a gallery, it featured a passenger car suspended beneath the fire brazier. This brazier was fitted within a ring or hoop, supported by leading lines from the balloon, and to this the car lines were attached. This was the first appearance of a method of suspension that would soon become standard on all hydrogen balloons. Relief from the heat of the fire was claimed to be the advantage of this arrangement, but it is obvious that it had two serious disadvantages. Had the envelope taken fire as a result of over-enthusiastic stoking the aeronauts could not have extinguished it, while hot ashes falling on them from the grate must have been an inconvenience to say the least. However, all went well on a flight lasting twenty minutes.

On the 20th May four ladies [1] ascended in a captive Montgolfière from the Faubourg St Antoine in Paris, but the honour of making the first free flight by a woman fell to the young and personable Madame Thible. Accompanied by a Monsieur Fleurant, this intrepid lady, singing like a bird, ascended in a Montgolfière from Lyons on the 4th of June. The balloon reached a height of 8,500 ft

---

[1] They were the Marchioness of Montalembert, the Countess of the same name, the Countess de Podenas and Mademoiselle de Lagarde.

in a flight lasting 45 minutes. The ascent was watched by the King of Sweden and the balloon was named *Le Gustave* in his honour.

For height and distance, the most remarkable of these early Montgolfière flights was made by Pilâtre de Rozier with a passenger named Proust on the 23rd June. In the balloon *Marie Antoinette* they took off from Versailles in the presence of the Royal family and the King of Sweden, rose to a height of 11,700 ft and landed 45 minutes later in a field at Luzarche, 36 miles away. This was a quite exceptional performance. Of the many Montgolfière ascents at this time, the majority were of very short duration and more than one balloon was destroyed by fire; this despite the provision made on later Montgolfières for releasing the fire basket before landing. It is remarkable that no fatalities occurred, for on many balloons that returned to earth safely the scorched state of the fabric revealed all too clearly that the margin of safety was in fact minimal. Thus while all honour is due – and was paid – to the brothers Montgolfier as pioneers, it became increasingly obvious during 1784 that for sustained flight the hydrogen balloon was far superior to its large, unwieldy and dangerous rival. At the outset, the speed and certainty with which a Montgolfière could be inflated told heavily in its favour, but as the process of generating hydrogen was improved, this advantage was lost. Moreover, a Montgolfière was usually damaged beyond repair after one flight, whereas the smaller and more durable envelope of the hydrogen balloon could be folded and stowed for further flights.

On 19th September, 1784, a remarkable flight by Cadet Robert, accompanied by M. Collin-Hullin, set the seal on the triumph of the hydrogen balloon. Taking off from Paris at noon they landed at Beuvry, near Bethune, 150 miles away, at 6.40 p.m. To be more precise, they came down in the grounds of a chateau where the owner, the Prince de Ghisthelles, was holding a fête for his tenantry. The Prince was about to release a small Montgolfière for their amusement when Robert descended from the skies and, after narrowly missing a mill building, landed safely in their midst. This unexpected bonus must have made the fête a never-to-be-forgotten occasion.

This memorable year also saw the first ascent by a man who would speedily become the most famous of early aeronauts – Jean

Pierre Blanchard. The most celebrated of his many ascents was made from Dover, however; so to keep this account of events in proper perspective we should precede Blanchard to England and return later to the career of this great aeronaut.

CHAPTER FOUR

Balloons over England

Lunardi's balloon rose in the air amain
Turned about, took a route and safely came down again.
The sky being clear a fine sight we did obtain,
Success to Lunardi and his air Balloon
London Street Ballad, 1784

THE AFFECTED INDIFFERENCE with which the news of the successful French balloon experiments was received by the Royal Society in London was undoubtedly due to sour grapes made all the sourer by the enmity between the two countries. The fact that Britain's traditional enemy had been the first to turn to such spectacular account the discoveries of Cavendish and Priestley was understandably galling. But this was the collective 'official' attitude; as individuals, many English scientists were keenly interested in the French experiments and kept themselves as fully informed as possible. Sir Joseph Banks, President of the Royal Society, had as his informant the United States Ambassador in Paris, the elderly and eminent Benjamin Franklin. Armed with a telescope, Franklin had watched the ascent of Charles and Robert from his carriage and had at once despatched to Sir Joseph an admirably detailed and accurate account of the occasion. More liberally minded than their London confrères, the members of the celebrated Lunar Society of Birmingham, who included Boulton, Watt and Priestley, watched the progress of events in France with a keen interest quite untinged by jealousy.

Popularly, British opinion was divided. Thus the *Morning Herald* for 27th December, 1783, called upon 'all men to laugh this new folly out of practice as soon as possible.' A few years later, the *Gentleman's Magazine* flew to the opposite extreme by describing the balloon as 'infinitely the most magnificent and most astonishing discovery made . . . perhaps since the creation.' Many intelligent laymen would not commit themselves either way, an attitude Horace Walpole explained when he wrote in June 1785:

'How posterity will laugh at us one way or the other! If half-a-dozen break their necks, and balloonism is exploded, we shall be called fools for having imagined it could be brought to use: if it should be turned to account, we shall be ridiculed for having doubted.'

Earlier, Walpole had expressed the opinion that ballooning was as childish as the kite-flying of school boys, yet on two occasions he could not resist the temptation, urged upon him by his servants, to go into his garden at Strawberry Hill in order to watch a balloon sail overhead. The fact was that when balloons appeared in English skies even the most sceptical succumbed to their fascination.

This uncertain attitude towards ballooning helps to explain why both the first small scale experiments and the first successful manned ascent in England were made by foreigners although Englishmen did not lag far behind.

Credit for making the first successful balloon experiment in England goes to an adventurous Italian sailor of fortune, Count Francesco Zambeccari. Born at Bologna in 1752 and educated at Parma, Zambeccari served as a mercenary with the Spanish fleet in actions against the Moors and off the American coast until, on returning to Spain, he got into trouble with the Inquisition and had to flee the country, making first to Paris and thence to England. It was in Paris that he learned with fascinated interest about Joseph Montgolfier's balloon experiments and determined to repeat them. Arrived in London, he encountered a fellow countryman named Michael Biaggini, a maker of artificial flowers in Cheapside, who helped him to make two small trial balloons. Even so recent an historian of flight as J. E. Hodgson describes these as 'hot-air' and 'inflammable air' balloons in the space of one paragraph, but from their performance it is safe to say that they were filled with hydrogen.

The first balloon was only 5 ft in diameter and was launched privately without any publicity, but it caused quite a stir as it floated over Highgate and was eventually picked up at Waltham Abbey. This was on 4th November, 1783. The second was double the size of the first, made of oiled silk and gilded. Filled with air, it was

exhibited at the Lyceum in the Strand, before being released from
the Artillery Ground at Moorfields before a large crowd on 25th
November. A northerly wind carried the little balloon over Sussex
until it came down at Graffham, a village under the escarpment of
the South Downs to the south-west of Petworth. The shrewd Sussex
farmer who discovered it, unlike the terror stricken peasants of
Gonesse, did not destroy the balloon but bore it away to his barn
where he exhibited it to wondering villagers at a penny a peep.

On the very next day, the celebrated Swiss scientist and friend of
Matthew Boulton, Aimé Argand, demonstrated a small hydrogen
balloon to George III and his family at Windsor. The King was
delighted with the new toy and invited Argand to stay for two
days and give further demonstrations.

In the early months of the following year small hydrogen balloons
were released from London, from a number of provincial cities in
England and from Aberdeen and Cork. Among the largest of these
were the 30 ft diameter balloon released by James Sadler, soon to
become the first English aeronaut, from the gardens of Queen's
College, Oxford on 9th February and the 25 ft balloon with 'triumphal
car' attached which was sent up from Astley's Hippodrome on
12th March.

On 24th February a contemporary press report from Ross stated
that 'a noted old English Jew Barber' of that town had ascended in
a balloon to a height of 116 yards. This balloon, we are told, 'then
descended gradually and brought the old Jew down unhurt to the
great surprise of more than a thousand spectators.'[1] Although this
account of what was evidently a Montgolfière reads circumstantially
enough, it has never been confirmed and is not generally accepted.
Credit for making the first manned ascent in the British Isles is
commonly awarded to James Tytler although his pioneer efforts
were singularly unsuccessful and luckless.

Tytler cuts a strange and tragic figure. Son of a poor Scottish
minister, he was born at Fearn in Forfar in 1747. After studying for
the medical profession under Dr Black at Edinburgh he made a
voyage to Greenland as ship's doctor on a fishing vessel, but on his
return he failed to qualify. He then entered into partnership with an

---

[1] The original press cutting is in Vol. 10 of the Norman Collection. Hodgson, on page
103 f., renders the height attained wrongly as 115 ft.

Edinburgh chemist named Scott and also became a hack writer. He is said to have edited the second edition of the *Encyclopaedia Britannica*, writing the greater part of it himself for the miserable pittance of 17s a week. How or why he became interested in balloons is not known, but he may originally have been inspired by Dr Black's knowledge of the properties of 'inflammable air'.

On 12th March, 1784, Scott and Tytler released a small balloon $3\frac{1}{2}$ ft in diameter from Heriot's Garden, Edinburgh. What type this was we are not told, but since it was picked up at Haddington, twenty miles away, it was most probably filled with hydrogen.

Scott and Tytler then proceeded to construct a large Montgolfière of a singularly crude and clumsy form. Shaped like a huge barrel, it was 40 ft high and 30 ft in diameter and it was cumbered by a furnace which alone weighed 300 lb. Tytler first attempted to ascend in this crazy construction from the Comely Gardens, near the King's Park, on 7th August. During the process of inflation the base of the balloon caught fire with the effect that the chains supporting the heavy furnace broke away and the gallery was also damaged. After hasty repairs, the balloon was inflated again the following evening, but just as Tytler was about to ascend a violent gust of wind caught and overset the balloon causing serious damage. In his own account, Tytler says that the wind entered the balloon driving out the hot air and this may well be true for the balloon had no neck, the size of the opening at its base being almost as great as its maximum diameter.

According to one press report, the exasperated crowd, convinced that they had been tricked by a charlatan, seized and burned the gallery. Whether this be true or no, Tytler, still doggedly determined to vindicate himself, made the desperate decision to dispense with both gallery and furnace and ascend suspended beneath the balloon 'like a log or piece of ballast', as he put it. Such a flight must necessarily be brief, but at least he might get himself airborne. When the balloon had been repaired and revarnished, Tytler did at last succeed in making two brief flights in this way on 25th August and 1st September and it is on the strength of these that his claim to the title of 'first British Aeronaut' rests. Tytler himself refers to them only as 'leaps' and the height attained – from which he landed heavily but without injury – was not more than 500 ft, but although this may be a slender claim, Tytler richly deserves the title for his courage and for his determination in the face of misfortune and derision.

Following these ascents, Tytler built a new gallery and furnace before making yet another attempt on 29th September, but owing to a strong wind this was completely disastrous. First, the suspension rope broke during inflation allowing the balloon to collapse onto the fire from which it was rescued with difficulty and re-hoisted. Two men then climbed one of the masts to secure the tackle whereupon the mast broke, the whole apparatus fell with a crash and the balloon was blown into some nearby trees. One man fell to the ground and was seriously injured; the other was carried into the trees with the balloon.

Even after this fiasco, Tytler would not admit defeat. He tried again on 11th October, but the balloon was visibly leaking from every seam and did not have the power to raise him from the ground. Tytler had to suffer the jeers of the crowd who taunted him for cowardice. Finally, the balloon was released without him, rose to 300 ft and then collapsed, never to rise again. The 'Grand Edinburgh Fire Balloon' made a final appearance on 26th July, 1785, when it was completely destroyed by a violent storm which broke over the ground just after the fire had been lit.

Scorned and ridiculed by his countrymen, this most unhappy of aeronauts retired from the stage into a life of poverty and obscurity. His expression of republican sympathies forced him to flee to Ireland in 1792 and three years later he emigrated to America, settling at Salem, Massachusetts. There he wrote scientific works and lived as an eccentric recluse until January 1804, when he perished miserably by falling into a salt-pit when drunk.

In England we should expect to find Count Zambeccari leading the way to the skies. He did indeed propose a 50 ft diameter hydrogen balloon in January 1784, with which he planned to ascend from Hyde Park, but he failed to raise the necessary funds. Indeed, the Count became so financially embarrassed that he was forced to leave England for a time, thus leaving the way clear for his fellow countryman, Vincenzo Lunardi, to succeed where he had failed.

Vincent Lunardi, as he was called in England, was born at Lucca on 11th January, 1759 and spent his early years in the East Indies.

The first manned hydrogen balloon: Charles and Robert ascending from the Tuilleries Gardens, 1st December, 1783

Charles landing at Nesle after
his successful flight from Paris,
December, 1783

The first cylindrical balloon:
The Duc de Chartres and the
brothers Robert about to make
their second ascent from the
Parc de Meudon, 25th July,
1784

Soon after his return to Italy he entered the service of Prince Carami-
nico, Neapolitan Ambassador to the Court of St James's, and so
came to London. In his subsequent writings, Lunardi describes
himself as Secretary to the Ambassador, whereas it is doubtful
whether, in fact, he was ever more than a servant or clerk at the
Embassy. This little self-aggrandisement gives us a key to Lunardi's
character. He was a vain and flamboyant exhibitionist who seized
upon the balloon as the best of all possible band-wagons. One
moment exalted and the next cast down in the depths of despair,
his was a mercurial Latin temperament. He was far too impulsive
ever to acquire that coolness and judgement which makes the truly
great aeronaut. The Comte de la Vaulx, asked to account for
his success as a balloonist, once replied briefly: 'Sang froid, toujours sang froid!', but Lunardi's blood was never cold. Yet his
faults are so transparent in his writing that they become endearing.
He was a completely honest man and what he lacked in skill and
judgement was recompensed by great courage. Gallant and generous
to a fault, young and extremely handsome, addicted to glittering
uniforms, Lunardi was irresistible to women.

He first obtained permission from the Governor, Sir George
Howard, to make an ascent from the grounds of Chelsea Hospital.
In return he promised to divide any profits among the pensioners.
This was in July 1784 and a subscription was next launched to cover
the cost of making a hydrogen balloon. Subscribers would be entitled to admission to the Lyceum, Exeter Change, in the Strand,
where the balloon would be built and exhibited, and to a special
enclosure at Chelsea. Sir Joseph Banks, President of the Royal
Society, was the first to subscribe, but despite this influential lead
the money came in slowly and it was not until mid August that
enough had been raised to complete the balloon. 33 ft in diameter,
giving a capacity of 18,200 cubic feet, it was duly admired by the
subscribers as it hung, filled with air, under the dome of the Lyceum.
Constructed from 520 yards of oiled silk in alternate gores of red and
white, it was judged mightily handsome.

In his advertisement of the coming ascent, Lunardi claimed that
his balloon was constructed 'on a plan entirely novel, and which has
originated in this Metropolis, from the ingenuity of a Gentleman,
who is to ascend with it.' Whether for 'Gentleman' we should read

5

Lunardi or his friend and patron George Biggin, who planned to ascend with him, is not clear. Biggin was an Etonian, a distinguished patron of the arts, an amateur chemist and the inventor of a coffee percolator. Certainly whoever designed the balloon deserves credit which past historians have been singularly reluctant to award. They dismiss Lunardi as an inexperienced amateur when compared with the Montgolfiers or Charles. It is true that in one respect Lunardi's balloon was inferior to that of Charles in that it had no valve at its north pole. This made it impossible for the pilot to descend at will by releasing gas; it was also dangerous, for the issue of gas from the neck was the only means of relieving the pressure caused by expansion under heat or at high altitude. But in other respects the English design revealed the latest French practice. For the net of Lunardi's balloon covered two-thirds of the envelope and terminated in 45 cords supporting a small wooden ring – which Lunardi himself called a hoop – below the balloon. To this hoop the car lines were attached, an arrangement first used on a hydrogen balloon by Blanchard on 2nd March, 1784. Moreover, the car was no baroque, boat-like object but a simple, functional, rectangular basket consisting of a light framework over which netting was stretched. These were considerable improvements.

So far all had gone smoothly, if slowly, for Lunardi, but there was trouble ahead. During this August, two attempts were made to forestall him. A gentleman described as the 'learned Chevalier de Moret, a genius for distinguished discoveries' announced his intention of ascending from Five Fields Row, Chelsea, on 4th August in a 'Grand Aerostatic Globe of the immortal M. Montgolfier, just arrived in this Capital from Paris in its progress to the University of Oxford'. This was a fantastic affair in the shape of a Chinese temple and it should have been obvious to the most gullible that the so-called Chevalier was a charlatan. After a postponement of a week this quack busied himself about his crazy aerial temple for three hours, consuming much straw but producing no apparent result whatever. Convinced that they had been defrauded, the enraged crowd broke through the barriers and a major riot ensued from which de Moret was lucky to escape with his life. The balloon was burnt, its remains torn to fragments and a great deal of damage done to surrounding property.

The second attempt, though honest, was equally ineffectual. Its originator was Dr John Sheldon, a distinguished but somewhat eccentric anatomist whose collection of anatomical specimens included the embalmed corpse of his departed spouse, an exhibit which his guests found somewhat disconcerting. One of the first English balloon enthusiasts, the doctor ordered Allen Keegan, an umbrella maker in the Strand, to construct a Montgolfière for him. When finished, this was 80 ft in diameter and 84 ft high, the largest balloon so far made in Britain. The 7 ft diameter fire basket was fitted with a hinged lid to act as a monster snuffer in case of emergency. At its first trial in Lord Foley's grounds in Portland Place on 16th August the balloon was damaged after one very modest captive ascent and the crowd dispersed, grumbling angrily. No further attempt was made until 29th September when the balloon was completely destroyed by fire, snuffer notwithstanding.

Although these failures left the field clear for Lunardi, they prejudiced his project seriously. Their effect was to make the London public completely cynical about balloon ascents and to turn the authorities against them for fear of further riots. Thus, three days after the de Moret fiasco, Lunardi received a letter from Sir George Howard withdrawing his permission to use the grounds of Chelsea Hospital. 'I am now sunk into the utmost depth of distress' he confided to a friend. However, the ladies who flocked to the Lyceum, ostensibly to inspect the balloon but in reality to dote upon their handsome hero, soon restored the spirits of the susceptible aeronaut. 'Many of them,' he wrote, 'wish I were not engaged to Mr Biggin that they might accompany me; and with that bewitching air of sincerity which is almost peculiar to the women of this country, and which I think more difficult to resist than the coquetry of my own, they express a tender regard for my safety which fixes my determination; and I will ascend, if I do it from the street.'

So, like a knight in tourney with a lady's gage upon his helm, the gallant Lunardi galloped once more into the fray. After a great deal of lobbying he managed to win the support of Sir Watkin Lewis, Captain General of the Honourable Artillery Company, who, after a violent debate, secured with his casting vote the agreement of the Court of Assistants to the use of the Company's training ground at Moorfields by Lunardi. The date of the ascent was fixed for the 15th of September, weather permitting. The Company would appear under arms to preserve law and order, aided by the City Militia and the Peace Officers who would guard the entrances.

No sooner had this difficulty been overcome, however, than further trouble arose. Although more than 20,000 people had been to see the balloon, the majority of whom had paid for admission, the proprietor of the Lyceum now put it under lock and key and refused Lunardi access unless he paid a royalty on the subscriptions he had obtained. Again Lunardi was instantly plunged into despair, so much so that he sent a letter of apology to the Artillery Company regretting that he could not fulfil his engagement. Feeling that it had been deceived, the Company demanded immediate payment of 100 guineas, otherwise the hydrogen generating apparatus, which was already on the ground, would be thrown out next morning. But help was at hand for the distracted aeronaut. Sir Watkin Lewis and a friend named Kirwan pacified the Artillery Company by standing surety, and Lunardi was granted a warrant for the removal of the balloon, if necessary by force. With the aid of a posse of police the balloon was seized from the Lyceum and taken under guard to Moorfields on the afternoon of 14th September. 'Behold me,' wrote Lunardi, 'exhausted with fatigue, anxiety and distress at the eve of an undertaking that requires my being collected, cool and easy in mind.'

The task of filling the balloon was entrusted to a Doctor George Fordyce, a general practitioner and chemist who had designed an 'improved' hydrogen generator. This consisted of two overhead cisterns of lead containing a mixture of sulphuric acid and water, the latter being pumped up to them as required by 'an engine'. From these cisterns the dilute acid gravitated into two large casks containing iron filings and zinc. The gas generated in the casks entered a receiver through a non-return valve and passed thence to the balloon through an alkaline solution to correct its acidity. This last feature was certainly an improvement, but the apparatus was evidently imperfect and generated at such a slow rate that, although the ascent was not advertised to take place until between noon and 1 p.m., it was decided to go on filling all through the previous night. Lunardi was determined to take no chances; his greatest fear was that he would suffer the fate of de Moret if the ascent was long delayed.

Doctor Fordyce superintended operations until midnight when he retired, leaving his henchmen in charge of the apparatus, but when he returned at 4 a.m. he found that they were hopelessly drunk and that no more gas had entered the balloon. It is doubtful whether the doctor himself was in much better shape for he was notoriously addicted to the bottle. Gossip related that when he was summoned one night to the bedside of a prostrate lady he found he was incapable of taking her pulse and muttered to himself, 'Drunk, by God!' Next day he received a handsome fee from the patient accompanied by a note confessing that his diagnosis was quite correct but begging him not to divulge the guilty secret. It was asking for trouble to entrust night-operations to a crew so fond of 'something to keep the cold out', and the loss of at least four hours filling time would have proved fatal to the venture had not Aimé Argand providentially arrived on the scene next morning. Describing the event in a letter to Matthew Boulton, Argand wrote: 'Yesterday for Lunardi's good fortune, I would go and be present at his going up in his balloon and put everything to rights of which he knew little, so that all was well . . .'

The weather that morning was perfect and an immense crowd estimated at 150,000 thronged the perimeter of the ground, though there were not many on the ground itself because of the fear that the proceedings might end in another riot. Certainly the situation hovered on the brink of chaos all morning. First the rumour that a mad bullock was loose caused a panic stampede. Next a wooden scaffold crowded with spectators collapsed with a rending crash. Then a furious affray broke out as people began pelting the occupants of coaches which had parked in front of them and blocked their view. There was more scuffling, shouting and excitement when a pickpocket was seized and ducked in a nearby pond.

In the midst of such a Hogarthian scene, poor Lunardi must have felt that he might soon suffer the fate of the pickpocket, if not something far worse, since no guards could restrain such a crowd if they once ran riot. For despite the skilful efforts of Argand to regain lost time, he could not perform miracles. One o'clock passed – half past one – and still the gay envelope was limp. The impatient muttering of the crowd became as ominous as distant thunder. The situation was perilous. Lunardi had not only his own safety to consider but that of the privileged group about the balloon which included the Prince of Wales and a number of members of Parliament. As two o'clock drew near it was agreed, after a hurried consultation with his co-adventurer George Biggin, that Lunardi should ascend alone in the still incompletely filled balloon. In view of the absence of any valve, perhaps this was just as well.

Accordingly, Lunardi stepped into the car. With him went a cat and a dog, a pigeon in a cage, a bottle of wine, a cold chicken and other eatables. He was also equipped with two 'wings' and two 'oars' with which he optimistically supposed that he could control his flight at will both horizontally and vertically by rowing.

In contrast to the Parisians, the temper of the London crowd was extremely sceptical. The commonality was convinced that ballooning was no more than an elaborate hoax and looked forward to another rough house; even the more intelligent believed that if Lunardi *did* ascend he would not be seen again alive. So it was that when the aeronaut gave the 'hands off' signal and the balloon rose in the air, all the gentlemen present followed the example of the Prince of Wales by removing their hats and standing in reverent silence. At the same time the King, who was in conference with his Ministers, broke off the meeting with the observation: 'We may resume our deliberations on the subject before us at pleasure, but we may never see poor Lunardi again.' Whereupon the King and Pitt followed the course of the balloon through telescopes until it passed out of sight.

Meanwhile the object of their anxious scrutiny was enjoying himself hugely. His evanescent spirits had soared up with the balloon. Unfortunately, in the excitement of departure, the foodstuffs had got mixed with the sand ballast, but he managed to rescue a leg from the chicken which he gnawed contentedly and, having drunk several glasses of wine, felt himself 'filled with calm delight'. There was really nothing better than ballooning, he decided. 'The broomsticks of witches', he wrote, 'Ariosto's flying horse, and even Milton's sunbeam conveying the angel to earth, have all an idea of effort, difficulty and restraint, which do not affect a voyage in a balloon.'

Wrapped in that breathless calm and silence which can only be experienced in a free balloon, the entranced Lunardi floated away over North London and into the fields of Hertfordshire while below him scepticism turned to incredulous wonderment. A jury hastily acquitted a prisoner so that they might rush from the court to see the balloon. Floating low over a group of harvesters, Lunardi hailed them cheerfully through his 'speaking trumpet' but heard only 'a confused noise' in reply. His cat now appeared to be feeling the cold so he decided to land. On his ascent he had broken and dropped one of his 'oars.' (He afterwards recounted with romantic relish that: 'A gentlewoman, mistaking the broken oar for my person, was so affected by my supposed destruction that she died a few days later.') No matter, despite this mishap Lunardi convinced himself that he had succeeded in rowing himself down into a cornfield belonging to a certain John Hunter Gubbins of North Mimms. Here, at 3.30, he landed the unhappy cat and discharged what remained of his sand ballast. He then shot up once more, cheerfully throwing out knives and forks, his empty wine bottle and a letter secured to a handkerchief with a corkscrew. In this way he achieved his greatest altitude. Again defying all the laws of aerodynamics, he finally rowed himself down into a large field near the farm of Thomas Read in the parish of Standon near Ware. The time was five minutes after four o'clock. Lunardi called out to the men who were working at harvest in the field to come and hold the rope he had thrown out, but they ran from him shouting that they would have nothing to do with one who came on the Devil's horse and it fell to a woman to put them to shame.

Elizabeth Brett was working in farmer Read's brewhouse and ran out when she heard the shouting because she thought the men were crying harvest home. It was a strange harvest indeed that she saw in the field, but the handsome young man under the great billowing globe of red and white silk was calling urgently for help and without hesitation she ran forward to seize the rope. The men sheepishly turned and followed her; Lunardi stepped out of the car; the first aerial flight in England was over. Soon his health was being toasted in the Bull Inn at Ware by those who had followed the balloon from London.

The field in which Lunardi landed was by some called Long Mead and by others Etna because of a great fire of hedge-timber that burned there at the time of the enclosures. In it there was erected a monument which stands to this day. It bears the inscription:

Let Posterity know
And knowing be astonished!
That
On the 15th day of September, 1784
Vincent Lunardi
of
Lucca in Tuscany
The First Aerial Traveller in Britain
Mounting from the Artillery Ground
in London
And traversing the Regions of the Air
For two Hours and fifteen Minutes
in this Spot
Revisited the Earth.
On this rude Monument
For Ages be recorded
That wonderous enterprize, successfully
achieved
By the powers of Chymistry
And the fortitude of man
That improvement in Science
Which
The Great Author of all Knowledge
Patronising by his Providence
The Inventions of Mankind
Hath generously permitted
To their Benefit
And
His own Eternal Glory

Lunardi's triumph was complete. If the world's acclaim had been his goal he certainly achieved it. In print his name was eulogized everywhere from columns in the newspapers to hastily produced street ballads. For several weeks the balloon (not forgetting the dog and cat) was exhibited in the Pantheon in Oxford Street. A special silver medal was struck. Testimonial subscriptions were opened in clubs and coffee houses. He was presented at Court. Modest ladies appeared in Lunardi bonnets and less modest ones in Lunardi garters. All this adulation caused some of those with a serious interest in 'aerostation' such as Cavallo to regard Lunardi somewhat sourly as a spoiled young man. But however true this may have been, at least he was not content to rest upon these laurels; instead they spurred him on to further efforts.

He proceeded to construct a bigger and better balloon and to decorate its envelope with the Union Jack in token of 'his regard and attachment to everything that is English.' After exhibiting this balloon during the winter, he announced that he would ascend from the Artillery Ground on 13th May accompanied, not only by the faithful George Biggin but also by a lady named Mrs Sage. But alas, the patient George was again disappointed and so was the lady for the balloon had insufficient lift and for the second time Lunardi went up alone. According to Mrs Sage the balloon was not fully inflated, but it was certainly defective, losing gas so fast that it came down near the Adam and Eve Gardens in Tottenham Court Road after a flight of less than thirty minutes.

The next ascent, from St George's Fields, Newington Butts before a great crowd on 29th June, was more successful although once again Lunardi misjudged his balloon's lifting power. He had announced this time that he would carry up three passengers, a Colonel Hastings as well as Biggin and Mrs Sage, but the balloon proved quite unequal to the task. This is not surprising, for although Mrs Sage is represented in contemporary pictures as a ravishing beauty, her charms were evidently of a very ample kind for on her own admission she weighed 200 lb or over 14 stone. A somewhat embarrassing situation was saved by the gallantry of Lunardi and the Colonel who stood down and left the car to Biggin and the lady.

With admirable composure 'The First English Female Aerial Traveller' noted down her impressions of the voyage in a book which she had brought for the purpose and subsequently published them in the form of 'A Letter Addressed to a Female Friend'. She expressed herself 'infinitely better pleased . . . than I ever was at any former event of my life.' The fact that her companion had never been airborne before either, makes the intrepid lady's sang froid the more admirable, though Biggin appears to have been as cool as she and to have handled the balloon with excellent judgement. As they floated gently over St James's Park and Piccadilly, the couple sat down to a lunch of chicken and ham washed down with 'Florence wine', throwing the empties nonchalantly over the side.

After flying for an hour, Biggin brought the balloon down to a good landing in a field near Harrow. He had planned to ascend again without the lady but was frustrated by the arrival of a furious farmer who accused them of damaging his crops. He was, wrote Mrs Sage, 'abusive and savage to a degree', but from this ugly situation they were rescued by the timely arrival of a party of boys from Harrow School.

After this, Lunardi left London with his balloon to make some provincial conquests. By the end of the year (1785) he had made ascents from Liverpool (twice), Edinburgh (twice), Kelso and Glasgow (twice). He wrote minutely detailed accounts of all these voyages which were subsequently ably summarized by J. E. Hodgson. He was widely praised for his courage in ascending under adverse weather conditions in order not to disappoint his public, but in this respect, like many another aeronaut after him, Lunardi was faced with a choice of evils and evidently preferred an angry sky to an angry crowd. By forcing aeronauts to take off ill prepared or under dangerous conditions, this fickleness of the public, whose cheers could in an instant turn to jeers, accounts for more accidents and tragedies than any other single factor in the history of ballooning.

Lunardi's second ascent from Liverpool was particularly venturesome, not to say foolhardy, for a north-west wind was blowing so strongly that even the exacting spectators relented, crying 'Don't let him go up, don't let him go up!' Lunardi, wearing a resplendant uniform, dramatically drew his sword and swore that he would cut off the hands that held down the balloon if his 'hands off' signal were not instantly obeyed. To avoid collision with nearby buildings he jettisoned a quantity of ballast, shot up 'swifter than a Rocket' and in four minutes had been blown out of sight of Liverpool. Little over an hour later he came down in a cornfield near Tarporley, but his anchor would not hold and he suffered the most terrifying and dangerous experience that can befall a balloonist – that of being dragged helplessly along, or a little above, the ground at the mercy of the wind. The balloon tore through hedges and trees, demolished the chimney of a cottage in the village of Tiverton and was finally brought to rest with the help of several countrymen in a lane near Beeston Castle.

After this adventure the balloon was taken to Chester where, on

8th September, Lunardi allowed a local man, Thomas Baldwin, to make a solo ascent from the yard of Chester Castle. Baldwin managed very well, making an intermediate landing near Frodsham and a final one on Rixton Moss, five miles from Warrington. He subsequently published a minutely detailed account of his adventure under the title *Airopaidia*. Its style is extravagant, prolix and boring, but it is remarkable for two things. First, it contains the first aerial views ever printed, representing drawings made by Baldwin from the car. Secondly, Baldwin suggests the use of a trail rope to control the altitude of a balloon. This idea is generally credited to the famous aeronaut Charles Green, and its function will be described later.

Nothing does Lunardi more credit than the respect and deference that he displayed towards the unfortunate Tytler when he visited Edinburgh. He followed Charles's courteous example by asking Tytler to release a small trial balloon before his ascent, and he may also have helped the unfortunate man financially. In return, the grateful Tytler penned some verses in Lunardi's praise. Perhaps it was as well that Lunardi thus set store in heaven, for his own nemesis was soon to come.

After a triumphantly successful ascent from Kettlewell's Orchard, near the Minster at York, on 23rd August, 1786, Lunardi proceeded to Newcastle-on-Tyne and it was here, when he was preparing to ascend from the Spital Ground before a large crowd that disaster struck. The balloon had been partially filled when an accident to the gas generator distracted the attention of those restraining the balloon, causing them to let go their hold. The balloon shot up, carrying with it a young man named Ralph Heron whose arm had somehow become entangled in the anchor rope. The balloon had risen above the height of the nearby church of St Nicholas when either the rope gave way or Heron lost his hold. He fell to earth with such force that he sank up to his knees in a flower-bed. He died shortly after in the presence of his parents who had witnessed this, the first fatal aerial accident in Britain.

Now although Lunardi was in no way to blame for a tragedy which deeply distressed him, it finished his aeronautical career in Britain. Flattery instantly turned to fury. He had much ado to escape from an angry, menacing crowd and he was bitterly attacked in the local press as an unscrupulous adventurer trading on popular credulity in order to line his pockets. He who had so lately been portrayed as an heroic figure now became the subject for cruel cartoons. One of these depicted him as a beggar with a balloon on his back and was entitled 'The Itinerant Aeronaut, or Aerostation out at elbows.' The ballad-mongers, too, quickly changed their tune:

> *Behold an Hero comely, tall and fair,*
> *His only food phlogisticated air,*
> *Now on the wings of Mighty Winds he rides;*
> *Now torn through Hedges, Dash'd in Ocean's Tides;*
> *Now drooping roams about from Town to Town*
> *Collecting pence t'inflate his poor balloon*
> *Pity the Wight and something to him give*
> *To purchase gas to keep his frame alive.*

Such is the fickleness of popular fame.

After making some experiments with an invention for saving life at sea, Lunardi left England never to return. He continued his aeronautical career by making a number of successful and adventurous balloon ascents, first in his native Italy at Rome, Palermo and Naples and finally in Spain and Portugal. Here he again won the acclaim that was so sweet to him. Once, when he landed at Horcajo in Spain the villagers took him for a saint come down from heaven and carried him in triumph to their church. In Portugal his health began to fail him and he died in a convent at Barbadinas, Lisbon, on 31st July, 1806.

As a courageous pioneer Lunardi deserves his place in the history of flight although, as has been said, he was not a great aeronaut being too impulsive, too concerned to cut a dashing figure to learn with patience the subtle art of ballooning. Thus although he publicized that art greatly he did not advance it. As the flights of Biddle and Baldwin showed, given good weather conditions it was perfectly possible for an intelligent novice to make a safe and successful flight; so also did the sheep, the cock and the duck at Versailles. The ability to hit an easy ball with a bat does not make a great cricketer. The ability, however, to sustain a long balloon flight under variable weather conditions and then make a safe landing calls for the greatest skill and judgement in the use of the valve and the ballast.

In order to understand why this should be so it is important to remember that a balloon is always submerged in an element of varying density – the atmosphere. When a balloon rises from the earth as an air bubble rises from the bottom of the sea the weight of the atmosphere surrounding it is progressively reduced until, in theory, it will reach a point of perfect equilibrium; an exact altitude at which, assuming no loss of gas through the fabric, it should be capable of floating indefinitely. In practice, however, such a state of equilibrium can never be achieved. The momentum of the balloon causes it to overshoot the point of equilibrium and this brings about an additional loss of gas through the neck due to expansion under reduced atmospheric pressure. Owing to this additional loss of gas, when the balloon does cease to climb it will not be in equilibrium but will immediately begin to descend. Obviously the more rapidly the balloon ascends the greater will be the margin above the equilibrium point and the more unbalanced it will be at the peak of its climb.

At this critical peak, the discharge of only a minute quantity of ballast will be sufficient to correct the unbalance and so bring the balloon to a state of equilibrium. But the balloon rapidly gains momentum as it descends with the effect that the longer this corrective action is deferred the greater will be the weight of ballast which must be discharged in order to prevent a precipitate return to earth. Such a delayed discharge of a substantial weight of ballast means that the balloon will again overshoot considerably before it reaches what might be called the critical trough and begins to ascend again. Then, having been so much lightened, it will climb with great rapidity, overshooting its critical peak by an even greater margin than before. The ascent may be so rapid that it becomes necessary to open the valve in order to check it, thus losing gas that a more prudent and skilful aeronaut would conserve.

It can be understood from this that a balloon flight undertaken by an unskilful pilot can speedily develop into a series of rapid ascents and descents, each more rapid and far-reaching than the last until loss of gas and ballast enforce a landing. Obviously a safe minimum of ballast must be retained for landing purposes in order to check the rate of descent on approaching the earth, another operation that calls for nice judgement.

The most skilful aeronaut is he who can keep his balloon as nearly as possible to a state of equilibrium although in practice the ideal of perfect balance can never be achieved because of other variables which operate upon the balloon. These are meteorological changes of atmospheric pressure and changes of temperature. A hot sun shining on the envelope rapidly expands the gas and so increases the balloon's lift and therefore its rate of climb, but if the sun, or the balloon itself, should be lost in cloud the effect will be equally rapidly reversed. For this reason it is easier to navigate a free balloon at night because it is not then subject to such wide and rapid variations of temperature.

The importance of checking the descent of a balloon at the earliest possible moment was soon appreciated by the pioneer aeronauts, but with a mercury barometer as their only measure of altitude this was easier said than done. Suspended in a breathless calm far above the earth, it was impossible to tell either from the barometer or from sensation or observation whether the balloon was rising or falling until it had attained a considerable velocity. The earliest check devised was that of throwing small pieces of paper or feathers out of the car and observing whether they appeared to rise or fall. Mrs Sage describes George Biggin doing just this on their flight over London and he must obviously have been briefed by Lunardi.

In fairness to Lunardi, these factors governing the art of ballooning were not fully understood by any of the pioneer aeronauts. They had to be learned in the hard school of experience and Lunardi was by no means the only man to fly by guess and by God or to cherish theories that time would prove quite false. That his countryman, Count Zambeccari, was equally misguided is revealed in his narrative of a perilous flight from London on 23rd March, 1785.

Zambeccari had returned to London in the autumn of 1784 and had completed his balloon before the end of the year. He advertised his ascent from Tottenham Court Road with Admiral Sir Edward Vernon and a Miss Grist, but, like Lunardi, he had misjudged the lift available and the lady had to be removed from the car with what the Count called 'gentle force'. This was just as well in view of what was to follow. The wind was so strong that the balloon was damaged in its ascent and, in carrying out hurried repairs to the neck, the cord controlling the valve was lost inside the envelope. Next, when the balloon was well above the clouds, three of the cords suspending the car broke, whereupon the Admiral expressed a 'Desire of approaching nearer to the Surface of the Earth'. The Count's illogical response to this was promptly to throw overboard the last remaining sack of ballast, arguing that since he was unable to use the valve, this would make the balloon lose gas more rapidly. What the Admiral thought of this manoeuvre the Count does not record. It was probably not printable for the loss of a whole sack of ballast caused the balloon to shoot up so high that they soon found themselves in the thick of a snowstorm. To add to their discomfort, the balloon began to revolve like a tee-to-tum. After all these unnerving happenings they were very lucky to make a safe landing in a ploughed field near Horsham, an hour after leaving London.

Although an Italian was first into the English air, an Englishman was not far behind him. On 4th October, 1784, less than three weeks after Lunardi's first flight, James Sadler ascended from Oxford in a Montgolfière in the early hours of the morning. The son of Thomas Sadler, a pastrycook and confectioner in the High Street of Oxford, this first of English aeronauts was a remarkable man, a skilful and daring pilot and an ingenious inventor. It would seem that instead of an open fire basket his Montgolfière was fitted with a form of stove having a damper by means of which he could control the admission of hot air or shut it off entirely. Into the calm air of an autumn dawn, Sadler rose successfully to a height of 3,600 ft. He had hoped that light airs would carry him as far as Woodstock, but he had the misfortune to drop his firing fork overboard with the result that the stove burned low and the balloon floated gently down to land between Islip and Woodeaton.

Evidently Sadler decided not to repeat his Montgolfière experiment, for his next ascent was made in a hydrogen balloon from the Physic Garden, Oxford on 12th November in the same year. This time he went up at 1 p.m. in the presence of a large crowd and a strong southwesterly wind swept him very rapidly over Otmoor and Thame. Only seventeen minutes after take-off, Sadler came down to a very rough landing on the estate of Sir William Lee at Hartwell, near Aylesbury, fourteen miles away. The balloon dragged for some distance and finally blew into a tree where it was completely destroyed, but luckily Sadler escaped injury.

On his next ascent from Moulsey Hurst on 5th May, 1785, Sadler was accompanied by the statesman William Windham, then M.P. for Norwich, who prudently made his will and left a letter to be opened in the event of his death. Sadler had not yet mastered the art of balloon management, for the flight consisted of a series of violent ascents and descents accompanied by the discharge of a great deal of ballast. They finally landed near the mouth of the Medway where the balloon escaped them and was blown out to sea. It was subsequently picked up by a Sunderland-bound collier off the Nore. From the grounds of Strawberry Hill, Horace Walpole had observed the balloon as it drifted down the Thames valley looking 'not bigger than my snuff-box.'

Sadler made four more ascents in 1785, two from Manchester in May and two from Worcester in August/September. On his second Manchester ascent he rose to 13,000 ft and travelled fifty miles to a landing at Pontefract. On this occasion he was badly injured when the balloon dragged him for two miles and eventually escaped him. It was later recovered from a field near Gainsborough.

His first flight from Worcester ended in a safe landing at Stretton Grandison in Herefordshire, but his second was very alarming. A strong southerly wind swept him up to Lichfield where he attempted a landing under most difficult conditions. The balloon dragged him for no less than five miles across country until he finally fell out of it whereupon the balloon shot upwards and was never seen again.

Perhaps it was this terrifying experience, coupled with the loss of his balloon that determined Sadler to stay on terra firma and devote his energies to the improvement of the steam engine. He patented a rotary engine and experimented with the application of steam-power to road vehicles. It was the latter activity, never a popular one with James Watt, which led Watt to dismiss him as 'a hunter of shadows'. Undeterred, however, Sadler, in collaboration with Thomas Beddoes, designed a very remarkable single-acting tandem compound rotative winding engine which circumvented the Watt patent and was used with success by the Coalbrookdale Company. In 1796 he joined the Board of Naval Works as a chemist and soon afterwards superintended the erection of the first steam engine at Portsmouth Dockyard. But the call of the air proved too strong for this remarkable man for, as we shall see, in 1810, twenty-four years after his

"The First Female Aeronaut": Madame Thible ascends from Lyons in the Montgolfière *Le Gustave*, June, 1784

First flight in Italy: Count Paolo Andreani ascends from Milan in a Montgolfière, February, 1784

First to fly in England: Vincent Lunardi, from the
portrait miniature by Cosway

Lunardi's balloon displayed in the Pantheon, 1784

accident at Lichfield, Sadler returned to ballooning, this time with his two sons.

Nothing if not ambitious, in the late autumn of 1784 Sadler had determined to fly across the English Channel from Dover, and for this purpose he constructed a new balloon which he calculated should remain in the air for twelve hours. In December he consigned it by barge down the Thames to London but, alas, the barge was held up by bad weather for more than a fortnight and when it finally arrived Sadler found to his dismay that the fresh varnish had stuck the folded fabric of the envelope together inextricably. A few days after this heartbreaking discovery he learned that he had been forestalled; the Channel had been conquered by the French aeronaut Blanchard.

CHAPTER FIVE

Peril on the Sea

I T SOON BECAME EVIDENT that there was money in ballooning. Not only would people pay to witness an ascent from close
quarters, but there were wealthy enthusiasts prepared to finance
a flight and reward the pilot handsomely in return for a place in the
car. So there came into being a class of professional aeronauts. Jean
Pierre Blanchard was the forerunner of these professionals and one
of the most celebrated.

Born of poor parents at Les Andelys in Normandy in 1753, Blanchard had little formal education but soon began to display a natural
aptitude for mechanics. At the age of sixteen he constructed a
'velocipede', in other words an ancestor of the bicycle. He then
became fascinated by the problem of flight and after studying the
flight of birds he constructed what he called a 'Vaisseau Volant'. This
weird and wonderful machine was an aerial adaptation of his velocipede in which two foot treadles and two hand levers were used
to actuate four flapping wings. Beneath the wings of this ornithopter the athletic pilot sat in a completely enclosed buoy-shaped
cockpit.

Although this device was quite incapable of leaving the ground,
it was seriously reported that Blanchard had succeeded in raising
himself 80 ft into the air. One public demonstration was in fact
staged, but 'rain stopped play' and Blanchard merely read a paper
about his invention in which he claimed for it a speed of 75 miles
an hour. This must have been disappointing for the spectators but
very much easier and safer for Blanchard.

Then came the successful experiments of the Montgolfiers and
Charles. Blanchard decided he would adopt the balloon for lift
but retain his flapping wings for propulsion. On his first balloon he
also introduced as a safety measure a parachute between the envelope
and the car. In experimenting with parachutes Blanchard was a

pioneer, but this particular application was unsound. It was subsequently found by experience that if a balloon burst in the air and the lower part of the deflated envelope was allowed to fly up into the net, the balloon became a parachute capable of bearing its passengers to earth, violently perhaps, but not fatally. Had such a misfortune befallen Blanchard, his small parachute would have been more of a hindrance than a help.[1]

Blanchard's first ascent in this curious vessel from the Champ de Mars on 2nd March, 1784, got off to a bad start. He had intended to ascend with a Benedictine monk named Pesch but an over-enthusiastic young man named Dupont de Chambon insisted that he must accompany them. Exasperated by Blanchard's repeated refusals, the impetuous de Chambon leapt into the car, drew a sword, wounded Blanchard in the left hand, slashed at the rigging and broke one of the wings before he could be restrained. After making extempore repairs, Blanchard ascended alone and made a short flight ending at Billancourt. So confident was he in the power of his wings to control his flight that he had announced his intention to land at La Villette, but an unkind wind carried him in the opposite direction.

This failure, however, could be blamed upon the damage caused by de Chambon and on his next two ascents from Rouen on 23rd May and 18th July Blanchard stubbornly persisted in his wing flapping. On the second of these flights he was accompanied by a M. Dominique Boby and in his account of it Blanchard wrote: 'I therefore struggled against the wind in presenting to it the convexity of my wings which I agitated with great force. This enabled me to turn to the west, after which I shifted my wings inversely and found with pleasure that we had escaped the current . . .' He also claimed that he was able to land without valving gas or using ballast. Thus Blanchard, like Lunardi – who doubtless took the idea from him – deluded himself that he could in fact control his flight by rowing with his 'wings'.

These ascents by Blanchard failed to win the attention and acclaim he had hoped for. In France, the honours had been fairly won

[1] It has been suggested that Blanchard may have intended to release the balloon and then propel the car and parachute with the wings. This is most unlikely, though such an experiment was tried in 1853–4 by the Frenchman François Letur and in 1874 by the Belgian, Vincent de Groof. Both were killed when demonstrating their 'dirigible parachutes' at Cremorne Gardens.

by the Montgolfiers and Pilâtre de Rozier, by Charles and the brothers Robert. Blanchard was but one of a number of aeronauts so after one more flight from Bordeaux on 26th July, he packed up his balloon and journeyed to London in August 1784, to seek fame in a country where competition was not yet so keen. Here he quickly became the focal point of a small group of balloon enthusiasts consisting of Lord Foley, the Duchess of Devonshire, Major Gardner, Lord Orford, Major Money, Dr John Sheldon and Dr John Jeffries. The last named was an American, born at Boston in 1744, who took his medical degree in England and subsequently practised here for about ten years before returning to Boston in 1789 where he remained until his death in 1819. Associated with the celebrated surgeon, John Hunter, Jeffries was a man of considerable means who was living in Cavendish Square at this time. He was noted for his scientific interests, particularly in the field of meteorology.

In fact if not in name, this little coterie became a 'Balloon Club', extending a welcome to any visiting aeronaut. Faujas de Saint-Fond and Count Paolo Andreani were both entertained in 1784 and early in 1785 no less a person than Pilâtre de Rozier paid them a visit. He and Blanchard were dined and wined at Strawberry Hill by Horace Walpole and Lord Orford.

Blanchard was as much of an exhibitionist as Lunardi, but he lacked the latter's endearing frankness and generosity. He was indeed a ruthless egotist, a mean-spirited and jealous man, a prima donna of the air who begrudged others the smallest share of his limelight. But though his personality was unattractive, the courage and skill of this small, slight man was such that even men like Sheldon and Jeffries, who suffered much from Blanchard, forgot his defects of character in their admiration for his ability as an aeronaut.

On his first ascent in England Blanchard was accompanied by Sheldon who paid all the expenses of the flight. This took place from Lochee's Military Academy, Chelsea on 16th October, 1784. The boat-shaped car was loaded with provisions, a basket of pigeons, a quantity of scientific instruments brought by Sheldon and the aeronaut's lap dog. Thus encumbered, the balloon rose too sluggishly to clear surrounding trees and buildings whereupon Blanchard, piqued, it is said, by having to share the honours with Sheldon, promptly threw out all the latter's instruments. Having been so expensively lightened, the balloon rose, floating away on an easterly wind over Hammersmith, Chiswick and Twickenham. On this occasion Blanchard was not only carrying his useless wings and a rudder but what he called his *moulinet* or rotating fan. Although this hand-operated device was no more able to influence the course of the balloon than the wings, it was the first application of a screw pro-peller to an aircraft. 'During the voyage,' wrote Blanchard, 'the fly, acting on the air as a screw, appeared to me as the most simple and efficacious mode which an aeronaut can adopt to advance in a calm.'

Blanchard landed Sheldon at Sunbury and, having added ballast to within 20 lb of his companion's weight, took off once more and eventually came down at Romsey, seventy-three miles from London. Blanchard's accounts of his flights are apt to resemble the tales of Baron Munchausen. On this one he claimed that he dropped his flag but by valving gas was able to descend so fast that he recovered the flag before it landed. He also claimed, as on his first flight from the Champ de Mars, that he reached an altitude 'never before attained by man'. This may be doubted. Sheldon never ascended again. He wrongly claimed to have been the first Englishman to fly, presumably unaware that he had been forestalled by James Sadler.

It was now the turn of Jeffries to pay for the privilege of a flight with Blanchard. They ascended from Mackenzie's Rhedarium be-tween Park Lane and Park Street, Mayfair on 30th November in the presence of the Prince of Wales and a distinguished company. Again the balloon had difficulty in clearing the surrounding trees and buildings, but Jeffries seems to have been able to manage the can-tankerous aeronaut with more success than Sheldon, for he con-trived to hang on to his scientific paraphernalia. This included vacuum flasks presented to him by Cavendish with the object of collecting specimens of the upper air. After a voyage of two hours they landed on Stone Marsh near the village of Ingress in Kent.

For both these flights Aimé Argand planned and operated the hydrogen generator and made an excellent job of filling the balloon. After the October flight he boasted to Matthew Boulton: 'I was very successful in filling the balloon in two hours and half the expense.'

It was immediately after their first ascent together that Blanchard

and Jeffries began to plan the most famous of all Blanchard's achievements, the first crossing of the English Channel by air. It may well
have been Jeffries who first suggested the adventure; he certainly
made all the arrangements and covered the whole cost of the voyage,
a substantial sum exceeding £700. Yet notwithstanding this generous sponsorship, Blanchard did his utmost to deny his patron a place
in the car so that he might reserve the glory for himself alone.

At the end of the year 1784 the balloon, with its generating
apparatus, was transported to Dover Castle where extraordinary
scenes took place when Blanchard literally entrenched himself and
denied Jeffries access. Recruiting a strong-arm squad of sailors,
Jeffries laid siege to the Castle until, thanks to the tactful mediation
of the castle's Governor, an amicable truce was agreed between the
two aeronauts. Yet Blanchard still had another card to play. The
balloon was inflated by Blanchard with the assistance of the London
aeronaut and balloon maker James Deeker who, a few months later,
would make an eventful ascent from Norwich in a thunderstorm.
When the moment came for the 'weighing on' it appeared that the
slight Blanchard had mysteriously put on a remarkable amount of
weight since his last ascent and Jeffries discovered that he was
wearing a belt weighted with lead under his clothes.

That good relations between the two men were not destroyed
by these manoeuvres and that Jeffries could still refer to Blanchard
as 'my gallant little captain' speaks volumes for the Doctor's philo-
sophy and good humour. He appears to have accepted Blanchard's
perversities as no more than the waywardness of a spoiled child.

On the morning of 7th January, 1785, a fine clear morning after
a frosty night with only a light air blowing from the North North
West, the balloon was carried to the edge of Dover cliff and at 1 p.m.
it was launched away. Cumbered once again with a great deal of
gear including the useless wings, rudder and *moulinet*, the balloon
rose sluggishly over the harbour and it seemed unlikely that it
would ever reach the coast of France unless the wind freshened.

Jeffries subsequently published a long and detailed account of this
historic flight which has often been quoted, but it lacks the graphic
immediacy of a less well known version written very soon after the
event.[1] In this the Doctor wrote:

[1] The copy quoted is in the Poynton Collection.

'Heaven crowned my utmost wishes with success: I cannot describe to you the magnificence and beauty of our voyage. . . . When two-thirds over, we had expended the whole of our ballast. At about five or six miles from the French coast we were again falling rapidly towards the sea, on which occasion my noble little captain gave orders, and set the example, by beginning to strip our aerial car, first of our silk and finery: this not giving us sufficient release, we cast one wing, then the other; after which I was obliged to unscrew and cast away our moulinet; yet still approaching the sea very fast, and the boats being much alarmed for us, we cast away, first one anchor, then the other, after which my little hero stripped and threw away his coat (great coat). On this I was compelled to follow his example. He next cast away his trowsers. We put on our cork jackets and were, God knows how, as merry as grigs to think how we should splatter in the water. We had a fixed cord, &c to mount into our upper story; and I believe both of us, as though inspired, felt ourselves confident of success in the event.

'Luckily, at this instant we found the mercury beginning to fall in the barometer and we soon ascended much higher than ever before, and made a most beautiful *entré* into France exactly at three o'clock. We entered rising, and to such a height that the arch we described brought us down just twelve miles into the country, when we descended most tranquilly[1] into the midst of the forest *De Felmores*, almost as naked as the trees, not an inch of cord or rope left, no anchor or anything to help us, nor a being within several miles. My good little captain begged for all my exertion to stop at the first tree I could reach. I succeeded beyond my comprehension, and you would have laughed to see us, each without a coat of any sort, Mr. Blanchard assisting at the valve, and I holding at the top of a lofty tree, and the balloon playing to and fro over us, holding almost too severe a contest for my arms. It took exactly twenty-eight minutes to let out air (i.e. inflammable air) enough to relieve the balloon without injury. We soon heard the wood surrounded by footmen, horsemen &c and received every possible assistance from them. I was soon well mounted and had a fine gallop of seven miles. . . .'

So ended man's first oversea flight, the first of the many that would be made by adventurous men in the years to come, some triumphant, some tragic, but none quite so richly serio-comic as this pioneer achievement. At the end of their seven miles gallop, the

[1] Having thrown out everything they could including their clothes, the Doctor relates elsewhere that they resorted to what he discreetly terms a 'curious expedient' in a final effort to lighten the balloon and so check its rate of descent.

victorious aeronauts were hospitably entertained at the chateau of a
Monsieur de Saudrouin who later despatched them to Calais in 'an
elegant chariot and six horses'. It was midnight before they arrived
there, but news of their achievement had gone ahead of them, the
city gates were specially opened and they received a tumultuous
welcome. The car of their balloon is still preserved in the Calais
museum and a balloon-topped marble monument, appropriately
inscribed, was erected at their landing place at Guisnes which was,
appropriately enough, near the celebrated Field of the Cloth of
Gold. The aeronauts were later presented to Louis XVI who rewarded Blanchard with a prize of 12,000 livres and a life pension.
Jeffries, who had inspired and financed the enterprise, got nothing
but a little reflected glory, but he evidently accepted this as philoso-
phically as ever.

Two pieces of cargo which the aeronauts did not jettison were a
small bottle of brandy and a parcel of letters tied up in a bladder –
the first air mail. The only item in this historic mail which has
survived is a letter from William Franklin addressed to his son
Temple, now preserved by the American Philosophical Society.
The letters addressed to Louis XVI and Benjamin Franklin have
perished.

When Blanchard returned to London he decided to capitalize his
fame and expend part of his reward on building a Balloon School
or 'Grand Aerostatic Academy', as he called it, in Stockwell Road,
Vauxhall. Here he advertised such entertainments as 'the Diversion
of Hawking with a Balloon' and parachute descents by animals. The
descent of a dog in June 1785 ended fatally but a cat was luckier. In
advertising his own ascents he claimed that he was the only aeronaut
who had succeeded in returning to the exact spot from which he
had ascended and was therefore 'no vain pretender to the noble
science of Aerostation'. This claim rested upon an ascent which
Blanchard made on a calm day in May accompanied by a young
French girl named Simonet. After landing, the aeronaut and his fair
companion were towed back to their starting point by two gentlemen on horse-back. Thus the balloon returned by virtue of a long
length of rope and not by the agency of wings and moulinet as
Blanchard encouraged his readers to believe.

Blanchard evidently expected his Academy to prove a great draw, for his advertisements end with a note on parking arrangements which has a strangely modern ring:

'The road leading to the ground is wide and open on all sides so that several thousand carriages may be ranged in the adjacent ground with the greatest ease. N.B. The Company are particularly requested to order their Coachmen, after having set them down close to the door, to drive on and follow the directions of proper persons, posted at the Gates for that purpose.'

These extravagant hopes were disappointed. The attendance did not come up to expectations and when an attempt to lower a sheep by parachute failed, Blanchard had to give the disgruntled spectators their money back. The end came when a fraudulent Italian, who had announced that he would descend by parachute playing a violin, jumped a mere ten feet. The crowd responded by wrecking the establishment, and Blanchard returned to France.

Back in Europe, Blanchard scored a remarkable number of first ascents in different countries. These were Germany (Frankfurt), Holland (The Hague) and Belgium (Ghent), all in 1785; Switzerland (Basle) 1788, Poland (Warsaw) and Czechoslovakia (Prague) in 1789. His Swiss ascent was particularly dramatic for, finding that he had insufficient gas, he detached the car and ascended hanging from the hoop by four cords. After an ascent from Lille in August 1785 with the Chevalier de L'Espinard, Blanchard travelled 300 miles, a long distance record at that time. For his ascents at Warsaw and Prague, Blanchard used a Montgolfière, but thereafter he returned to the hydrogen balloon. Soon after the French Revolution broke out, Blanchard was accused by the Austrian Government of spreading revolutionary propaganda and was arrested at Kufstein in the Tyrol. He contrived to escape to America where, at Philadelphia on the 9th January, 1793, he made the first aerial flight in the new world – his 45th ascent.

On his return to France in 1798, Blanchard continued his aeronautical career, styling himself in his advertisements 'Adopted Citizen of the Chief Towns of the Two Worlds and Aerial Pensionary of the French Republic.' On an ascent from the Tivoli Gardens, Paris, with the astronomer Lalande he claimed, with undoubted exaggeration, to have reached a height of 32,000 ft. In February

1808, Blanchard made his 60th and last ascent from The Hague in a Montgolfière. When in mid-air he collapsed with a heart attack and landed heavily. Although he subsequently managed to travel back to Paris, he never fully recovered and died on 7th March, 1809. Despite his unloveable character and the extravagant claims he made for himself, Blanchard was unquestionably the most skilful of the first generation of aeronauts.

Pilâtre de Rozier also planned to fly the English Channel, indeed he had hoped to be the first to do so. He was too large and generous a man to begrudge Blanchard his triumph and he is known to have been present at one or more of the latter's ascents from London in May 1785. It was at this time that Pilâtre became engaged to a young Yorkshire girl named Susan Dyer whom he had first met at Boulogne where she attended a finishing school. She begged him not to fly again, but although he had been forestalled by Blanchard, Pilâtre refused to give up his Channel project. He assured her, however, that this would be his last flight.

Who first suggested combining a hydrogen balloon or 'Charlière' with a Montgolfière for this Channel attempt is not known. This risky idea is commonly credited to Pilâtre, indeed the type is sometimes referred to as a 'Rozier', although it could equally well have stemmed from either the Comte de Provence who sponsored the enterprise or Jules Romain who constructed and exhibited the *Royal Balloon*, as it was called, in Paris. Certainly Pilâtre seems to have harboured doubts about the balloon from the start, although he felt himself in honour bound to the Count and Romain to fulfil his undertaking to fly it.

The reasoning behind the notion of combining both types of balloon was that the Montgolfière portion would make the craft self-regulating, and despite the dangers involved this was attractive at a time when the pilots of hydrogen balloons had not mastered the art of using and conserving their ballast to the best advantage. Construction of the balloon was slow and difficult, involving drastic modifications. As completed, it consisted of a spherical hydrogen envelope 33 ft in diameter with a cylindrical Montgolfière below it made of green silk lined with paper, 24 ft high and 12 ft in diameter. This was very much smaller than the Montgolfière section originally designed and its calculated useful lift was only 60 lb. Its regulating power was therefore so limited as to be almost valueless and indeed when he ascended, Pilâtre carried sand ballast as well as faggots and charcoal on the gallery. This annular gallery surrounded the Mont-golfière cylinder and was suspended by cords extending from the rim of its 3 ft high balustrade to the net enclosing the upper hemis-phere of the hydrogen envelope. The iron furnace pan was normally suspended 8 ft below the gallery but could be lowered further at will.

Some contemporary prints of the balloon show its two portions united, its appearance resembling that of a gigantic button mush-room, but the account in which the above dimensions are given states that the Montgolfière cylinder was suspended 5 ft below the hydrogen envelope, an arrangement which sounds more logical since it would prevent the direct transfer of heat from one envelope to the other. For obvious reasons the line controlling the valve at the north pole of the balloon could not pass through its centre in the normal manner but had to travel round its periphery. This was an unsatisfactory arrangement because, when it was pulled, the valve line, instead of overcoming the resistance of the valve springs, would tend merely to deform the envelope at its equator. Finally, the neck of the hydrogen envelope was extended in the form of a long tube terminating well below the furnace. Thus, it was argued, any gas passing through the neck due to expansion as the balloon ascended would be exhausted sufficiently far beneath the fire to be safely dissipated. As it was intended that the valve would be opened only to initiate a descent, no risk of fire was envisaged from this source.

Pilâtre planned to ascend with Romain from Boulogne, a difficult starting point, for if there was any west in the wind it would drive the balloon out into the North Sea instead of across to the English coast. Many weary weeks were spent in waiting for suitable con-ditions during which de Rozier's spirits sank lower and lower. His friends joined Susan Dyer in imploring him to abandon so desperate a venture, but Pilâtre would not hear of it. In reply to one he burst out passionately: 'For God's sake don't mention such a thing! It is now too late; give me encouragement for I would rather take a knife and pierce my heart than give up the attempt which I have engaged in, although I was certain of meeting with death.'

To add to Pilâtre's anxieties, one of his dearest friends, the Marquis de la Maisonfort, begged persistently to be allowed to ascend with him instead of Romain. Unwilling to accept his friend's repeated refusals, the Marquis tried to bribe Romain to give up his place. He offered 100 livres and was refused; he doubled his offer and Romain reluctantly accepted. However, at ten o'clock, on the night before the flight Pilâtre finally succeeded in dissuading his friend.

At 7.15 a.m. on the morning of 15th June, 1785, the balloon at last took off from Boulogne and rose swiftly into the air. An eye-witness described the ascent as 'horribly majestic and daringly august'. But the same onlooker also noticed that the gallery was at least a foot out of balance and that the balloon looked 'crazy and ill contrived'. At first the balloon appeared to be drifting out to sea, but at a height of 5,000 ft it evidently encountered a contrary air current for it began to float back over the land. Then, before the horrified gaze of the spectators, disaster struck, swift and deadly.

What exactly happened has been the subject of much debate. The accounts of eye-witnesses were confused and in some cases conflicting. With one exception, however, they all agreed that the balloon caught fire and this led those who were not on the spot to assume too readily that the disaster was due to the risky combination principle. The Marquis de la Maisonfort alone insisted that there was no fire at all. Subsequently, however, the Marquis became convinced that he had been wrong in this, an error he acknowledged in a letter now preserved among the Montgolfier papers in the Paris Musée de l'Air. According to an eye-witness account preserved in the Norman Collection (Vol. II), Pilâtre tugged repeatedly at the valve line as the balloon ascended and at the same time the Montgolfière fire basket, normally 34 ft below the base of the hydrogen balloon, was lowered still further. At a height of about 5,000 ft this same witness 'perceived a column of smoke ascending from the top of it' and goes on to declare that the next instant he saw the two portions of the balloon part company and fall in different directions. This separation was not confirmed by others and is almost certainly incorrect, but the origin of the fire at the top of the hydrogen balloon was corroborated, not only by other witnesses but by Blanchard who afterwards paid a special visit to Boulogne to inspect and report upon the balloon. He found the evidence of burning confined to a 15 ft circle of the fabric and net around the valve.

From these statements it seems evident that the neck, with its overlong extension pipe, proved incapable of sufficiently relieving the balloon of pressure when the gas expanded on a rapid ascent. The balloon may have been overfilled to start with, while heat radiated from the Montgolfière portion below would increase the expansion rate. Pilâtre immediately sought to remedy this situation by opening the valve, at the same time ordering Romain to lower the Montgolfière fire-basket as a precautionary measure. Owing to the tortuous path taken by the valve line he had considerable difficulty in getting the valve to open, but when he at last succeeded the escaping gas immediately caught fire. The theory advanced by the Boulogne physicist Duriez that the gas was ignited by a spark produced by a sudden discharge of static current is almost certainly correct. The valve was of copper and the envelope, elaborately decorated with thin sheets of gold, would all too readily act as a condenser. Moreover, the friction of the external valve line on the envelope during the aeronaut's efforts to open the valve may have helped to induce the static charge, as would the rush of gas through the valve. The rapid fall of the balloon thereafter would naturally limit the fire to the area immediately round the valve.[1]

Susan Dyer was among the shocked and silent crowd at Boulogne who saw the wrecked balloon plummet down the sky until it disappeared below their horizon. So overcome was she by the sight that she collapsed and died soon after. The aeronauts crashed to earth at Huitmile Warren near the town and – ironically enough – not far from the scene of Blanchard's triumphal landing after his channel crossing barely six months before. Just before the end of their fearful fall, one of them shouted through a speaking trumpet, alerting some men who were working nearby. Running to the spot and lifting the pitiful heap of crumpled silk that was all that remained of the Royal Balloon, they found them. Romain had breath enough left to whisper 'O, Jesu!' but Pilâtre de Rozier was already dead. So perished the world's first aeronaut in the world's first aerial disaster.

[1] Between the two world wars, the crew of three of a French Naval balloon, fitted with a metal valve and flying free, unknowingly re-enacted the de Rozier disaster, though fortunately without tragic consequences. On valving at 1,000 ft preparatory to landing, a static spark fired the gas as it escaped through the valve. This was seen from the ground, but the crew remained unaware that the balloon, which landed quite normally, was on fire. When they ripped the balloon, however, the remaining gas went up in a great sheet of flame. – Information supplied by M. Charles Dollfuss in a letter to the author. Hence the use of wooden valves and non-static fabrics.

The effect of this calamity was to cause a serious setback to ballooning, particularly in France. The unwarranted fears that had preceded the first manned ascents from Paris had too soon been succeeded by an equally unjustifiable optimism. In the first flush of enthusiasm so many ascents were made all over France by men who were necessarily novices at the first essay yet suffered no more hurt than a few bruises on landing, that an illusion of perfect safety had been created. Now that illusion was shattered, and the fact that the victim of the disaster was no raw novice but the great Pilâtre de Rozier himself, the man who had first showed the world the way to the skies, made its impact far greater. Those who had argued that God never intended man to fly now saw the fate of the First Aeronaut as the just punishment for his presumption; a sign of the wrath of a heaven sore provoked by the insolence of man's invasion. A few bold spirits carried on, Blanchard among them, but the effect of the de Rozier disaster and the French Revolution which followed it was that ballooning did not regain a wide popularity until the early years of the nineteenth century. Throughout England a number of ascents were made until the end of 1785, some of them highly dramatic, but subsequently ballooning lapsed here also until the end of the century.

Apart from those who, like Blanchard and de Rozier, deliberately set out to make a sea crossing, there was always the risk that an incautious aeronaut, ascending near the coast, might be blown out to sea by an unexpected shift of wind. The first aeronaut to suffer this alarming experience was the English ballooning enthusiast Major (later General) John Money on the second of his three ascents.

On 22nd July, 1785 Money went up alone in Zambeccari's hydrogen balloon from Norwich in a light north easterly air. Unfortunately he subsequently encountered what a contemporary account called 'an improper current' which began to bear him rapidly to the south-east. The Major prepared to descend but found that he could not open the valve because, it was afterwards alleged, a piece of silk had been sewn over it during inflation. In the early evening the balloon was seen to cross the coast at Pakefield, near Yarmouth, at a high altitude and to disappear over the sea. Boats at once put out from Lowestoft and Southwold, but their crews failed to find any trace of the balloon and as dusk fell they returned to port convinced that Money had been drowned.

Meanwhile Money had come down into the sea at 6 p.m. twenty miles offshore. For five hours he fought for his life. Twice before darkness fell his hopes were raised when he sighted craft which appeared to be coming towards him, but they bore away. The car sank so that he had to climb into the hoop and as the balloon gradually lost gas so the water rose about him. With a refinement of torture the balloon was drowning him by inches. Money confessed afterwards that at this time he wished that providence would grant him the swift fate of de Rozier rather than such a lingering death. By 11.30 p.m. the water was nearly up to his chin and he was so weak that he could scarcely keep his hold on the suspension cords, but at this eleventh hour the balloon was sighted in the moonlight by the revenue cutter *Argus* and Money was lifted from the sea. After several glasses of grog, which he described as 'more delicious than champagne', the aeronaut quickly revived. He was landed at Lowestoft early next morning where he received a tumultuous welcome. The popularity of two highly dramatic mezzotints of the incident, one from a drawing by P. Reinagle and the other by an unknown artist, made this the best known of all the early balloon adventures.

On 7th October, 1785, the people of Yarmouth saw another balloon pass over and head out to sea at a great height. Its car contained the Rev Peter Routh, Mr Robert Davy and a Mrs Hines who had ascended from Beccles. Again the balloon was given up as lost, but the trio were picked up off the coast of Holland by a Dutch ship whose Master, Captain Andrew Van Swieten, had sighted the balloon scudding over the sea with its car in the water. On their return to Beccles the lucky aeronauts were paraded through the streets wearing laurel crowns inscribed in gilt letters with the legend 'The Favoured of Heaven'.

On his second Edinburgh ascent of 20th December, 1785 Vincent Lunardi came down into the Firth of Forth near the Fidra Rock and was driven rapidly through the water towards the Island of May near the north shore. He had made some provision for such an emergency by equipping his car with inflated bladders and cork floats, but even so he had been forced to climb into the hoop by the time he was rescued by the crew of a small fishing boat. In the excitement of the rescue the balloon escaped and was never recovered. It was typical of Lunardi that when a revenue cutter subsequently came up and offered to take him aboard he refused out of gratitude to his humble rescuers who eventually landed him near North Berwick.

Notwithstanding the fate of Pilâtre de Rozier, the idea of the 'combination' balloon continued to attract, particularly in Italy where at least two aeronauts, Olivari (Orleans, 25th November, 1802) and none other than Count Zambeccari, lost their lives as a result.

After an adventurous spell of service in the Russian Navy in the course of which he was shipwrecked and taken prisoner by the Turks, the intrepid Zambeccari returned to his native Bologna in 1800 and resumed his aeronautical career. Balloons had never been out of his thoughts for he had beguiled the two-and-a-half years of his imprisonment by writing a treatise on the subject. He now evolved a combined hydrogen and hot-air balloon in which the latter was inflated by a form of 'lamp', as the Count called it, burning spirits of wine instead of by a solid fuel furnace.

On an early ascent in this device from Boulogne the balloon caught in the upper branches of a tree just after take-off causing the spirits of wine to spill, and setting fire to the Count's clothing. This blaze increased the balloon's lifting power and enabled it to free itself. The horrified crowd, which included Zambeccari's young wife and her children, saw the balloon sail into the sky with its pilot surrounded by flames. However, the Count managed to extinguish the fire and landed safely.

Undeterred by this hair-raising experience the Count took off from Bologna with two companions, Andreoli and Grassetti on the 7th October, 1804. Many exasperating delays and difficulties, including forty-eight hours of continuous rain, made Zambeccari determined to ascend although by the time it was possible to do so the three men were already tired out, it was midnight and the weather was cold and threatening. 'The lamp, which was intended to increase our ascending force, became useless', writes the Count, but the hydrogen portion alone proved sufficient to lift them to a very high altitude. Here the effect of the height, the darkness and the bitter cold on men who had worked all day without food was stupefying. 'I fell upon the floor of the gallery in a profound sleep that was like death,' says Zambeccari. The same thing happened to Grassetti, but Andreoli, who had had a meal and fortified himself

Unsuccessful Competitor: The burning of Keegan's balloon in Lord Foley's garden, 1784

The first aerial voyage in England: Lunardi ascending from Moorfields

with rum before starting, managed to keep alert although suffering greatly from the cold.

It was 2 a.m. before Andreoli managed to rouse his companions. It was evident by this time that the balloon was losing height but in the darkness they could not read their barometer. Eventually they managed with great difficulty to light a small lantern by means of flint and steel, but by then it was too late. A distant, ominous murmur rapidly grew into the unmistakeable roar of an angry sea. The Count promptly threw out a whole sack of ballast, but the balloon had by now gained too much momentum and at a little after 3 a.m. it plunged into the Adriatic.

Immediately great waves began to sweep over them and in this nightmare situation the desperate men threw all their remaining ballast and everything that was portable into the sea. Thus lightened, the balloon suddenly shot upwards to such a height that it became difficult to breathe. The Count was violently sick, Grassetti began bleeding from the nose and all three became temporarily deaf so that they shouted to each other in vain. They became covered in ice as their sea-soaked clothing froze upon them. 'I could not,' wrote Zambeccari, 'account for the reason why the moon, which was in its last quarter, appeared on a parallel line with us, and looked red as blood.'

For half an hour they remained suspended between this devil of a deathly cold and the deep sea. Then the balloon began gently to descend again and at 4 a.m. it fell once more into the sea. The balloon was now so much deflated that the strong wind flattened the lower portion of the envelope into a sail and drove them before it through a heavy swell which often submerged them completely. They had no idea of their position for it was pitch dark, but somehow they clung on and survived that terrible night. When dawn broke at last they found to their joy that Pesaro lay straight ahead of them, not more than four miles away, but just as they were congratulating themselves on their escape the wind changed. Blowing off the shore, it swept them out into the open sea once more and they were soon out of sight of land. The few boats they sighted appeared deliberately to avoid them until their only faint hope was that they might reach the Dalmatian coast. It was 8 a.m. before help came at last. The master of a passing ship, more enlightened than the others, realized that the

7

strange object in the sea was a fallen balloon and lowered a longboat. The sailors lifted the aeronauts on board, but the balloon escaped them, shooting into the air to be seen no more. They were landed and taken to Ferrara, but all three were suffering severely from exhaustion and frostbite, so much so that Zambeccari had to have his fingers amputated while Grassetti was in such a state that he only just survived.

After such an experience as this most men would have called it a day, but not the indomitable Zambeccari. He continued to fly and is said to have come down in the Adriatic on another occasion, though not with such dire consequences. Moreover, he still favoured the dangerous combination balloon and it was this which eventually caused his death. Coming in to land near Boulogne on the 21st September, 1812, the Count's grapnel caught in the branch of a tree, jerking and tilting the car. This overset the lamp and in a few seconds the balloon became a mass of flames. The Count and his companion, Signor Bonaga, jumped for their lives from tree-top height. Bonaga, though seriously injured, survived the fall, but Zambeccari was killed on the spot.

If he was not the greatest of the pioneer aeronauts, Zambeccari was certainly the boldest. No difficulty or disaster could break his iron nerve or could daunt his determination to fly. Yet his name was undeservedly forgotten and if it was remembered at all it was often rendered incorrectly. Nevertheless, such a man can often influence the distant future in mysterious ways. Otto Lilienthal read of the Count's adventures in a little book called *The Travels of Count Zambeccay* and was inspired by them to begin the historic experiments with gliders that ended in his own death, but not before he had paved the way for successful powered flight.

The crossing of the Irish Sea was another exploit to attract the aeronauts at an early date, but although the prevailing winds favoured such a voyage from the Irish side it was not achieved for many years. The first attempt was made on 17th June, 1785 by a Dr Potain, a Frenchman then living in Dublin, in a balloon equipped, like Blanchard's, with wings, rudder and moulinet. These aids proved of no avail; indeed the winds were so contrary that the Doctor never got over the sea at all but made a very rough landing in the hills near Powerscourt, sixteen miles from his Dublin starting point.

The next to make the attempt was the first Irish aeronaut, Richard Crosbie. Crosbie's second ascent – if such it can be called – from Dublin was pure farce. He had proposed ascending with a young army officer named Richard McGuire, but Crosbie was a large and heavily built man and the balloon proved incapable of lifting him, let alone a passenger. McGuire, who was a lighter man but completely inexperienced, then took Crosbie's place, but the latter changed his mind, pushed McGuire out and ordered more gas to be put into the balloon. In vain; still the balloon would not budge. The last move in this Cox and Box comedy was that McGuire again leapt into the car and precipitately departed, narrowly missing a neighbouring chimney. He was blown straight out to sea where, nine miles off Howth Head, the balloon burst, McGuire having broken the valve line. When the balloon hit the sea, McGuire was thrown out of the car but his ankle became entangled in a rope and as the balloon then rose slightly he found himself suspended head downwards just above the waves. From this predicament he managed to free himself and after floating and swimming for half an hour he was rescued by a Dublin wherry which also retrieved the balloon. For this foolhardy and ridiculous exploit McGuire was knighted by the Lord Lieutenant.

No doubt Crosbie felt that his thunder had been most unfairly stolen on this occasion for it was two months later, on the 19th July, 1785, that he rose from Merrion Square, Dublin, on a deliberate attempt to cross the Irish Sea. Like McGuire he was soon water-borne instead of air-borne, but he had prudently equipped the car with bladders which kept him afloat until he was rescued by a certain Captain Walnutt in a Dunleary barge. No knighthood was forthcoming on this occasion, nor were any further attempts made on the crossing until the veteran aeronaut, James Sadler took up the challenge on the 1st October, 1812.

Sadler returned to ballooning with an ascent at Oxford in July 1810 and he followed this with an ascent from Bristol in September accompanied by a chemist, William Clayfield. This ended in the Bristol Channel four miles off the Somerset coast at Combe Martin. Fortunately the sea was calm and after floating about for an hour they were picked up by a boat from Lynmouth. Of his several flights during the following year, that from Birmingham on the 7th

October accompanied by a Mr Burcham was the most exciting. A gale swept the balloon 112 miles in eighty minutes, almost certainly the fastest journey man had ever performed at that time. In attempting to land in Lincolnshire Sadler was thrown out and the balloon carried Burcham for a mile and a half over land until it became entangled in an ash tree and was torn to pieces. Each aeronaut gave the other up for dead so they were delighted to encounter each other in the nearby village of Heckington, near Spalding.

For his Irish Sea attempt a year later, James Sadler built himself a new balloon of large size, 55 ft diameter giving a capacity of 87,114 cubic feet which enabled him to carry 11 cwt of ballast when he went up from Belvedere House, Drumcondra and still make a rapid ascent with the balloon only two-thirds inflated. It is clear from this that Sadler appreciated that large capacity was the key to prolonged flight. It enabled him to carry an ample reserve of ballast with an envelope only partially filled to allow for expansion without loss of gas. Nevertheless, his attempt was defeated, partly by variable air currents and partly because he was too ambitious.

When he was directly over Ireland's Eye a rent appeared in the valve cord tube, but the resourceful Sadler improvised a ladder from his grapnel rope, climbed up and stopped the leak by tying his neck-cloth round the tube. The south-westerly wind in which he had set off carried him along the south-east coast of the Isle of Man. He then discharged ballast, climbing until he encountered a north-easterly current. This bore him in the direction of Anglesey which he soon sighted. Passing to the south of the Skerry lighthouse he sailed directly over Anglesey at a height of three-and-a-half miles. Had Sadler continued on this course he would almost certainly have achieved his aim, but, alas, he over-estimated his ability to pick his destination by playing the air currents. He argued that if he now descended he would again encounter the south-westerly wind and might in this way reach Liverpool. At first this plan looked like succeeding; at 4.30 p.m., four hours after leaving Ireland, he was just off the Great Orme's head and right on course, but then the wind shifted to the southward and began to blow him out to sea. He sought for a better current by varying his altitude but in vain and as dusk was falling he valved and came down in the sea just astern of two ships. They failed to see him, however, so he discharged ballast and rose again, seeing the sunset for the second time like the pioneer Charles.

Soon after this the balloon was sighted and signalled by the Douglas herring trawler *Victory*, Master John Lee, who hoisted a Manx flag. Sadler again came down in the sea at 6 p.m. and tied most of his clothing to his grappling iron so that it would the better act as a sea-anchor and enable the trawler to overhaul him more rapidly. By a pretty piece of seamanship, Captain John Lee managed to run the bowsprit of the *Victory* through the balloon and Sadler was picked up.

Sadler afterwards estimated that in this attempt he had travelled 43 miles over land and 237 over water. His account of the voyage shows how greatly he had advanced in the art of balloon management compared with the pioneers. He only failed indeed because his expertise made him over-confident and in spite of this experience he continued to maintain that a skilful aeronaut should be able to direct the course of his balloon wherever he wished by adjusting his altitude to different air currents.

James Sadler's elder son, John, made a number of ascents both in the company of his father and solo, but it was his younger son Windham Sadler who became a professional aeronaut. At the age of only seventeen Windham made his first solo ascent from Cheltenham on 7th September, 1813. He encountered a heavy snowstorm at high altitude and this made it difficult to open the valve, but he managed to land safely at Chadlington bridge, near Chipping Norton. Four years later, on 22nd July, 1817, the veteran aeronaut had the satisfaction of seeing his son succeed where he had failed. With the help of his father, Windham took off from Portobello Barracks, Dublin at 1.30 p.m. and, after an uneventful flight, made a perfect landing in Anglesey at seven o'clock.

Unfortunately the conqueror of the Irish Sea did not live long to enjoy his success. On the 29th September, 1824, Windham and his servant James Donnelly ascended from Bolton. In attempting to land in a strong wind the grapnel broke, the balloon was dashed against the chimney of a house at Foxhill Bank, between Blackburn and Haslingden, and Windham was thrown out. For a few fearful moments he hung suspended by his legs in mid-air before plunging to the ground. He died a few hours after. His father survived him. The only one of the pioneer aeronauts to live on into the age of the great professionals, James Sadler died at Oxford on 26th March, 1828 and was buried in the churchyard of St Peter-in-the-East. Though much defaced by the weather he braved so often, his tombstone still stands. It is the only monument to the first English aeronaut.

CHAPTER SIX

The Great Showmen

WHEN ONE WHO WITNESSED the birth of the hydrogen balloon in Paris questioned its utility, the aged Benjamin Franklin made the classic rejoinder: 'Of what use is a new born baby?' In the first flush of victory in a new element the pioneer aeronauts believed with Franklin that their helpless babe would very soon grow into a controllable aerial ship, mastering, instead of mastered by, the currents of the air. As we shall see in a later chapter, the first tentative steps that ultimately led to the successful dirigible were taken at this time, but they were frustrated by the lack of suitable motive power. Blanchard and Lunardi with their flapping wings and oars were only two of the many who drew a false analogy between the boat which moves in two elements and the balloon which moves only in one and who vainly sought control not only by means of oars but by paddle wheels or even sails. Another school believed, with Sadler, that aerial currents, like the great ocean currents, were regular and predictable; that when they had been learned and charted the aeronauts could ride them to reach any destination.

When it was realized that 'the wind bloweth where it listeth' carrying the free balloon with it and that all manual efforts to prevail against it were vain, disillusionment succeeded the first fine, careless rapture of aerial conquest. It was not to be so easy or so complete a conquest after all, and this disappointment helped to bring about the temporary eclipse that followed the de Rozier disaster.

The revival of ballooning in the nineteenth century was due to men who followed the example set by Blanchard when he founded his 'Aerostatic Academy' but with much greater success; men who accepted the limitations of the free balloon but who frankly exploited its spectacular qualities and earned a comfortable livelihood thereby. The best of these professionals were great showmen, but because in this as in any other show business 'the show must go on', they were also very courageous men and great aeronauts. Not only their own lives but those of others depended on their skill and judgement, for they took up many passengers in their large balloons. They accumulated a wealth of experience of the ways of the air to the unacknowledged benefit of their better equipped successors. Technically, their greatest contribution to the future was the parachute although by their contemporaries this was regarded simply as a risky stunt. That the parachute would one day become as indispensable in the air as a life-jacket at sea was not foreseen.

No fête or celebration was complete without a balloon ascent. From the pleasure grounds and squares of the cities of Europe and America, from the Tivoli Garden or the Hippodrome in Paris, from London's Vauxhall and Cremorne and from the Castle Garden, New York the aeronauts rose majestically in their resplendent balloons. In France the stars were Madame Blanchard, who inherited the mantle of her husband, Tétu-Brissy, a veteran of the early days, Poitevin, Duruof, Etienne Robertson and his son Eugene, the two great ballooning families of Garnerin and Godard and Francisque Arban, first to cross the Alps from Marseilles to Stubini, near Turin.[1] In England the best known professionals were George and Margaret Graham, John Hampton, Richard Gypson, George Gale, Charles Green, the greatest of all English aeronauts, and, of a later generation, Henry Coxwell and the Spencer brothers. In America, the foremost pilots were Charles F. Durant, John Wise, Thaddeus S. C. Lowe, John La Mountain and Rufus Wells. In the true tradition of show business, American aeronauts favoured the title of 'Professor', Wise and Lowe especially being commonly referred to in this way.

Some of these aeronauts did not confine their activities to their own countries; the French aeronauts travelled widely in Europe while both Eugene Robertson and Godard visited the United States; Gale made ascents in France and Coxwell in Germany; perhaps the most widely travelled of them all was the American Rufus Wells who visited South America, Australia, Egypt, India, Java and Japan as well as Britain and countries in Europe, making ascents in both hydrogen and hot-air balloons.

These were the leaders of the new profession. There were many

---

[1] On 7th October, 1849, a month after his trans-alpine flight, Arban was lost over the Mediterranean after an ascent from Barcelona.

lesser figures and enthusiastic amateurs. At the bottom of the scale were the acrobats and trapeze artists who performed their feats suspended from balloons at country fairs. They commonly used a cheap form of Montgolfière devised and popularized by two French aeronauts Lartet and Kirsch. This carried no stove but was quickly filled from a very hot fire and as quickly released, remaining aloft just long enough for the performer to complete his act.

When straightforward ascents began to pall, even the top-ranking professionals had to indulge in risky aerial feats in order to satisfy a sensation-loving public. Parachute descents were the first spectacular attraction; then followed night ascents, often accompanied by the discharge of fireworks – a particularly risky affair in a hydrogen balloon – and ascents on horseback or with other animals. It was Tétu-Brissy who made the first-ever night ascent in a balloon on the 18th June, 1786 from Paris. He remained aloft for eleven hours, successfully riding out a violent storm. Twelve years later. Tétu-Brissy made two ascents from Meudon on horseback, the horse standing on a platform suspended from the balloon. His example was soon followed by others with variations that included wild animals.

The greatest French aeronaut to follow Blanchard was unquestionably André Jacques Garnerin (1770–1825) and during his flying career he was ably abetted by his wife Jeanne and his niece Elisa. Young Garnerin made his first ascent from Metz in 1787, but the Revolution soon interrupted his flying career. 'Citizen Garnerin', as he was then called, joined the army on the northern front where he fought bravely until he was taken prisoner by the English. He was handed over to the Austrians who imprisoned him in the fortress of Buda in Hungary for nearly three years. Garnerin knew of Blanchard's experiments with parachutes. No doubt, too, he had heard of Sebastian de Normand's jump with a 14 ft parachute from the tower of Montpellier Observatory in December 1783. During this long confinement Garnerin dreamed of constructing a parachute and using it to escape from the fortress. This wild scheme came to nothing, but he resolved to make a parachute descent when he achieved his liberty.

It will be recalled that Blanchard had dropped animals by parachute at his short-lived Aerostatic Academy. It has been said that Blanchard himself made a descent before Garnerin, but this is very doubtful and if he did so it was from so modest a height as to be not worthy of record. Such few parachute descents as were advertised by others proved either fraudulent or futile. That advertised by the Englishman Stuart Amos Arnold belonged to the latter category. In a large balloon named *Royal George* Arnold ascended – or rather attempted to ascend – from St George's Fields on the last day of August 1785. With him in the car was his young son and beneath it an intrepid tar named George Appleby was suspended in a parachute. Lacking lift, the balloon first struck against some high railings, detaching the parachute so that Appleby fell to the ground. The car of the balloon next struck a cart and this time the car itself fell off, carrying with it Arnold senior and all his ballast and equipment. Thus doubly relieved of its burden the balloon shot into the sky with Arnold junior clinging desperately to the hoop. Young Arnold was given up for lost, the more so when the balloon, which had been grossly over-inflated, spectacularly burst. However, the descending balloon plunged the youth into the waters of Execution Dock at Rotherhithe, whence he was promptly fished out, none the worse, by a Mr Jackson of Leigh Street, Red Lion Square, who was fortunately passing by in a boat at the time. Although Arnold failed to fulfil his promise to send 'a Gentleman down by a Parachute, when a mile high', he certainly provided the large crowd with plenty of excitement. Nor was this absurd affair completely abortive since it demonstrated for the first time that a burst balloon could itself act as a parachute and so bring an aeronaut to earth in safety.

Such was the state of the art when Garnerin was released and returned to Paris resolved to resume his aeronautical career and to make his bold experiment. On the 22nd October, 1797 he ascended from the park of Monceau in the tiny car of his furled parachute which was attached to a hydrogen balloon. When opened, the parachute resembled a huge umbrella, 30 ft in diameter (flat), made of canvas. At a height of 3,000 ft this courageous man cut the suspension cord. Some accounts say that the balloon, relieved of his weight, shot upwards and burst, others that Garnerin's release arrangement incorporated a device which ripped the envelope of the balloon. Meanwhile the parachute opened perfectly, but as it was made of impervious fabric it could not spill the wind. It therefore descended in a series of oscillations becoming ever more violent, swinging the little car like a pendulum so that Garnerin had to hold on for dear life. However, he landed safely if somewhat roughly, on the plain of Monceau where, mounting a horse, he rode in triumph back to the park.

In 1802, Garnerin came to England where he made a number of ascents from London and the provinces including a rapid passage from Chelsea Gardens to Colchester in 45 minutes. On the 21st September in this year he repeated his parachute performance over London,[1] taking off from St George's Parade, North Audley Street. This time he rose to 10,000 ft before releasing himself from the balloon. Descending from this much greater height, the oscillations of the parachute became even more violent. From the ground the sight was so frightening that those who saw it feared the worst, expecting either that the parachute would collapse or that Garnerin would be flung out of the car. Rushing to the field near St Pancras where the parachute was seen to fall they found Garnerin somewhat bruised and very sick from the motion of the car but otherwise in good heart. Among the first to arrive on the scene were the Duke of York and Lord Stanhope who congratulated him heartily. His feat also earned the approval of the ballad mongers, one of whom wrote:

> *Bold Garnerin went up*
> *Which increased his Repute*
> *And came safe to earth*
> *In his Grand Parachute.*

These were but two of many parachute descents made not only by Garnerin himself, but by his wife Jeanne-Geneviève, the first woman to make a parachute descent, and by his niece Elisa Garnerin who became the first professional woman parachutist. Later descents became less alarming as their technique was improved by experience. At the suggestion of the French astronomer Lalande, the friend of both Garnerin and Blanchard, a hole was made in the centre of the parachute to spill the wind. This reduced the oscillation considerably, but it was many years before it was realized that the true answer to parachute stability was to make its fabric permeable by air. Garnerin also fitted a counterweight at the north pole of the balloons used to raise his parachutes. As soon as the parachute was released this weight

---

[1] This was Garnerin's fifth parachute descent.

inverted the balloon so that the gas was rapidly discharged through the neck, allowing the balloon to descend undamaged.

In the course of his career Garnerin visited Italy, Germany and Russia and it was after his return from Russia that, with the true showman's touch, he styled himself 'The Great Aeronaut of the North'. In Paris he became famous for his night ascents, frequently bearing aloft coloured lamps or fireworks. He was probably the first aeronaut to appreciate the advantages of flying by night when the balloon is not subject to daytime variations of temperature, for these ascents carried him far afield, to Simmern, near Frankfort, to Aix la Chapelle, to Mont Tonnerre (where he landed, most appropriately, in a thunderstorm) and to many remote parts of France.

As the No. 1 aeronaut of France, Garnerin only once blotted his copybook so far as officialdom was concerned, though this was really no fault of his. He was asked to contribute to the lavish festivities in Paris that marked the coronation of Napoleon Bonaparte on the 16th December, 1804. These included a mammoth display of fireworks, with set-pieces intended to represent the crossing of Mont St Bernard, which was staged on floats in the river between the Isle of St Louis and the bridge of Notre Dame. As the display began, Garnerin released his contribution from the gates of Notre Dame. This was a very large hydrogen balloon bearing in letters of gold on its elaborately decorated envelope the inscription: 'Paris, 25^{ieme} Frimaire, an.XIII., couronnement de l'empereur Napoléon, Ier par S.S.Pie VII.' It bore aloft a huge gilded crown decorated with coloured lanterns. Everything went without a hitch and the balloon stole the show as it sailed majestically into the night sky; the sequel, however, was not so happy.

Next morning the citizens of Rome were astonished to see a large balloon bearing down upon them at a very low altitude. By a chance in a million Garnerin's balloon had made a remarkable pilotless flight between the two capitals. The balloon skimmed over the dome of St Peter's and the Vatican, descended to ground level, rose again and finally disappeared in the waters of Lake Bracciano. All this was well enough, indeed more gratifying than otherwise, but it was presently discovered that in its momentary descent the balloon had, with singular tactlessness, deposited part of the gilded crown upon the tomb of Nero. Now, like all absolute dictators, or 'men of destiny' as they prefer to call themselves, Napoleon was a superstitious man. He was not at all amused, particularly when the Italian press made great play with an incident that no Frenchman dared to mention. The balloon was retrieved from the lake and preserved in the vaults of the Vatican until the 1814 campaign when it was seized and brought back to France. Meanwhile poor Garnerin fell into official disfavour and ballooning was discouraged except at great public fêtes or celebrations where Madame Blanchard was appointed to supervise ascents.

Madame Blanchard was small and slightly built like her husband and emulated him by becoming the first professional aeronaut of her sex. She was not a handsome woman, her features being described as sharp and bird-like, but she made herself popular with the French crowds by her plucky ascents in small balloons equipped with equally small and fragile cars of an elegant boat shape. Truly bird-like, this strange little woman seems to have felt more at home in the air than upon earth. She liked to ascend in the still air of dusk when she would frequently remain aloft all night sleeping, it was alleged, in her tiny car. She hated returning to earth where the slightest noise frightened her. A ride in a carriage terrified her, so great was her fear that it would overturn. It was just as well that she was not born into our modern world; one feels she would have been the first to volunteer for a flight to the moon.

Unfortunately, when Garnerin temporarily fell from favour in France, Madame Blanchard adopted his practice of ascending at night with lights or fireworks and it was this which ultimately brought about her downfall at the Tivoli Gardens on the 7th July, 1819. The skilfully stage-managed scene on that still summer night was typical of those far-off days; typical, too, not only of the Tivoli but of the pleasures of Vauxhall and Cremorne. In the lantern-lit, shadowy walks the crowd waited expectantly for the maroon that would signal the ascent. The moment it crashed out, all the trees in their heavy leaf were suddenly lit by the smokey glare of Bengal lights as, to the accompaniment of a triumphant fanfare from an unseen orchestra, Madame Blanchard soared into the air, trailing beneath her car a great star of silver fire. Tremendous applause. Now brightness falls from the air. Madame has lit bombs of gold and silver rain, sending them floating earthwards on miniature parachutes.

Renewed applause, presently redoubled as a great jet of flame shoots out of the balloon. Alas, this was no part of the performance, as was soon apparent. The port-fire Madame was using to ignite the fireworks had set light to the gas issuing from the neck of the ascending balloon. For a few moments the unhappy woman tried, with great presence of mind, to extinguish the flames. Then, finding herself falling rapidly, she threw out all her ballast. The rush of the descent drove the flames back into the balloon and, according to some eyewitnesses, extinguished them. Had the balloon fallen into the gardens all might still have been well, but instead it landed upon the roof of a nearby house, the car colliding with a chimney stack and overturning. With a despairing cry of 'A moi!', 'A moi!', Madame Blanchard slid helplessly down the steeply pitched roof and plunged to her death upon the pavement below.

Twenty-eight years later, a similar night ascent with fireworks from Vauxhall Gardens was followed by one of the most terrifying descents in aeronautical history although in this case the balloon did not catch fire. The balloon was that of Richard Gypson who took with him three passengers, a Mr Pridmore, Albert Smith, a popular writer of the day, and Henry Coxwell, then a young man who had still to establish his reputation as an aeronaut. Coxwell subsequently wrote a graphic account of the affair in his reminiscences.

The day – 6th July, 1847 – had been hot and sultry with an occasional ominous rumble of distant thunder. By the time darkness had fallen and the balloon was ready to ascend, lightning was flickering over London, but after some discussion it was agreed to go ahead. A frame carrying no less than 60 lb weight of 'Darby's Fireworks' was attached beneath the basket and to the customary accompaniment of maroons, music and Bengal Lights the balloon rose. As he was the youngest member of the party, Coxwell had clambered into the hoop. It was his first night ascent. The fireworks below the car, petards, Roman candles, gold and silver rain, were putting up a brave show to the audible delight of the crowd below when nature joined in with a vivid flash of lightning quickly followed by a deafening peal of thunder. The burning of the fireworks had the effect of a continuous discharge of ballast, causing the balloon to rise ever more rapidly into the heart of the storm. Soon it had reached 4,000 ft, lightning flashed repeatedly round them, the thunder roared and the fireworks had still not exhausted themselves. Young Coxwell was in a fearful dilemma. From his place in the hoop he could see more clearly than the others in the glare of the lightning that the balloon had become dangerously distended in its rapid ascent and needed immediate relief from the valve. The valve line was within his reach and his fingers itched to pull it, but as he was the junior member of the party he felt he dared not take such a liberty. Instead, he tried, as tactfully as he could, to persuade Gypson to valve gas, but for reasons best known to himself the aeronaut ignored him. At last he shouted desperately: 'if the valve is not opened the balloon will burst!' Too late. Suddenly and sickeningly the car dropped some six or eight feet. A rent sixteen feet long appeared in the envelope and in a moment the balloon was falling headlong right onto the west end of London. The lines of gas lamps became visibly larger and brighter every second and still the thunder roared. It was a miracle that the escaping gas did not ignite, for as they plummeted down the glowing cases of spent fireworks rushed past them.

In this extreme peril the niceties of protocol were forgotten. Without hesitation Coxwell cut the cord that was holding down the neck of the balloon. At once the wildly flapping fabric shot up into the net and the car lines tautened. The rate of descent had been effectually checked. Even so the adventure might still have ended tragically had they landed on some roof-top like poor Madame Blanchard. As it was they were lucky enough to come down in a newly formed street off the Belgrave Road in Pimlico where the net, by becoming caught in some scaffold poles on a building site, helped to break their fall. The only casualty was Coxwell who, entangled in the net, received a cut on the hand from the knife of an over-enthusiastic rescuer.

With the balloon stowed on the roof of a cab, the adventurers returned to Vauxhall where they found the spectators, who included Albert Smith's brother, blissfully unaware that anything had gone wrong. 'Good gracious, Albert,' exclaimed the latter, 'I could have declared I saw you go up in the balloon.' 'So you did,' replied Albert, doubtless with considerable feeling. A week later Gypson, accompanied by Coxwell, ascended again from Vauxhall in the repaired balloon carrying double the weight of fireworks. 'Mr Albert Smith,' writes Coxwell tactfully, 'was again invited, but a certain pressure, exercised perhaps wisely, by his friends prevented him from

ascending again. Mr Pridmore, too, although as brave as need be, did
not join us. . . .'

With the object of making the aerial discharge of fireworks less
hazardous, Lt George Burcher Gale, R.N. designed and constructed a
special balloon with dual cars, each consisting of a light canvas-
covered framework, which fitted into each other like Chinese boxes.
When aloft, the outer of the two cars could be lowered some twenty
to thirty feet by rope tackle, whereupon the intrepid aeronaut
descended by rope ladder and discharged the fireworks from the
lower car. Quite apart from the fireworks, this spectacle of the aeronaut in transit gave the crowds an extra thrill. As an additional precaution, Gale provided two small auxiliary balloons, these being
connected to the neck of the main envelope so that they would act as
reservoirs for gas escaping from the neck. Apart from the safety
aspect, Gale argued that these auxiliaries would enable him to rise
higher without losing gas and that, on descending the gas would pass
back from the auxiliaries into the main envelope.

Gale was a man of parts and a showman in more senses than one.
Born at Fulham in 1794 he first went onto the stage and is said to have
played the name part in *Mazeppa* at the Bowery Theatre, New York,
for 200 performances. He then returned to England where he joined
the Coastal Blockade Service of the Royal Navy for a time before
becoming a professional aeronaut. Unfortunately he was addicted to
the bottle, a perilous weakness in an aeronaut. On the 8th July, 1850
he crossed the channel in his balloon, ascending from Cremorne
Gardens, and began a tour of France. He was said to have been in-
toxicated when he ascended from Bordeaux on the 8th September
seated on a pony. Although he landed safely and the pony was
removed by some helpful peasants, Gale was somehow carried aloft
clinging to the rigging lines. When his body was found some days
later it was evident that he must have fallen from a considerable
height.

By far the most accident-prone of all the well-known aeronauts of
the period were the Grahams, husband and wife. They had no need
to indulge in spectacular stunts; their advertisements could be relied
upon to draw a sensation-loving crowd, expecting trouble and rarely
disappointed. It would be difficult to say whether the couple were
unlucky to have so many accidents or lucky to escape so often with

Doctor Jeffries equipped for his channel flight

Blanchard and Jeffries setting out from Dover on their successful cross-channel flight, January, 1785

De Rozier's ill-fated 'Combination' balloon

'The Perilous Situation of Major Money'

their lives. There could scarcely have been a bone in either of their bodies that remained unbroken. On balance it would seem that luck was on their side as their efforts were more remarkable for courage than for skill.

George Graham got away to an unpromising start, for his first attempt to ascend from the White Conduit House Tavern, Pentonville, in August 1823 was a fiasco. The envelope of his balloon, which was made of lawn, proved so permeable that although it was of large size it refused to budge. Finally the disgruntled aeronaut cut the balloon adrift, but not in time to prevent the riot that was almost inevitably the price of failure. His second effort from the same place was little better, for as it took off the balloon was torn by fouling one of the poles from which it had been suspended during inflation. Leaking badly, the balloon only managed to lift Graham 400 ft before it deposited him in a flooded gravel pit, 20 ft deep, in a field not half a mile away. And so it went on. An ascent from Plymouth led to a ducking in Plymouth Sound, while another from the gardens of the 'Yorkshire Stingo' at Paddington ended precipitately and painfully at Reigate Hill when their grapnel hit an iron bridge, overturning the car and tipping out the Grahams along with their passenger, Mr Warwick. In August 1836 Mrs Graham rose from the Flora Tea Gardens, Bayswater, with the mad Duke of Brunswick as passenger. This flight ended in the usual debacle, this time at Kelvedon wood, near Brentwood where the Duke jumped out prematurely, the balloon shot up and the lady aeronaut, losing her balance, fell out of the car from a considerable height.

In June 1838 the Grahams contributed to the coronation festivities of that year by ascending from Green Park. On this occasion their grapnel dislodged a coping stone from a house in Marylebone Lane. This fell upon the head of an unsuspecting passer-by with fatal results. After this, ascents by George Graham became rarer. Considerably the older of the pair, he evidently decided he had tempted providence far enough, but his amazing wife continued her headlong career, bearing George a long succession of progeny in the intervals and styling herself 'Her Majesty's Aeronautè' or 'The Only English Female Aeronaut'. However, they both celebrated the Great Exhibition year of 1851 by ascending in a new balloon named *Victoria and Albert* and but narrowly avoiding a head-on collision with the

Crystal Palace. Frantically discharging ballast to the discomfort of those below, the balloon skimmed the great glass roof and sailed away to the east, still only at roof-top height, leaving a trail of ruin and consternation behind it as its dangling grapnel savaged the buildings en route. Finally it hit the front of Colonel North's house in Arlington Street, Piccadilly, demolished a large section of the cornice and left the Grahams, insensible, upon the roof. Even this was not the end, for Margaret Graham survived a similarly destructive roof-skimming exploit over Dublin in 1853. The really amazing thing is that Margaret Graham should have soldiered on in this way for no less than thirty years without, it would seem, becoming any more skilled in the art of balloon management, and yet have survived to die in her bed. Many better pilots have lost their lives through a single mistake.

The operation of landing a balloon calls for great skill and judgement and in the early days, no matter how expert the aeronaut might be, it was a very risky undertaking if the wind was strong. In such weather conditions the aeronaut would try to pick a landing place in the lee of a wood or some other effective wind-break, but if this was not possible, everything depended on the grapnel. If this broke or failed to find a secure hold the aeronaut would be dragged helplessly through bush and through briar at the mercy of the wind. Even if he managed to keep a hold upon the valve line, which he was frequently unable to do, the balloon would take some minutes to deflate and during those critical minutes it would possess the strength of ten and behave like a mad elephant. In such circumstances the wicker basket proved wonderfully strong, being both shock resistant and shock absorbent. For this reason, with but rare exceptions such as Gale's dual cars, the wicker basket soon became, and remains to this day, the standard form of balloon car. Nevertheless, rough landings were the most frequent cause of injury and were sometimes fatal. We have already seen how Windham Sadler met his death in this way and in 1852 the aeronaut James Goulston was killed in identical circumstances – also in the Pennines – following an ascent from Belle Vue, Manchester. With fifty-one ascents to his credit, Goulston, like Sadler, was no tyro but a skilful professional aeronaut.

It is easy for the historian to fall into the error of hindsight by being wise after the event, but in this case the remedy for the peril of the dragging balloon was so simple that, reading the endless accounts of protracted landing accidents, often resulting in the total destruction of the balloon if nothing worse, it does seem astonishing that it was not applied much sooner. Perhaps the delay may have been prolonged by the fact that the first man to grasp the principle of the remedy failed to apply it successfully with a fatal result.

Little is known of Thomas Harris. He was not a professional aeronaut, though he may have aspired to become one. He accompanied George Graham on one of his early flights from London in September 1823 which terminated – safely for once – at Rochester. Fired by this, Harris then proceeded to construct a large balloon of his own which he named the *Royal George*. Harris had concluded quite correctly that the remedy for the peril of the dragging balloon was to provide a means for deflating it instantaneously the moment the car touched down. In the north pole of the *Royal George* he fitted a valve so large that it could discharge all the gas from the envelope in a matter of seconds. The normal small valve used to relieve pressure was incorporated within the diameter of the large one, there being dual control cords.

Harris exhibited his balloon at the Royal Tennis Court, Great Windmill Street, Haymarket, in the spring of 1824 and on the 25th May he took off from the Eagle Tavern, City Road on his maiden flight accompanied by an eighteen-year-old London girl named Stocks. It was said afterwards that Harris made a first attempt to land at Dobbins Hill, near Croydon, but ascended again on finding he had forgotten his grapnel. Minutes later, a gamekeeper in Beddington Park, Croydon, saw a balloon falling from the sky at a fearful speed. Breaking a large limb from an oak tree as it came, the balloon landed with a sickening crash. The keeper found the unfortunate girl lying badly injured on the ground. 'Oh Lord!' she groaned, 'Where am I? Have I fallen out of the Car?' The body of Harris was found beneath the wreckage of his *Royal George*. He had been killed instantly.

French accounts of the accident expressed the belief that Harris had gallantly jumped out of the balloon before it landed in order to lighten it and so save the life of his companion, but this romantic notion seems doubtful. The girl did recover, but her account of Harris's last moments was not very precise or coherent. She spoke of 'the cords becoming entangled' and remembered Harris crying

'Good God protect me!' as the balloon started to fall. In his evidence
at the inquest, George Graham expressed the opinion that Harris,
intending to valve gas in order to descend, had mistakenly pulled the
wrong cord and so opened his large valve. This explanation was
generally accepted at the time, but what seems more likely is that
Harris had tied the end of the large valve line to some part of the car
without leaving sufficient slack in the line. Loss of gas from the
balloon would cause the car to drop relative to the envelope, thus
tautening the line and automatically opening the valve. The girl's
reference to tangled cords may have been prompted by Harris's
frantic efforts to correct his mistake by freeing the line. The fact
that Harris had just previously valved gas in order to make his attempted descent at Dobbins Hill makes this explanation the more
probable.

As a consequence of this tragedy English aeronauts did not pursue
poor Harris's perfectly sound idea of quick deflation. It was left to the
great American aeronaut, 'Professor' John Wise to re-introduce it in
a somewhat different form. Instead of an over-large valve, Wise
equipped his balloon with a sewn-in panel in its upper hemisphere
which could instantly be ripped out by pulling a cord. Wise first
used the ripping panel on 27th April, 1839 and it is surprising that so
many years elapsed before it was widely adopted in the old world.
The rip cord is always painted red to distinguish it clearly from the
valve line. Moreover, the rip cord is lightly attached intermediately
to the lower part of the envelope in such a way that an ample amount
of slack is determined and the cord cannot be tautened by any
lowering of the car due to loss of gas. In these precautions the fate
of the *Royal George* is recalled to this day.

Because of prevailing south-westerly winds a balloon taking off in
the London area was most commonly carried in the direction of the
Essex marshes where it was essential to land in order to avoid being
blown out to sea. Despite the spread of railways, such was the in-
sularity of rural England that the descent of a balloon in any other
part of the country could still strike terror and dismay. Henry Coxwell told how the 'Hampshire Hogs', as he called them, fled from him
when he landed on the downs near Basingstoke in 1853. Such a
reaction was embarrassing for the aeronaut who, in the days before
ripping panels, badly needed outside assistance but frequently found

that his shouts for aid merely provoked a more rapid retreat. A landing in Essex could be equally embarrassing, but for a quite different reason. The Essex farmers had become all too familiar with balloon descents on their property. Crops were trampled, hedges damaged and stock terrified. Hence the natives became decidedly unfriendly. Passengers who had paid handsomely for the privilege of a place in a balloon car and had sailed into the sky from Vauxhall or Cremorne with the cheers of the crowds ringing in their ears came down to earth with a vengeance when they found themselves looking down the business end of a blunderbuss. By 1853 the farmers in the most balloon-frequented parishes of East Ham, Plaistow, Leyton, Wanstead and Ilford had become so exasperated that they issued a printed proclamation headed 'Balloon Descents' and threatening 'Aeronauts and others' with dire penalties for trespass.

Because of the high cost, ballooning could never have reached such a pitch of popularity as this had inflation with hydrogen remained the rule. Experience had made the process of generating hydrogen more reliable, while aeronauts recouped a proportion of the outlay by the sale of the by-product. So early as 1786 the announcement of one of Lunardi's ascents advertised: '7 tons of Residuum or green liquor which will make the finest copperas. Will sell the whole for Eight guineas to any person who will send casks to contain it and a proper person to pass it from the cistern into the casks while warm and before it crystallizes.' Nevertheless, hydrogen production was still very costly and embarrassingly slow for an aeronaut beset by restive crowds.

The idea of using carburetted hydrogen, generated from coal, in balloons was first suggested by the Belgian scientist, J. P. Minielers, in 1784, and in the following year Cavallo declared 'that pit-coal is the substance which may be most advantageously used for the production of inflammable air in aerostation.' But, as Cavallo pointed out, the specific weight of coal-gas was greater than that of pure hydrogen so that, in order to lift a given weight, a balloon intended to be filled with the former would need to be of greater capacity. Some experiments with small balloons filled with coal gas were subsequently made upon the Continent, but so long as the use of either gas required the installation of a special generating plant on the launching site, the aeronauts not unnaturally continued to favour hydrogen with its

superior lifting power. By the end of the second decade of the nineteenth century, however, the situation had entirely altered as a result
of the inventive achievements in coal-gas generation of two em-
ployees of Boulton & Watt, William Murdock and Samuel Clegg.
The London Gas Light & Coke Company was founded by F. A.
Winsor in 1812 and by the end of 1816 the Company had laid twenty-
six miles of gas mains. Thereafter the use of coal-gas for commercial
and domestic purposes in London and the provinces spread very
rapidly. The ease with which a balloon could now be inflated merely
by connecting it to a gas main was an advantage which far out-
weighed the loss of lifting power.

The man who pioneered the use of coal-gas in balloons was
Charles Green, certainly the greatest English aeronaut and one of the
most skilful and successful balloon pilots that the world has ever seen.
Green claimed four advantages for coal gas as compared with hydrogen; first, ease and speed of inflation; secondly, cheapness. He calculated that at this time (1821) he could inflate a balloon six times
with coal-gas for the cost of one filling with hydrogen; thirdly, he
claimed that coal-gas was less damaging to the silk fabric and fourthly
that it did not penetrate the fabric so readily as hydrogen.

There is yet another advantage of coal-gas that Green evidently
failed at first to appreciate. Whereas the specific heat of hydrogen is
lower than that of common air, coal-gas has a higher specific heat
than air. In practice this means that coal-gas is less susceptible to
changes of temperature, reacting less rapidly by expansion and contraction on a day of alternating sunshine and cloud, for example.
Consequently if two balloons of equal lifting power, one filled with
hydrogen and the other with coal-gas, were sent off together, the
latter would fly further.

The serious snag that had to be set against these advantages was
not so much the loss of lifting power as the unpredictable and widely
variable quality of the gas produced commercially at that time.
Before he made his first ascent, Green made some experiments, using
small balloons, and found that the gas given off at the beginning of
the distillation process, though the best illuminant, was heavier and
therefore less suitable for balloons than that produced at the end
which burned with an almost invisible flame. In fact, with the
generating technique then used the specific gravity varied widely,

being anything from 340 to 790. When, as frequently became the case, a balloon was filled at the works of a well disposed gas company, the operatives could ensure that the gas was of the best quality for the purpose, whereas if an aeronaut simply tapped a main he took a gamble on the amount of lift he would obtain.

In the days of hydrogen, aeronauts left prospective passengers behind either through gross miscalculation or because an impatient crowd forced them to ascend with a balloon only partially filled. In the period with which we are now concerned, such disappointments were generally due to gas of indifferent quality. The Grahams' roof-skimming exploits and suchlike misadventures may often have been due to an over-optimistic faith in the theoretical lifting power of the balloon which failed to take into account the effect of poor quality gas.

The difference in lifting power between hydrogen and coal-gas was difficult to estimate when the quality of the latter was so variable. At the end of the century when the supply had become more stable it was reckoned that the average weight of 1,000 cubic feet of gas was $37\frac{1}{2}$ lb[1] as compared with 5 lb for hydrogen and 75 lb for common air at sea-level. The effect of this difference on a balloon of 40,000 cubic feet capacity would be as follows:

Pounds	*Hydrogen*	*Coal-gas*
Weight of air displaced	3000	3000
Less weight of gas	200	1500
Less weight of balloon and gear	600	600
Useful lift at sea-level	2200	900

This substantial difference makes it easy to understand why the use of coal gas in the nineteenth century led to larger balloons.

By the 1830s, aeronauts were complaining of exploitation by London gas companies who were charging them 20s per 1,000 cubic feet, compared with the domestic charge of 5s. Nevertheless, the saving was still very considerable for it was estimated in 1836 that a 70,000 cubic foot balloon cost from £70 to £80 to inflate with coal-gas as against £250 for hydrogen. Even £70 was a substantial sum in those days, however. No wonder the aeronauts, having once inflated,

[1] Modern mains gas is of higher calorific value but higher weight and is therefore less suitable for balloons than that used in the early years of this century.

could rarely be dissuaded from taking off even under very adverse weather conditions; no wonder, too, that those who wanted a trip in a balloon had to pay handsomely for the privilege.

The great Charles Green was born in London on the 31st January, 1785. He was the son of a fruiterer in the Goswell Road and on leaving school he joined his father in the business. It is said that his experiments with gas, and the interest in ballooning to which these led, originated in a plan to make an apparatus for lighting the shop by gas. A bluff, massively built man with a heavy, rubicund face, Green looked more like a prosperous yeoman farmer than a London shopkeeper or an aeronaut. He could have sat as a model for the original John Bull. Genial and talkative on the ground, he became a taciturn martinet in the air, imposing an iron discipline and insisting upon absolute obedience no matter how much his passengers may have paid for the privilege of accompanying him. This was seldom resented for he inspired a confidence that was never misplaced. He had the prime qualities that make a great balloon pilot: a coolness that no emergency could ruffle combined with lightning-quick reactions. Had he been born in our own day he would have been a 'natural' as a racing driver. If Henry Coxwell is to be believed, he became somewhat jealous of his supremacy in his old age. Like an old bull, Green seems to have scented a potential rival in Coxwell and, unlike Gypson and Gale, would give the eager young man no help or advice.

Green made his first ascent – and the first ever to be made with coal-gas – from Green Park on 19th July, 1821 in celebration of the coronation of George IV. The balloon was decorated with the royal arms and the inscription 'George IV, Royal Coronation Balloon'. It was of a little under 16,000 cubic feet capacity[1] and was filled from the Piccadilly gas main. The ascent was completely successful, the balloon rising to 11,000 ft, though Green's landing near Barnet was a rough one, the balloon dragging for nearly a quarter of a mile. In all his subsequent ascents, Green only once used hydrogen.

Green did not at once become a master of the skies. On many of his early ascents he suffered the usual misfortunes that beset the inexperienced aeronaut, landing in trees, hitting a chimney stack at

---

[1] '100,000 gallons' was the figure given at the time. Hodgson quotes Green as saying that the balloon contained 1,200 cubic feet, whereas 12,000 was obviously the correct figure.

Oxford gas works, falling in the sea off Brighton. But by far the most alarming of these 'prentice flights' was that made from Cheltenham on the 1st August, 1822 when he was accompanied by a *Cheltenham Chronicle* reporter named Griffith. In the moment of ascent Green realized to his horror that at least one of the car lines had been maliciously cut with a razor or a very sharp knife by someone in the crowd that had pressed about the car just before their take-off from the London Hotel yard. This placed them in a nightmare situation; the car was thrown out of balance, and all but one of the remaining car lines parted so that they were forced to cling to the hoop. Then the meshes of the net began to fail with a sound like a succession of pistol shots and it seemed likely that the balloon would escape through it. Part of it did so, the balloon then resembling an hour glass. Needless to say, Green made an early descent a mile and a half from Salperton, but the grappling iron failed to hold and they were dragged for some distance before the balloon struck a tree, broke through the net and exploded, flinging both men heavily to the ground in a field at Notgrove.

Perhaps because of the injuries he received and the damage to the balloon, Green did not make another ascent until June of the following year. He maintained that the car lines had been cut by 'black legs' from London, claiming that no less than £20,000 had been wagered on the distance he would fly, most of it placed in London.

In his early days Green also indulged in the usual stunts, ascending on horse-back or with fireworks, but in later life when he had reached the pinnacle of his fame he could afford to put such frivolities behind him. The vehicle that brought him that fame was the most celebrated and long-lived of all free balloons, the *Royal Vauxhall* or, as it was later called, the *Nassau*. This great balloon and its master pilot formed the most outstanding combination in the history of nineteenth century aeronautics.

In his *Royal Coronation* balloon and its similar successor Green had, by 1835, made 200 ascents and travelled some 6,000 miles in 240 flying hours. He then planned a new balloon of much greater size and superlative construction embodying all the fruits of his experience. Lacking the necessary capital, the balloon was built at the expense of Messrs Gye & Hughes, the owners of Vauxhall Gardens so that, although they treated him very fairly by allowing him complete freedom in its design, Green did not become a free agent in the use of the balloon until 1840 when he bought it from Gye & Hughes for £500.

To make the envelope of the *Royal Vauxhall*, 2,000 yards of the finest silk was imported from Italy in the raw state and made up by Sopers of Spitalfields. The seams uniting the alternating gores of crimson and white were not sewn but cemented with a special preparation invented by Green which he claimed would be stronger and more durable than any stitching. The longevity of the balloon proved him right, as would much later experience with airship gas bags. The balloon had a capacity of 70,000 cubic feet and when inflated with car attached stood 80 ft high. The hoop was 6 ft in diameter and the original wicker-work car was boat-shaped, 9 ft long by 4 ft wide, with gilded eagles' heads at prow and stern. The performance of the balloon so far exceeded expectations, however, that a more roomy circular car was subsequently fitted for the balloon's second ascent. To reduce landing shocks the grappling iron was fitted with an 'Indian rubber cord' made by Sievier of Paris.

The maiden flight of this splendid balloon was made from Vauxhall on the 9th September, 1836 and was watched by Lord Palmerston, Count D'Orsay and many other notables. It was estimated that with hydrogen the balloon would have had a lift of no less than 4,982 lb and even with coal-gas the restraining power of forty-one 56 lb weights and thirty-six policemen had to be supplemented by twenty workmen hurriedly recruited from the gardens to hold the balloon down. The ascent was delayed by rain until 6 p.m. Then Green, his wife, his brother James, Robert Hollond, M.P. for Hastings, and five others climbed aboard and to the accompaniment of a roar of applause the *Royal Vauxhall* soared majestically into the air. Notwithstanding the weight of nine people and four hundredweight of ballast, the lift was so great that Green estimated that he had to valve 15,000 cubic feet of gas to check the rate of ascent. Even so the balloon rose to 13,000 ft in five minutes, bursting through the heavy clouds that hung over London into brilliant evening sunshine. To bring this untried monster down through the clouds to a safe anchorage on an invisible earth must have been a supreme test of Green's nerve and skill, bearing in mind the disasters that had befallen much smaller and more manageable balloons in such circumstances. But just as dusk was falling, Green brought the *Royal Vauxhall* down to a perfect landing near the village of Cliffe, five miles beyond Gravesend.

On his third flight with the big balloon, one of Green's passengers was the Irishman, Thomas Monck Mason, flute player, patron of the Opera, and lessee of Her Majesty's Theatre. As a result of this flight, Mason became an ardent balloon enthusiast. So impressed were Robert Hollond and Monck Mason with the performance of the new balloon that they conceived the idea of making a long-distance flight that would surpass anything achieved before. Hollond was prepared to finance the venture, Green consented to act as pilot while Messrs Gye & Hughes very sportingly agreed to the use of their balloon without any prior publicity or advertisement.

Most elaborate preparations were made for this flight. Green equipped the balloon with a thousand foot 'guide-rope' or trail rope complete with a small winch to control it. As mentioned earlier, Baldwin had suggested the use of such a device many years before but Green was the first to use it on a balloon. The principle was simple. Assuming the rope to be extended to its full length below the car, at an altitude of less than 1,000 ft part of the rope would trail upon the ground thus relieving the balloon of the weight of that part. This, like the discharge of ballast, would produce a tendency to ascend, but this would be checked when the balloon again took the full weight of the rope. Thus the trail rope conserved ballast by acting as an automatic height regulator. In addition, Green claimed that it would greatly reduce the risk of running into high ground when flying at low altitude by night. Green also equipped the trail rope with specially designed copper floats so that it would function in the same manner on the sea.

In 1809, the engineer John Woodhouse had employed exactly the same principle, but using chains instead of a rope, to balance the caisson and counterweights of England's first vertical boat lift on the Worcester & Birmingham Canal at Tardebigge. Whether there was any transmission of ideas from Baldwin and Woodhouse to Green may never be known. Green claimed originality, but may have done so in innocence. The idea of his great balloon sweeping across Europe trailing a rope behind it sounds pretty alarming for those below, but this aspect of the matter seems to have caused him little concern. At least there was no 'wire-scape' in those days.

Other special items of equipment were a means of heating coffee by quick lime, a lamp that could be lowered over the side when gas was being released, and Bengal lights attached to small parachutes to be used for signalling or in the event of a night landing. Green estimated that with their 4 cwt of ballast the balloon might be capable of staying aloft for three weeks and on the strength of this a prodigious amount of food and drink was stowed aboard. The weighing on list included 40 lb of ham, beef and tongue, 45 lb of fowls and preserves, 40 lb of sugar, bread and biscuits and two gallons each of sherry, port and brandy of a total weight of 61 lb. Excluding the aeronauts but including sand ballast the equipment and stores weighed altogether 2,763 lb.

Thus amply provisioned, the three adventurers rose from Vauxhall at 1.30 p.m. on the 7th November, 1836. Carried by a north-westerly breeze, the balloon passed over Kent, crossed the Medway near Rochester and was within two miles of the towers of Canterbury shortly before 4 p.m. Here a letter addressed to the Mayor was dropped by parachute. It was duly delivered. By now they were flying at low altitude and the balloon was tending to bear too much to the eastward towards the North Sea. Green therefore discharged ballast, hoping that by rising the balloon might pick up a more northerly current that would take them over the Channel. This manoeuvre was completely successful. Passing directly over Dover Castle and right on course for Calais, the balloon crossed the shore line at 4.48 p.m. Below them the harbour lights sparkled through the gathering dusk and in their soundless passage they could hear the beating of the waves upon Dover beach. They had prepared the trail rope and floats for the sea crossing but this proved unnecessary for the balloon continued to travel at about 25 m.p.h., the lights of Calais soon came up and they crossed the French coast an hour later at a height of 3,000 ft.

The copper floats were now removed from the trail rope which was then lowered to its full extent. As it was now quite dark the lamp was lit and the three aeronauts ate a hearty supper, spreading out their meal on the central division of the car, toasting their friends at home and making laboured puns about the high flavour of the food as their great balloon flew onwards upon its noiseless way across Europe. A glow of light on the horizon ahead proved to be the iron-works surrounding Liege, a dramatic inferno of furnaces and flame-lit smoke over which they passed directly, prudently raising their trail rope as they did so. Here Green inadvertently dropped the quick-lime coffee heater overboard, so, as this made the spare barrel of lime useless it was jettisoned, being attached to a small parachute out of consideration for those below.

The night was moonless and from this region of light they passed into a darkness so total that no circumstance of the voyage seems to have impressed the travellers so much. Monck Mason described it as 'an unfathomable abyss of darkness visible' and wrote: 'we could scarcely avoid the impression that we were cleaving our way through an interminable mass of black marble in which we were imbedded, and which, solid a few inches before us, seemed to soften as we approached. . . .' They again lowered the trail rope and assumed, rightly or wrongly, from variations in the barometer reading that it was working effectively. It became bitterly cold but, as other aeronauts have observed before and since, they did not feel the cold severely thanks to the absence of any current of air.

After hours of blindness, the first pale dawnlight was very cheering. Green discharged ballast and the *Royal Vauxhall* rose to 12,000 ft, the greatest altitude attained on the voyage. They were at this height when they saw the sun rise in great splendour. At first the earth below was still in shadow, but as the sun climbed the sky it revealed a vast tract of hilly country, the higher ground covered in snow. They had not the faintest notion of their whereabouts and believed they might be in Poland or Russia. Having cleared the snowfields and finding themselves over a region of thickly wooded hills and narrow, fertile valleys they decided to attempt a landing. This was not easy in such a terrain especially as the wind currents near the ground proved treacherously unpredictable. Twice they had to throw out ballast and rise again, but at the third attempt the skill of Charles Green brought the big balloon down to a safe landing on the edge of a wood. From the countrymen who soon appeared on the scene and who could not believe that they had left London the previous afternoon, the adventurers learned that they had landed near the town of Weilburg in the Duchy of Nassau. The time was 7.30 a.m. and they had covered

480 miles in eighteen hours, the greatest flight that man had ever
accomplished. Curiously enough they had come down at Dillhausen
Mill on the Elbern, almost the exact spot where Blanchard had landed
after an ascent from Frankfort in 1785.

The aeronauts received a hero's welcome at Weilburg where they
were lavishly entertained by all the local notables for several days.
There was an endless round of balls, dinners and concerts; there was
an elaborate christening ceremony, with barons and baronesses playing godfathers and godmothers, when the balloon, inflated with air
for the occasion and occupied by Green and eight young ladies, was
named 'The Great Balloon of Nassau'. Green was crowned with
laurels and addressed with odes in German and Latin composed by
the learned doctors of the College of Weilburg. In translation, one of
these reads:

> *In former days the Gallic Blanchard came*
> *To Weilburg's humble shores, in search of fame.*
> *But short his flight, and brief his bold career,*
> *From Frankfort and the Maine transported here.*
> *But who is he that now, with bolder span,*
> *Flies from the Thames to settle on the Lahn,*
> *O'erleaping empires in his daring flight,*
> *Regardless of the sable frowns of night?*
> *Yield, Romans; yield, Greeks; Frenchmen, quit the throne;*
> *The crown of Daedalus is Green's alone.*

All these pomps and pageants, these heady sweets of triumph, were,
however, followed by the inevitable anti-climax. Hollond had to
return to London leaving Green and Monck Mason with the difficult
problem of transporting the balloon to Paris where its owners had
arranged to exhibit it. In Coblentz they purchased a second-hand
carriage, removed the body, fitted the balloon car with a temporary
seat and an oil-cloth tilt-cover and lashed it to the frame. To the
wonder of all beholders they set off in this remarkable equipage
drawn by four horses. Alas, the weather which had hitherto held fair,
now broke into violent storms; gales threatened to overturn the whole
crazy outfit; the oil-cloth cover failed to keep out torrential rain so
that they were soaked to the skin and to complete their misery the
seat suddenly collapsed, precipitating them into the bottom of the

basket. Repairs and improvements were made at the village of Thionville and after six arduous days and nights of travel the bedraggled aeronauts finally reached Paris where Green made two ascents before returning with the balloon to England.

The most remarkable subsequent event in the career of Charles Green and the *Nassau* balloon (as it was now called) was his ascent with Robert Cocking and his parachute on the 24th July, 1837. Robert Cocking, the son of an Irish clergyman, was a professional watercolourist and an amateur scientist. As a young man he had witnessed Garnerin's London parachute descent of 1802 and he had since devoted thirty-five years of thought and experiment to the development of an improved form of parachute which would not oscillate as Garnerin's had done. Influenced perhaps by the writings of Sir George Cayley, Cocking came to the conclusion that a stable parachute should be in the form of an inverted cone and proved this to his own satisfaction by experiments with models. He then constructed a full-scale man-carrier on the same lines which was of very large size. Three hoops, the uppermost of block tin and the other two of copper, determined the form of the inverted cone, with angles of 30°, the top hoop being 107 ft 4 in circumference and the lowest 4 ft, the height between them being 10 ft. Ten light timber spars and bracing lines connected the hoops to complete a framework which was covered with Irish linen. Including the basket slung below, the parachute weighed 223 lb to which was added Cocking's substantial weight of 170 lb. Earlier balloons would have been incapable of lifting such a weight, but the advent of the *Nassau* had solved this problem for Cocking and he persuaded the proprietors of Vauxhall Gardens to allow him the use of the balloon, with Green as pilot, for his experiment – the first parachute attempt by an Englishman.

Green viewed the whole project with the gravest misgivings, but he was not then his own master where the *Nassau* was concerned. So doubtful was he about Cocking's parachute that he agreed to the venture only on condition that he should not be responsible for releasing it. A trigger mechanism was therefore designed so that Cocking could release himself. In accepting the hazardous assignment Green also realized that the sudden loss of a weight of nearly 400 lb would place the balloon and its occupants in as great a peril as the parachutist. Such a feat had never been essayed before and it was clear that it would be a supreme test of Green's courage and skill. Nevertheless, the risk did not deter Edward Spencer, a close friend of Green, from volunteering to accompany him. Spencer was a Barnsbury solicitor who made a number of ascents with Green in the *Nassau* and whose son, Charles Green Spencer, founded the once famous firm of C. G. Spencer & Sons of Highbury, manufacturers of balloons and parachutes.

Green prepared for the ascent with the greatest care. Not only did he install an extra large valve 3 ft in diameter at the north pole of the *Nassau*, but he fitted a second valve 2 ft in diameter below to supplement the neck, the object being to relieve the balloon of as much gas as possible as soon as the parachute was released in order to check its rate of ascent and prevent it bursting. He also provided an air bag of 500 gallons capacity equipped with two breathing tubes as he reasoned that he and his companion might otherwise be asphyxiated by the great volume of gas so suddenly realeased. A long canvas pipe was fitted to carry discharged sand ballast clear of the parachute and means were contrived to enable Cocking to climb up to the balloon car if arrangements went wrong and the *Nassau* was forced to land with the parachute unreleased.

Efforts were made to persuade Cocking, then in his sixty-first year, to abandon his experiment, but these were in vain so at 7.30 p.m. on a perfect summer evening the *Nassau* rose from Vauxhall with the parachute attached. When the balloon had reached 5,000 ft, Green advised Cocking that with such a weight he could rise no higher. From his place in the parachute basket 50 ft below the car Cocking called back: 'Then I shall very soon leave you, but tell me whereabouts I am.' 'We appear to be on a level with Greenwich. Are you comfortable?' Green asked. 'Yes, I never felt more comfortable or more delighted in my life', replied Cocking and then, after a pause, he added: 'Well, now I think I shall leave you.' On hearing this Green called back: 'I wish you a very good night and a safe descent if you are determined to make it and not use the tackle.' Then, as Cocking called 'Goodnight Spencer, good night Green', the two aeronauts placed the air tubes in their mouths and crouched down in the bottom of the car, Green grasping the two valve lines. After a preliminary jerk, they felt the parachute leave them and what followed next is best told in Green's own words:

James Sadler ascends from Dublin on his attempt to cross the Irish Sea, 1812

Death of Madame Blanchard,
1819

Death of Thomas Harris, 1824

'The effect upon us at this moment is almost beyond description. The immense machine which suspended us between earth and heaven, whilst it appeared to be forced upwards with terrific violence and rapidity through unknown and untravelled regions, amidst the howlings of a fearful hurricane, rolled about as though revelling in a freedom for which it had long struggled but of which until that moment it had been kept in utter ignorance. It at length, as if somewhat fatigued by its exertions, gradually assumed the motions of a snake working its way with astonishing speed towards a given object. During this frightful operation, the gas was rushing in torrents from the upper and lower valves, but more particularly from the latter, as the density of the atmosphere through which we were forcing our progress pressed so heavily on the valve at the top of the balloon as to admit of comparatively but a small escape by the aperture.'

For nearly five minutes both men were completely blinded by the escaping gas. When they recovered their sight the barometer read 13.20 representing an altitude of 23,384 ft by Green's calculation. The fact that by this time the balloon was already falling rapidly and that it had lost an estimated 30,000 ft of gas, led Green to believe that the maximum height had been considerably greater than this,[1] perhaps the greatest yet attained by man at that time. Despite the great loss of gas and an experience that would have unnerved most men, Charles Green, cool and skilful as ever, brought the *Nassau* down to a perfect landing in deep twilight at Offham, near Town Malling, Kent, at 8.45 p.m. This meant throwing out everything portable, for the balloon had lost a third of its gas and resembled a parachute with the basket dangling nearly 60 ft below the envelope.

Green and Spencer spent a pleasant night with the rector of Town Malling who turned out to be the son of that pioneer aeronaut Major Money, and it was not until they reached Wrotham next day that they learned of the awful fate of Robert Cocking. Horrified watchers below had seen the unfortunate man's parachute collapse in the air soon after its release. Beneath a useless cloud of wildly flapping fabric, poor Cocking had crashed to earth in a field at Lee Green only three minutes after his release. He was still alive when found, but he never spoke and died as he was being carried on a litter to the Tiger's Head

---

[1] In a letter to Mrs Hutton, of Bennetts Hill, Birmingham, now in the Poynton Collection, Green claimed to have reached 27,000 ft on this occasion, though in view of later ascents with the *Nassau* this seems a little doubtful.

9

Inn at Lee. He lies buried in Lee churchyard. So ended the aspiration of a lifetime.

Both Green and Mrs Graham subsequently made 'benefit' ascents in aid of Cocking's widow. Mrs Graham released two miniature parachutes of Garnerin's and Cocking's designs and it was observed that the latter was much the steadier of the two. In fact the Cayley and Cocking theory of the inverted cone was by no means so absurd as it might seem at first thought, and it is clear that Cocking's death was due to mechanical rather than aerodynamic failure. Cocking had insisted upon metal hoops in face of his friends' efforts to persuade him to use ash and according to eye-witnesses it was the large upper hoop of block tin that first gave way.

Although a Polish aeronaut, Jordaki Kuparento, is said to have made a successful parachute escape from a blazing Montgolfière over Warsaw in 1808, the Cocking disaster simply strengthened the view, particularly in England, that the parachute was merely a useless vehicle that pandered to a morbid public desire for sensational stunts and ought to be banned. However, this hostility could not shake the determination of the aeronaut John Hampton to become the first English parachutist and at Cheltenham on the 8th October, 1838 he achieved his great ambition. Hampton, like Gale, served in the Royal Navy before turning professional aeronaut. Born in 1799, he made his first ascent in June 1838 and had completed well over a hundred flights in his *Albion* and *Erin-go-bragh* balloons before he retired in 1852. His small but significant contribution to the balloon was the substitution of wooden toggles for knots as a method of securing the car lines. For two days before his Cheltenham adventure he exhibited his parachute in the Montpellier Pumproom. This was of the Garnerin 'umbrella' pattern, 15 ft in diameter, the canvas envelope being stretched over a framework of whale-bone ribs and bamboo stretchers. A copper tube formed the 'stick' of the umbrella and to this the small wicker car was attached.

Hampton's project met with great opposition in Cheltenham; so much so that the local magistrates were asked to prohibit the ascent but, although they were sympathetic, these worthies ruled that it was not within their power to do so. There was one way of stopping Hampton, however, and that was to deny him the use of the town gas supply. Nevertheless, the somewhat simple-minded townsfolk finally relented on condition that Hampton would only give a demonstration by ascending captive. To this the aeronaut and his sole confidant, Grenville Fletcher, readily agreed. The balloon was inflated, the parachute was brought from the Pumproom to the Montpellier Gardens and attached; Hampton took his place in the basket and under Fletcher's direction the balloon was allowed to rise to a height of 300 ft on a rope. At this moment, as the conspirators had arranged, Hampton cut the rope and with a gasp of dismay the spectators saw the aeronaut soar into the sky. At 6,000 ft Hampton released his parachute from the balloon. The latter is said to have burst and its rapid fall horrified many spectators who thought they were seeing another Cocking tragedy. Hampton, however, came safely to earth in a field at Badgeworth owned by a Mr Hicks. His descent had taken 12m 40s, representing a falling rate of about 500 ft per minute and his parachute appears to have been more stable than that of Garnerin. The total weight of the parachute and its occupant – 328 lb – included 56 lb of ballast which Hampton discharged shortly before landing, thus checking his descent. This was not only the first successful parachute descent ever made by an Englishman but the first to be made in England for 36 years. In June of the following year, Hampton repeated his performance at Cremorne Gardens and altogether he made seven parachute descents in the course of his career.

With his *Erin-go-bragh* balloon, which was second only in size to the *Nassau*, Hampton became Charles Green's greatest rival. But the pre-eminence of that old master of the air and his famous balloon was too secure to be challenged. He had now no need to indulge in stunts for there was never any lack of patrons prepared to pay handsomely for the privilege of a place in the car of the *Nassau*. At the end of July 1844 Green wrote[1] in reply to a 'fan' letter from a Mrs Hutton that he had at that date made 299 ascents, thirteen of them at night, and that he had carried 548 passengers including twenty-eight women. Thereafter, despite his advancing years, Green continued to make frequent flights, mostly from Vauxhall, with the obvious intent to set up a record of 500 ascents. He reached this target in 1852 and in that year, in the true tradition of the great showman, a number of

[1] The original, dated 30th July, 1844 and addressed to Mrs Hutton, is in the Poynton Collection.

'farewell ascents' and 'positively last appearances' were advertised from
Vauxhall. His last flight on the 12th September, 1852 was advertised
as his 500th, though estimates of the actual number of ascents he
made vary from 504 to 527. Thereafter Green retired to his home at
Aerial Cottage, Highgate, though he continued to take an active
interest in matters aeronautical. Born in the year of Lunardi's first
flight, this grand old aeronaut lived to become a member of the
(Royal) Aeronautical Society, founded in 1866. He attended a number of the early meetings of the Society before he died of heart failure
on the 26th March, 1870 at the ripe old age of eighty-five.

What was it really like to travel with Charles Green in the car of
the *Nassau* balloon? Accounts of contemporary balloon voyages are
legion, but most of them are prolix and few truly articulate. Most
fortunately for posterity, however, one of Green's passengers on his
last flight from Vauxhall was none other than Henry Mayhew, that
indefatigable recorder of life in Victorian London. His graphic
account[1] of his adventure makes a most appropriate postscript to this
chapter.

'I had seen the great metropolis under almost every aspect. I had dived
into holes and corners hidden from the honest and well-to-do portion of
the Cockney community. I had visited Jacob's Island (the plague-spot) in
the height of the cholera, when, to inhale the very air of the place was
almost to breathe the breath of death. I had sought out the haunts of beg-
gars and thieves, and passed hours communing with them as to their
histories, habits, natures and impulses. I had seen the world of London
below the surface, as it were, and I had a craving to contemplate it far
above it – to behold the immense mass of vice and avarice and cunning, of
noble aspirations and humble heroism, blent into one black spot; to take,
as it were, an angel's view of that huge city where, perhaps, there is more
virtue and more iniquity, more wealth and more want huddled together
in one vast heap than in any other part of the earth; to look down upon the
strange, incongruous clump of palaces and workhouses, of factory chim-
neys and church steeples, of banks and prisons, of docks and hospitals, of
parks and squares, of courts and alleys – to look down upon these as the
birds of the air look down upon them, and see the whole dwindle into a
heap of rubbish on the green sward, a human anthill, as it were; to hear
the hubbub of the restless sea of life below, and hear it like the ocean in a
shell, whispering to you of the incessant strugglings and chafings of the

[1] Written for the *Illustrated London News*, 18th September, 1852.

distant tide – to swing in the air far above all the petty jealousies and heartburnings, and small ambitions and vain parades, and feel for once tranquil as a babe in a cot – that you were hardly of the earth earthy; and to find as you drink in the pure thin air above you, the blood dancing and tingling joyously through your veins, and your whole spirit becoming etherealised as, Jacob-like, you mounted the aerial ladder, and beheld the world beneath you fade and fade from your sight like a mirage in the desert; to feel yourself really, as you had ideally in your dreams, floating through the endless realms of space, sailing among the stars free as "the lark at Heaven's gate"; and to enjoy for a brief half-hour at least a fore-taste of that elysian destiny which is the hope of all. To see, to think, and to feel thus was surely worth some little risk, and this it was that led me to peril my bones in the car of a balloon.

'. . . I gladly availed myself of a seat in the car which Mr Green had set aside for me. At about a quarter to seven o'clock, six of us and the "veteran aeronaut" took our places in the large deep wicker-work basket of a car attached to the Royal Nassau Balloon, while two gentlemen were seated immediately above our heads, with their backs resting against the netting and their legs stretched across the hoop. . . . There were altogether nine of us – a complete set of human pins for the air to play at skittles with – and the majority, myself among the number, no sylphs in weight. Above us reeled the great gas bag like a monster peg-top, and all around the car were groups of men holding to the sides of the basket, while the huge iron weights were handed out and replaced by large squabby bags of sand.

'In the course of about ten minutes all the arrangements for starting were complete; the grapnel, looking like a bundle of large iron fish-hooks, welded together, was hanging over the side of the car. The guide-rope, longer than St. Pauls is high, and done up in a canvas bag, with only the end hanging out, was dangling beside the grapnel, and we were raised some fifty feet in the air to try the ascensive power of the machine that was to bear us through the clouds. Then, having been duly dragged down, the signal was at length given to fire the cannons, and Mr. Green loosening the only rope that bound us to the Gardens, we shot into the air – or rather the earth seemed to sink suddenly down, as if the spot of ground, with all the spectators on it, and on which we ourselves had been lately standing, had been constructed on the same principle as the Adelphi stage, and admitted of being lowered at a moment's notice. The last thing that I remember to have seen distinctly was the flash of the guns, and instantaneously there appeared a multitude of upturned faces in the Gardens below, the greater part with their mouths wide open, and a *chevaux-de-frise* of hands extended above them, all signalling farewell to us.

Then, as we swept rapidly above the trees, I could see the roadway immediately outside the Gardens, stuck all over with rows of tiny people, looking like so many black pins on a cushion, and the hubbub of the voices below was like the sound of a distant school let loose.

'And here began that peculiar panoramic effect which is the distinguishing feature of a view from a balloon, and which arises from the utter absence of all sense of motion in the machine itself. The earth appeared literally to consist of a long series of scenes, which were being continually drawn along under you, as if it were a diorama beheld flat upon the ground, and gave one almost the notion that the world was an endless landscape stretched upon rollers, which some invisible sprites were revolving for your especial enjoyment.

'Then, as we struck towards the fields of Surrey, and I looked over the edge of the car in which I was standing, holding on tight to the thick rope descending from the hoop above, and with the rim of the wicker-work reaching up to my breast, the sight was the most exquisite delight I ever experienced. The houses below looked like the tiny wooden things out of a child's box of toys and the streets like ruts. . . . As the balloon kept on ascending, the lines of buildings grew smaller and smaller, till in a few minutes the projections seemed very much like the prominences on the little plaster models of countries. Then we could see the gas-lights along the different lines of road start into light one after another all over the earth. . . . The river we could see winding far away, undulating, as it streamed along, like a man-of-war's pennant, and glittering here and there in the dusk like grey steel. All around the horizon were thick slate-coloured clouds, edged with the orange-red of the departed sun; and with the tops of these we seemed to be on a level. So deep was the dusk in the distance, that it was difficult to tell where the earth ended and the sky began; and in trying to make out the objects afar off, it seemed to be as if you were looking through so much crepe. . . .'

At this juncture Mayhew could not help reflecting upon 'the awful havoc there would be if the twigs of the wicker car were to break and the bottom give way'.

'On what sharp church-steeple, thought I, should I be spitted? and as I looked down the beauty of the scene once more took all sense of fear from my mind, for the earth now appeared concave with the height, and seemed like a huge black bowl – as if it were the sky of the nether regions. The lights of the villages scattered over the scene were like clusters of glow-worms, from the midst of which you could here and there distinguish the crimson speck of some railway-lamp.'

Some of Mayhew's companions had, in his own words, 'supplied themselves with an extraordinary stock of courage previous to starting' which made them 'more noisy than agreeable', but they were presently silenced by Green, who reminded them that the balloon was now descending rapidly and that it was time they considered their safety. The aerial idyll, alcoholic or otherwise, was over and the passengers faced the inevitable anti-climax of the return to earth, in this case a distinctly brutal one.

'A bag of ballast was intrusted to one of the passengers to let fall at a given signal, while Green himself stood with the grapnel ready to loose immediately he came to a fitting spot. Presently the signal for the descent of the ballast was given, and as it dropped it was curious to watch it fall; the earth had seemed almost at our feet as the car swept over the fields, but so long was the heavy bag in getting to the ground that, as the eye watched it fall and fall, the mind was filled with amazement at the height the balloon still was in the air. Suddenly the sound as of a gun announced that the bag had struck the soil, and then we were all told to sit low down in the car and hold fast. Scarcely had we obeyed the orders given than the car was suddenly and fiercely jerked half round, and all within it thrown one on top of another; immediately after this, bump went the bottom of the car on the ground, giving us so violent a shake that it seemed as if every limb in the body had been simultaneously dislocated. Now the balloon pitched on its side, and lay on the ground struggling with the wind, and rolling about, heaving like a huge whale in the agonies of death.

' "For Heaven's sake! hold fast," shouted Mr Green, as we were dashed up and down in the car, all rolling one on the other, with each fresh lurch of the giant machine stretched on the ground before us, and from which we could hear the gas roaring from the valve, like the blast of a furnace.

' "Sit still, all of you, I say!" roared our pilot, as he saw someone endeavouring to leave the car.

'Again we were pitched right on end, and the bottom of the car shifted into a ditch, the water of which bubbled up through the wicker-work of the car; and I, unlucky wight, who was seated in that part of which the concussions were mostly confined, soon began to feel that I was quietly sitting in a pool of water.

'To move, however, was evidently to peril not only one's own life, but that of all the other passengers, but still no one came to us; for we had fallen in a swamp, which we afterwards found out was Pirbright Common, situate some half-dozen miles from Guildford.

'Presently, however, to our great delight, some hundred drab-smocked countrymen appeared, almost as if by magic, around the edges of the car; for some little time they were afraid to touch, but at last they got a firm hold of it, and we were one after another extricated from our seats.

'To tell the remainder of the adventure would be tame and dull; suffice it that, after some two hours' labour, the aerial machine, car, grapnels and all, was rolled and packed up in a cart, and thus transported, an hour after midnight, to Guildford; the voyagers journeying to the same town in a tilted cart, delighted with their trip, and listening to the many curious adventures of the veteran aeronaut who had successfully piloted them and some hundred others through the air; and who, now that the responsibility of their lives rested no longer in his hands, seemed a thoroughly different man; before he was taciturn, and almost irritable, when spoken to; and now he was garrulous, and delighting all with his intelligence, his enterprise, his enthusiasm and his courtesy. Indeed, long shall we all remember the pleasant night we passed with the old ethereal pilot on his 500th ascent with the Royal Nassau Balloon.'

CHAPTER SEVEN

The Giants

FOR A CERTAIN TYPE of mind sheer size seems to exert an irresistible fascination. Although the lesson of history is that the biggest is seldom or never the best, ever since the building of the tower of Babel ambitious men have striven to create monsters to gratify their desire for power or fame. Fortunately, many of these monsters never got off the drawing board; of those that did the majority failed more or less spectacularly, attracting to their creators notoriety rather than the coveted fame.

Even the Montgolfier brothers fell a prey to this cult of giantism when they constructed their huge *Le Flesselle*, but at least its brief career seems effectually to have deterred others from following their example for more than fifty years. In the construction of such monsters there were no peculiar difficulties such as beset – and often defeated – monster-makers in other technological realms. The problem here, as *Le Flesselle* had shown, was to get such an unwieldy mass of fabric inflated and airborne and, having done so, to bring it safe to earth again. As the aeronauts soon learned by bitter experience, even the smallest balloon could become unmanageable when under restraint.

The rebirth of the giant balloon sprang from the belief that constant and predictable aerial currents would enable the skilled aeronaut to make flights of almost infinite distance and duration provided he was sustained by a sufficiently large reservoir of gas. The first manifestation of this train of thought was a design by the aeronaut Etienne Robertson, published in 1804, for a balloon which he claimed would be capable of sustaining a crew of sixty 'chosen by the academies' on a globe-trotting voyage of six months or more. Although the grandiloquent dedication to Volta would appear to have been written in all seriousness, the design of *La Minerva* is of such baroque extravagance that the conclusion that Robertson was either mad or

137

clowning is hard to resist. It depicts a large galleon with a balloon
150 ft in diameter in place of masts and sails. Dangling below the hull
and accessible by 'ladders of silk' suspended in space appear an enormous barrel for storing water, wine and foodstuffs and three small
buildings labelled respectively 'Medicine room', 'A room fitted up
for recreation, walking and gymnastics' and 'closets'. Looking at
those vertiginous ladders one feels that before they had voyaged far
the academic crew would be suffering acutely from want of medical
care, lack of exercise and constipation.

The next essay in this vein came from an Englishman, J. W. Hoar.
Though not so wildly bizarre as the first, it sailed perilously near the
lunatic fringe. In 1837 Hoar was instrumental in launching an 'Aeronautic Association' for the purpose of exploring Africa by balloon, a
project which, it was said, might require the explorers to remain aloft
for a month or two. The prospectus promised an ultimate profit of
200 per cent on the capital of £8,000 and announced that the project
would be superintended by Mr Graham (not perhaps the happiest
choice) who would lead a team of six aeronauts including a natura-
list, a geographer and a draughtsman on a flight over unknown territory. This scheme was undoubtedly inspired by the success of Green's
flight to Weilberg.

In the following year Hoar constructed an enormous Montgolfière,
130 ft high with a capacity of 170,000 cubic feet. It was made of
varnished lawn in alternate gores of red and white. There was no
net, suspension cords being sewn into the seams and attached to a
cane hoop 46 ft in diameter. A wicker-work car 15 ft long was supported by the hoop. A chimney extended from the stove into the
neck, but although the latter was said to be 'specially designed' it
burned the traditional Montgolfier mixture of wool, chopped straw
and faggots, so how the aeronauts could have hoped to remain aloft
for a day, let alone a month, is hard to conceive.

A maiden ascent by this monster was advertised to take place from
the Surrey Zoological Gardens on the 24th May, 1838, the birthday
of Queen Victoria. Claiming her 'immediate patronage' the pro-
moters named the balloon the *Queen's Royal Aerostat* and made
most elaborate preparations. A launching platform with suspension
masts was erected upon an island in the lake at the Surrey Gardens
and grandstands were built along the shore line. For hours the large

crowd watched with growing impatience while the aeronauts busied themselves about their great balloon, but for some obscure reason they totally failed to get it airborne. When six o'clock came without sign of success there was an ominous stamping of feet in the stands punctuated by cries of 'Let it off!' 'Off with it!' At seven o'clock, when these cries were renewed with greater vehemence, a small boat appeared on the lake bearing aloft a notice which read: 'The balloon cannot ascend but to compensate for the unavoidable disappointment an eruption will take place at dusk'. This referred to the miniature Vesuvius which was a regular feature of Surrey Gardens firework displays, but the notice provoked an immediate eruption of quite a different kind. There were furious shouts of 'Shame!' 'A Hoax!' and the men in the boat were forced to beat a hasty retreat under a withering fire of stones, bottles and other missiles. Once they were out of range, the balloon became the target and its envelope was soon as full of holes as a colander. Then the enraged crowd cut the guy ropes of the suspension masts, which were attached to the shore, causing the tattered balloon to collapse in ruin. So much damage was done in this riot that balloons were unpopular with the proprietors of the Surrey Gardens for a long while after.

Most men would have been discouraged by a fiasco of such magnitude, but Hoar must have suffered from giantism in a most acute and chronic form for he proceeded to make a second and even larger Montgolfière with which he planned to ascend from Beulah Spa, Norwood to celebrate the opening of the Croydon Atmospheric Railway. This occasion was just as disastrous, but Hoar must needs try a third time at Notting Hill racecourse in April 1839 with a still bigger Montgolfière of 215,000 ft capacity. The result was the same and after this we hear no more of J. W. Hoar or the Aeronautic Association.

The next proposal for long-distance flight was advanced in 1840 by no less a man than Charles Green, the project being to make an east to west crossing of the North Atlantic. His idea was that such a voyage should be made at low altitude using a trail rope equipped with copper floats and canvas buckets fitted with non-return valves to enable the aeronaut to pick up water ballast from the sea. Green also advocated the use of a clockwork driven propeller the axis of which could either be fixed horizontally or inclined upwards or

downwards in order to influence the course of the balloon in ascent
and descent as well as in forward motion. Unfortunately, shortly
after his scheme was announced, Green was badly injured in a very
rough descent in a gale in Essex and the project languished never to
be revived. Green had argued that by the use of the trail rope both
ballast and gas would be conserved, making a monster balloon unnecessary for an ocean crossing. Nevertheless his scheme has a
relevance in this chapter.

On the 13th April, 1844 Americans learned from a long article in
the *New York Sun* the very remarkable news that Monck Mason and
seven companions had just landed on the coast of South Carolina
after an adventurous three day voyage over the Atlantic from Britain
which was described in great detail. Much to the glee of rival newspapers, this article, needless to say, turned out to be a hoax perpe-
trated, it is believed, by Edgar Allan Poe. Whoever the author was,
his imagination was obviously inspired by the great Nassau flight and
Green's subsequent trans-Atlantic project. It undoubtedly stimulated
interest in the United States and thereafter schemes for Atlantic
flights became almost a monopoly of American aeronauts. This was
natural, because the prevailing westerlies made the eastern seaboard
of America the most favourable starting point.

In view of their pioneering enterprise in many other fields, Americans were remarkably late in taking to the air. The fact that from the
outset aeronautical developments in Europe were fully, accurately
and enthusiastically reported by Franklin, Jefferson and other intelligent American observers makes this the more surprising. The often
quoted story that a carpenter named James Wilcox ascended from
Philadelphia on the 28th December, 1783 using a cluster of small
balloons is based, like that of Monck Mason's ocean voyage, on a
hoax account. Some rather half-hearted native experiments were
made subsequently but, as mentioned earlier, credit for the first
authentic aerial voyage must go to Blanchard for his ascent from the
yard of the old Washington Prison, Walnut Street, Philadelphia on
the 9th January, 1793. Blanchard was followed to America by his
countrymen Louis-Charles Guille and Eugene Robertson, but these
'American tours' were not conspicuously successful from a financial
point of view. The disgruntled Frenchmen found that a thrifty and
sceptical American public would rather watch freely from a distance

than pay to enter the launching site enclosures. Eugene Godard fared better on his much later visit in 1850 because by that time the achievements of American aeronauts had popularized ballooning.

Trained in France by Eugene Robertson, 'professor' Charles Ferson Durant became America's first successful aeronaut, making his maiden ascent on his native heath from New York's Castle Garden on the 9th September, 1830. By his successful tours he did much to pave the way for others including those great 'professors', La Mountain, Wise and Lowe. These men were essentially showmen like their contemporaries in Britain and Europe and the chronicle of their careers follows a similar pattern of derring-do and sensational exploits. The great land mass of the United States and Canada gave them wonderful opportunities for extended voyages, though the great lakes were a hazard that sealed the fate of more than one aeronaut and there was always the risk of landing in uninhabited territory with its dangers of death from exposure or starvation. La Mountain and his companion once tramped for four days without food or adequate clothing after a landing in the wilds of Canada and were on the point of collapse when they reached the cabin of an hospitable Scottish settler.

The first American aeronaut to dream of an Atlantic challenger was a young English emigrant named Richard Clayton who had settled in Cincinnati as a watchmaker before he took up ballooning. In 1835 it was stated in the New York *Evening Star* that Clayton was actually constructing a mammoth balloon to be called *Star of the West* capable of carrying from twenty to thirty passengers over the Atlantic, but if it was ever completed it would seem that this great star never rose. There do not appear to have been any further schemes of this kind until after the Monck Mason hoax had kindled fresh interest.

In 1843 John Wise launched an unsuccessful appeal for funds for a balloon flight to Europe and it was not until 1859 that a wealthy enthusiast named O. A. Gager financed the building of the 50,000 cubic feet *Atlantic* with a lifeboat suspended beneath the car in case of trouble. In this year Wise, La Mountain, Gager and a reporter made a remarkable flight of 809 miles in this balloon from St Louis to Henderson in Jefferson County, N.Y. This was completed in 19 hours 50 minutes. At one stage a violent storm threatened to force them

down into Lake Erie, but instead of readying the lifeboat the aeronauts wisely decided to cut it adrift and so gain valuable lift. Their
situation must have appeared pretty desperate at this moment, for
Wise also jettisoned a bag of mail consigned to them by the United
States Express Company. This narrow escape from raging waters
may have caused Wise to temper his valour with more discretion for
his *Atlantic* never ventured over that ocean.

Wise's great rival, Thaddeus Lowe, also cherished the dream of a
trans-Atlantic voyage and in this same year (1859) he secured sufficient financial backing to enable him to construct an enormous balloon
which was at first named *City of New York* and later *Great Western*.
200 ft high and 130 ft in diameter at the equator, this giant had a
capacity of 725,000 cubic feet giving it an estimated lift of $22\frac{1}{2}$ tons.
Constructed from 6,000 yards of twilled muslin, it was thus by far
the largest hydrogen balloon that had ever been built. Beneath the
enclosed and windowed car of canvas-covered wickerwork was suspended a thirty-foot steam-powered lifeboat named *Leonine*, after
Lowe's wife. Lowe had obviously taken a leaf out of Charles Green's
book, for this craft's steam engine not only drove paddle wheels in
the normal manner but also an aerial screw having a moveable axis so
that it could be used to vary elevation as well as to assist the balloon's
forward motion.

The first attempt to inflate this giant was made in November 1859
in the grounds of the New York Crystal Palace between Fifth
Avenue and Forty-Second Street. The large crowd was disappointed
because the New York Gas Company could not supply gas in sufficient volume to complete the inflation. After this failure, Lowe took
his balloon to Philadelphia where the Point Breeze Gas Works had
guaranteed to provide enough gas, but owing to the onset of winter
further attempts were postponed until the following year. On the
28th June, 1860 Philadelphia succeeded where New York had failed
and its citizens were rewarded by the spectacle of the monster aloft
for the first time. By a coincidence, this maiden flight of the *Great
Western*, ending in a landing on the sand flats of New Jersey, coincided with the debut of another monster, the arrival in New York
harbour of Brunel's giant ship, the *Great Eastern* after her maiden
Atlantic voyage.

Encouraged by the success of this trial flight, Lowe began his preparations for the ocean voyage and the date was fixed for the 8th September. Alas, half an hour before departure time a sudden wind squall caught his all too vulnerable monster. The balloon burst and was completely destroyed. Lowe did not lose heart, nor did his Philadelphian backers desert him. He sought the advice of one of the most respected scientists in America, Professor Joseph Henry, Secretary of the Smithsonian Institution. Henry, who became a good friend to Lowe, pronounced the ocean crossing feasible, but suggested a trial flight from some point in the Middle West to the Atlantic seaboard in order to prove the prevailing westerly air current upon which success depended.

Lowe accepted the Professor's advice and decided to make the experiment from his home town of Cincinnati in his 20,000 cubic feet *Enterprise*. Notwithstanding the comparatively small size of this balloon Lowe considered this the first leg of his ocean flight as he was determined to make the attempt if the experiment was successful. On the night of 19th April, 1861, Lowe was being entertained at a banquet when news reached him that conditions were favourable. Without stopping to change his clothes, Lowe hurried straight to the boarded enclosure near the hospital where the *Enterprise* was housed and began its inflation. At 3.30 a.m. he took off in bright moonlight. The air at ground level had been dead calm, but as the balloon rose it encountered the hoped for westerly current. There must have been some north in the wind, however, for the balloon crossed the Appalachians into South Carolina.

After a flight lasting nine hours, Lowe came down a little to the west of the town of Unionville, only to find himself surrounded by a distinctly unfriendly group of planters and negroes who, despite the fact that he had descended from the heavens, evidently thought he was the devil. Perhaps they believed that, like Lucifer, he had been thrown out of heaven by the Almighty, but Lowe did not stop to reason why; he hastily discharged ballast and took off again. His second landing a few miles away met with exactly the same reception. This time there were threats of lynching and the aeronaut, now short of ballast, had to hold the hostile crowd at bay with his Colt revolver, a new and novel weapon which effectively overawed his assailants. Finally a truce was called and Lowe agreed to accompany them to Unionville where he was put into the gaol. Very fortunately the influential proprietor of the local hotel had made a captive ascent with Lowe a year before, recognized him, and procured his release. With his balloon safely stowed, the aeronaut took the train to Columbia where he was again arrested, this time as a Yankee spy. America was indeed on the brink of civil war at this time and in after years Lowe would boast that he was that war's first prisoner. Released after cross-examination, Lowe was able to continue his journey home, but soon after he offered his services to the forces of the Union and all thoughts of ocean flights were temporarily forgotten. So far as Lowe was concerned, the outbreak of war may have been providential. Had he ventured out over the North Atlantic with the *Enterprise* it is most unlikely that he would ever have been heard of again.

The virile new world rapidly recovered from the heavy losses and the havoc of civil war. Ballooning soon revived and with it the dream of the Atlantic crossing. A new generation of professional aeronauts came to the fore, W. H. Donaldson, Samuel King and the James Allens, father and son, but of the various schemes put forward it was that of the veteran John Wise which secured financial backing – from the *New York Daily Illustrated Graphic*. The *Daily Graphic* balloon, as it was called, had a capacity of 600,000 cubic feet. Its enclosed car, shaped like a diving bell, was two storeys high and was lavishly equipped with scientific apparatus. The now customary lifeboat was suspended beneath it and auxiliary balloons carried an extra gas supply. Unfortunately, Wise withdrew from the enterprise owing to a disagreement with his sponsors and his place was taken by W. H. Donaldson. Donaldson had become noted for his daring acrobatic feats in balloons and for his publicity stunts. An example of the latter was the aerial marriage solemnized at Cincinnati before – or rather above – 50,000 spectators who cheered lustily when Donaldson took off with the happy couple, their attendants, the minister and flowers. But, as a pilot, Donaldson lacked the experience of Wise and his attempted ocean voyage, with two novices as companions, on 6th October, 1873 ended ignominiously after a few hours when the *Daily Graphic* came down in the Catskill mountains. Presumably the balloon was damaged beyond repair for nothing more was heard of it. Two years later, Donaldson and a companion were lost when a storm forced their balloon down into Lake Michigan. Curiously

Cocking's parachute as it appeared before its collapse

Garnerin's first London Parachute descent, 1802

Perilous descent of Gypson's balloon, 1847

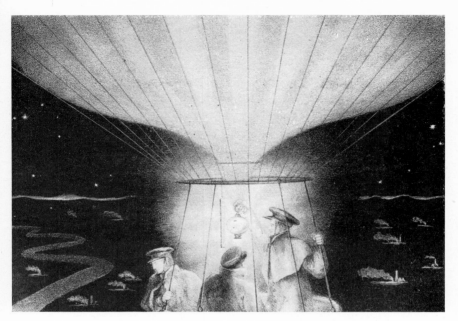

Night Flight to Nassau: Passing over the iron furnaces of Liege

Night Flight to Nassau: The landing in the Elreru Valley

A night ascent by Green's *Royal Victoria* from Vauxhall Gardens

The last flight of Green in the *Nassau* and a rough landing for Henry Mayhew on Pirbright Common, 1852

enough, John Wise, who might fairly be called the Charles Green of America, perished on Lake Michigan in identical circumstances on the 29th September, 1879.

Notwithstanding the abject failure of previous efforts, the notion of the Atlantic crossing still held an irresistible attraction, the latest champion to enter the lists being Samuel King. King was an aeronaut of great skill and long experience. He was also the first American to adopt the trail rope. Details of King's giant balloon are lacking, but if there is any truth in the report that one million cubic feet of hydrogen were required to inflate it, it was the largest balloon ever made. This inflation took place on the 16th September, 1881 at Minneapolis whence King and six companions planned to fly to the Atlantic coast as a first stage on their ocean voyage. A huge crowd watched this giant mount into the air, but the wind was wrong with the result that King and his companions landed only a short distance from the city. Once again, the attempt was never renewed and the air over the North Atlantic remained inviolate. The ocean would never be bridged by a free balloon.

The first and most celebrated of the great balloons to appear in Europe in the nineteenth century was Nadar's *Le Géant*. Nadar, whose real name was Félix Tournachon, was the greatest pioneer French photographer and the holder of several important photographic patents. In the early winter of 1858 he took the world's first aerial photograph from a balloon above the valley of the Bièvre. He developed a passionate interest in aeronautics, and his views on this subject are significant of the way the climate of opinion was changing. 'I have profound faith', wrote Nadar in 1863, 'that the screw will be our aerial motor' and he envisaged a form of helicopter, which he called an aeromotive, using screws for lift as well as for horizontal flight. His giant balloon was conceived solely with the object of raising funds to finance experiments with heavier-than-air flying machines.

The envelope of *Le Géant* was made from two layers of the finest white silk, no less than 22,000 yards being used. It had a capacity of about 212,000 cubic feet. The balloon stood 196 ft high and its estimated useful lift was 4½ tons. The car was probably the most remarkable wicker-work construction ever made, resembling a miniature bungalow, 13 ft long and 8 ft wide, with a balustraded balcony on its flat roof. Its interior was divided into six compartments, the captain's cabin with sleeping berth and space below for luggage storage, a passenger cabin with three berths, a lavatory and a provision store. The two remaining compartments housed apparatus for aerial photography and a printing press. To make recovery easier after a descent, this remarkable car was equipped with axles and four detachable wheels. The gores of the great double envelope were sewn together by hand, a force of 300 seamstresses being employed. Nadar adopted Gale's idea for conserving gas, but instead of the two small balloons beside the main envelope, he proposed a single 'compensator', as he called it, of 3,531 cubic feet capacity suspended beneath the car. It would appear, however, that this device was never used. The brothers Louis and Jules Godard were appointed to superintend construction. At this time the Godards, with their father Eugene, were the premier aeronauts of France and their ascents all over the country were so numerous that many Frenchmen referred to all balloons as 'Godards'.

The first two ascents of *Le Géant* from the Champ de Mars on the 4th and 18th October, 1863 caused more excitement in Paris and attracted greater crowds than any aeronautical event since the days of Montgolfier and Charles. On the first occasion the balloon carried a complement of fifteen, the Captain, Nadar, with the brothers Godard as lieutenants and twelve passengers. Nadar had ruled that there should be no women aboard, but the young and personable Princess de la Tour d'Auvergne, who was attracted to the balloon while driving down the Bois de Boulogne, so beguiled the susceptible Nadar that he agreed to take her. Inflation proved so slow and difficult that when at last the monster rose into the air at 5 p.m. the patience of the crowd was so exhausted that they looked on in sullen silence. The optimistic passengers had armed themselves with passports and documents in anticipation of a flight across Europe, but they were doomed to disappointment for the balloon came down prematurely at Meaux, only fifteen miles east of Paris. Moreover the landing was a violent one and before the monster could be subdued it dragged the wicker 'house' on its side for a mile with its occupants clinging desperately to the car-lines. This anti-climax was due, it was alleged, to the weight of the valve line holding the valve off its seat and so causing a serious and constant loss of gas. This may help to explain why the balloon took so long to inflate.

The second flight was more successful although it came to a

spectacularly violent and terrifying conclusion. This time six passengers including Madame Nadar accompanied the same captain and lieutenants and their ascent was witnessed by the Emperor Napoleon III and the King of Greece. Again it was five o'clock before the balloon rose over Paris and bore away to the north-east, but this time it was obvious that there was no lack of lifting power and in the light of the setting sun the enchanted passengers sat down to an excellent dinner on the balcony of their aerial house, broaching the six cases of 'wines of the finest quality' which had been presented to *Le Géant* by Messrs Courmeaux, the Paris wine merchants.

At 8.30 p.m., with her great white envelope still lit by a sun that had left the earth two hours before, the balloon passed over Compiegne at a height of 4,000 ft and Nadar dropped an 'All goes well' message by parachute. At midnight the Belgian frontier was crossed at Erquelines and those passengers who remained awake were rewarded by the same dramatic spectacle of flaring ironworks that Green and his companions had observed on their historic flight to Nassau. By the early hours of the morning the balloon had crossed Belgium and below them the aeronauts could just distinguish the dykes of Holland glimmering in the first pale dawnlight. Fearing that the balloon might be carried over the North Sea, the Godard brothers advised an immediate descent, but Nadar hesitated to bring the big balloon down in darkness and fortunately for him a shift of wind changed the course more to the eastward and so into Germany. There, in the sunlight of a brilliant morning the balloon entered Westphalia, crossed over the river Ems and the towns of Rheine and Ibbenburhen and then turned towards Hanover. At this juncture the decision was made to land because, it is said, the heat of the sun had so distended the balloon that Nadar feared it would burst. After the inevitable gas loss of so long a flight, this seems scarcely credible, but there was evidently considerable anxiety for a great volume of gas was valved causing the balloon to descend very rapidly. Whereas the balloon had been drifting in light airs it was realized too late that a violent wind was blowing near ground level. By this time too much gas had been lost and it was not possible for the balloon to rise again.

Pandemonium at once broke out as those who a few moments before had been idyllically afloat in the warm sunshine now found themselves clinging for their lives to the car lines. With the lower, deflated part of the envelope acting as a sail, *Le Géant* went berserk, tearing across country at a speed of thirty miles an hour or more and occasionally leaping fifty feet into the air. The cable of the first grapnel parted like pack thread; the second tore part of the roof from a house before breaking away. Sizeable trees and great branches were torn down by the flying car. To make matters worse, Nadar lost his hold of the valve line which coiled itself out of reach, but at the risk of his life Jules Godard managed at the third attempt to climb into the hoop and retrieve it. When a line of railway and an approaching train appeared ahead, the luckless passengers gave themselves up for lost, but fortunately the driver sighted the balloon and drew his locomotive to a grinding halt as the wicker car leapt across the tracks in front of his buffer beam, felling a telegraph pole and carrying with it a tangle of wires. Finally, the mad giant fetched up against a dense wood, neat the small town of Rethem, and burst. By this time only Madame Nadar remained on the car; the rest had either fallen out or jumped out and lay, more or less seriously injured, along the wreckage-strewn path of the balloon. They all counted themselves lucky to escape with their lives.

So ended a 400 mile flight, the longest ever made by *Le Géant*. After the big balloon had been repaired, ascents were made from the Hague, Brussels, Hanover, Meaux and Lyons, while Nadar also brought his monster to England and exhibited it at the Crystal Palace. The last three ascents of *Le Géant* were made from Paris in June, July and August, 1867 from the esplanade of Les Invalides, the Champ de Mars being occupied by the Great Exhibition of that year. De Fonvielle was a passenger on these flights, and, if his account is correct, they were little short of fraudulent. Passengers were encouraged to part with considerable sums of money in the expectation of a long flight whereas the patched-up envelope was in so leaky a state that such a flight could never have been sustained. The first flight ended in the suburbs of Paris, much to De Fonvielle's chagrin, and on the second he fared little better, while his temper was not improved when the cab he had hired to take him back to Paris dropped into a deep rut and overturned. As an additional source of revenue, Nadar had by this time taken to distributing advertising leaflets from the air, but the advertisers cannot have been very satisfied, for on at least one occasion the bundles of leaflets were simply dumped en masse as ballast to check the rate of descent. Despite all Nadar's efforts, *Le Géant* never fulfilled his expectations as a money-raiser. As other aeronauts discovered, too many people were content to watch balloon ascents freely from a distance and would not part with their money to enter the launching enclosures.

The vicissitudes of *Le Géant* illustrate the hazards of landing so large a balloon with no ripping panel to release the gas. The reason why its landings were always so precipitate, however, is not easy to understand. Its momentum in descent seems to have been habitually miscalculated as all passenger accounts describe the balloon coming to earth at a frightening speed. An uneasy command may have been partly responsible, for although Nadar was an authoritarian Captain whose word was law, he was not so experienced in balloon management as his two lieutenants.

The father of these two lieutenants, Eugene Godard, closely followed Nadar in building an enormous balloon. This was *L'Aigle*, a Montgolfière which was more than double the size of *Le Géant*, having a capacity of 500,000 cubic feet. The gallery of the balloon surrounded an impressive straw-burning stove, 18 ft in diameter and weighing 980 lb. This was encased in planished metal emblazoned with the eagle device. Godard patented this stove; also a curious fringe-like parachute that encircled the upper hemisphere of his balloon. Unlike Hoar's abortive efforts, *L'Aigle* appears to have been as successful as such an unwieldy monster could be. Godard brought his giant to England where he made two ascents from Cremorne in the summer of 1864. Among his passengers was the celebrated Colonel Frederick Burnaby of the Blues who subsequently became an enthusiastic and skilful aeronaut, crossing the Channel from Dover gasworks to a point 18 miles south-west of Dieppe in March 1882. The two flights of *L'Aigle* ended at Greenwich and Walthamstow, the balloon being damaged in a collision with a tree on the second occasion. This was the first and the last Montgolfière to be flown of a size comparable with *Le Flesselle*.

The next – and the last – French creator of giants was that brilliant engineer Henri Giffard. Giffard invented the injector for feeding locomotive boilers with water and we shall meet him again in a later chapter in his role of airship pioneer. Giffard's Flaud works, where he manufactured his injectors, were situated on the Avenue de Suffren close by the site of the Paris International Exhibition of 1867. Undeterred by the financial failure of Nadar's earlier project, Giffard decided to raise funds for aeronautical research by constructing a very large captive balloon for public ascents during the exhibition. A vacant plot on his works site was used for this purpose. Giffard did not overlook the fact that a captive balloon is subject to constant wind stresses such as no free balloon has to endure and he made the envelope of this balloon and its successors immensely strong. The material consisted of two layers of rubber, two of linen, one of muslin and one of shellac varnish followed by six coats of oil varnish. Though very strong, this envelope was naturally extremely heavy, so that although the capacity was 176,500 cubic feet, Giffard determined to use hydrogen in order to increase the payload of the circular car.

After experimenting with different methods of hydrogen generation, Giffard adopted the traditional one of sulphuric acid and iron, but he built at his works an improved generator which produced gas of excellent quality at a greater rate. In the centre of a shallow pit over which the car of the balloon could rest there was anchored a single pulley. The balloon cable was passed round this pulley and thence through a tunnel to a large steam winch carrying more than 1,000 ft of cable. Although this cable had a safety factor of four, as an additional precaution Giffard incorporated a dynamometer in the car-coupling. As might be expected of so able an engineer, these arrangements worked perfectly and the balloon was a popular attraction throughout the exhibition. Next year it was exhibited at the Paris Hippodrome until Eugene Godard, taking off from the same place in his free balloon *Ville de Florence*, was caught by a sudden squall and collided with the captive, seriously damaging it.

De Fonvielle next persuaded Giffard to construct a similar captive balloon for exhibition in London. This *Captive*, as it was named, was considerably larger than Giffard's first balloon, having a capacity of 350,000 cubic feet. It was built in Paris, shipped to England and installed in a great circular enclosure, walled with timber and canvas to the height of a five-storey house, on a site adjacent to Cremorne Gardens. Alas, the workmen assembling the balloon mistakenly greased the netting and the effect of this on the fabric of the envelope was so disastrous that the balloon had to be scrapped. Undismayed by this debacle, Giffard promptly replaced it by an even larger *Captive* of

424,000 cubic feet capacity. Instead of an open neck at its south pole, the balloon was fitted with a lightly loaded safety valve of large diameter. The control arrangements were the same as those used in Paris except that the winch barrel carried over 2,000 ft of cable, and the circular car could seat thirty passengers. Unfortunately Londoners proved far less eager than Parisians to make aerial excursions and the venture was a financial failure. It was finally doomed when, on the 28th May, 1869, the *Captive* escaped. Owing to a mistake on the part of the engineer controlling the steam winch, the rope overrode the pulley and was cut through by one of the pulley flanges. The *Captive* at once shot up to an estimated height of 12,000 ft. Wild rumours immediately circulated that the balloon had disappeared with a full complement of passengers, but in fact the car was empty at the time. The automatic safety valve prevented it from bursting and the runaway eventually touched down near Winslow. There a number of countrymen attempted to hold the monster but it defied them and rose again with one youth clinging to the net. Fortunately it eventually brought him down safely after an experience that no doubt earned him many a pint of beer thereafter. The *Captive* finally came to rest against an oak tree in Claydon Park.

After this, no Londoner was likely to venture his money in the balloon. De Fonvielle and his friend, the famous aeronaut Gaston Tissandier, persuaded Giffard to allow them to use his balloon for free ascents from Paris in aid of Gustave Lambert's north polar expedition. For this purpose the balloon was re-named *Le Pole Nord* and was fitted by Giffard with an enormous valve four feet in diameter. This was a bold scheme, for the balloon was twice the size of *Le Géant*, and its envelope alone weighed nearly three tons.

With two companions, the intrepid aeronauts took off from the Champ de Mars on 26th June, 1869, in the largest hydrogen balloon that had ever been flown freely in Europe. 'This marvellous aerostat,' writes De Fonvielle, 'was to other balloons what the *Great Eastern* is to other ships.' They must have anticipated a lengthy voyage for in addition to lavish supplies of food they carried sixty pints of wine and twenty pints of brandy. However, lack of ballast, uncertain winds and approaching darkness made the aeronauts decide that discretion was the better part of valour. To prove that it *was* possible to control a giant balloon, Gaston Tissandier brought *Le Pole Nord* down to a perfect landing in a field of rye near the village of Auneau. The balloon dragged for a short distance, but the gas escaped so rapidly through Giffard's huge valve that with the help of the villagers it was soon brought under control. In return for their help and for the damage to the rye, the aeronauts made the villagers free of the liquid contents of the car and there was a saturnalia which must have been remembered for many a year in Auneau as the pints of wine and brandy disappeared. The aeronauts, we are told, spent the warm summer night in the field beside their balloon. Perhaps, like the local representative of the Gendarmerie, they had become incapable of moving under their own power. After all this jollity it is sad to relate that the exploit was yet another financial failure, poor Joseph Lambert receiving no money for his expedition.

Giffard's last and greatest balloon was built for the Paris World's Fair of 1878. With the possible, but doubtful, exception of Samuel King's, this was the largest conventional balloon ever constructed, having a capacity of 883,000 cubic feet, giving a lift, when filled with hydrogen, of 27 tons. Its circular car held fifty-two passengers. Installed, with its huge steam-winch, in the Cour de Carrousel in the heart of Paris, the balloon was a great success. Though it was held a captive, Giffard's last giant probably did more to widen interest in aeronautics than any other balloon in history, for by the end of the Fair it had carried aloft no less than 35,000 passengers.

Of all the giant balloon projects that of Salomon August Andrée and his North Polar expedition with his *Ornen* (Eagle) balloon was the last, the most heroic and the most tragic in its conclusion. A Swede, born at Grenna on Lake Vetter in 1854, Andrée visited America in 1876 in connection with the Philadelphia International Exhibition of that year. There he met the great veteran aeronaut John Wise. Though he had abandoned his last Atlantic flight project three years before, it is clear that Wise still clung obstinately to his belief in the practicability of an Atlantic voyage, for young Andrée not only acquired from him a passionate interest in aeronatics but also a fervent belief in the idea of riding the air currents to reach a far distant destination. Back in Sweden he pursued first an engineering and then a scientific career. The latter led him to join a party of scientists on a visit to Spitzbergen in July 1882 to make a physical and meteorological study of the polar region. The ideas he had inherited from

Wise and his experience at Spitzbergen fused into a scheme for an expedition to the North Pole by balloon. His reputation as a scientist was now such that his views were taken seriously in Sweden and in 1893 he was granted money for the purchase of a balloon.

This balloon, the *Svea* (37,230 cubic feet), was made for him by Gabriel Yon, the Parisian balloon constructor and with it Andrée made a number of successful experimental flights including a crossing of the Baltic. Not only did he experiment with the trail rope but with another idea which Green had first advanced in 1846. This was that if by the resistance of a trail rope the speed of a balloon was reduced below that of the wind, then it would be possible to alter the course of that balloon by means of sails. It was on the experience thus gained with the *Svea* that the design of the polar balloon *Ornen* was based.

The enterprise was financed by a subscription to which Alfred Nobel contributed, and the *Ornen* was built by Lachambre of Paris under the supervision of the Swedish engineer Nordenfeld. As first made, the envelope was spherical but it was subsequently enlarged to an elliptical shape with a capacity of 170,000 cubic feet. The upper hemisphere was made of three layers of double Chinese silk and the lower of a single skin of the same material. Because of the danger of snow blockage there was no valve at the north pole of the balloon; instead two valves were inserted at different heights in the lower hemisphere. At the south pole a Giffard safety valve was fitted in the place of an open neck. To prevent snow or ice lodging in the interstices of the net, the upper hemisphere of the envelope was entirely covered by a smooth cap or 'calotte' consisting of a single layer of varnished silk. The enclosed, circular wicker car, 6½ ft diameter and 5 ft deep, contained three sleeping berths, and all the stores for the expedition including a canvas boat and three sledges. The whole car was canvas covered and its flat roof was protected by a canvas dodger. On this observation platform there was suspended at eye level an instrument ring and above the hoop, accessible by rope ladder, canvas storage pockets were attached to the leading-lines.

The *Ornen* carried three trail ropes, each 1,100 ft long and weighing altogether 16 cwt. These were attached to a swivelling block below the hoop. There were also eight 'ballast lines', each 230 ft long, weighing 880 lb. At very low altitude these 'ballast lines' would also act as additional trail ropes with the effect that, at zero feet, the balloon would rid itself of $18\frac{1}{2}$ cwt of rope. Three square sails of a total area of 800 square feet were rigged on horizontal spars of bamboo. These sails were fixed, the method of changing course being to adjust the swivelling block that anchored the trail ropes, thus altering the position of the latter in relation to the pull of the sails. All ropes and lines, including the net of the balloon, were specially treated to prevent water absorption.

Andrée, who planned every detail with meticulous care, showed a reluctance to make alterations at the suggestion of others, but he was persuaded to make one change that would prove unfortunate. In each trail rope he had provided a weak point incapable of sustaining the pull of the balloon. This was to avoid sacrificing the whole of a rope if it became jammed in the arctic ice. The portion of each rope attached to the balloon was of hemp, whereas the portion that would normally trail was of coconut fibre, and Andrée was persuaded to unite these two parts by quick-thread screw-connectors of the kind used to join drain-cleaning rods. Thus, it was argued, in the event of jamming, the balloon could be freed by twisting the upper portion of the rope.

The point Andrée selected for departure was the north shore of Danes Island at the north-western tip of Spitzbergen and here a large balloon-house 95 ft long and 100 ft high was built so that the *Ornen* could be inflated and await the required southerly wind, fully protected from arctic storms. When conditions were favourable, the north wall of this house was quickly removable so that the balloon could be within its protection until the moment of departure.

The balloon was installed in this house on the 30th June, 1896 but weather conditions were consistently unfavourable and after many frustrating weeks of waiting Andrée and his companions packed up the balloon and set sail for Stockholm in the expedition's ship *Virgo* on the 20th August, it being then too late in the year to make the attempt. It was over the following winter that the *Ornen* was enlarged, the weight of the envelope having proved greater than was expected.

On the 30th May, 1897 the explorers returned to Danes Island in the *Virgo* to find that the balloon-house had sustained little damage in the winter storms. The *Ornen* was again installed and inflated, the hydrogen generator being of the type used by Giffard. The envelope was tested for tightness by laying over it strips of white linen impregnated with lead acetate which turned black in the presence of hydrogen. More weary weeks of waiting followed, but in the early hours of the morning of 11th July, after a spell of flat calm, the mirror of Virgo Harbour was flawed by the first catspaws of a south-south-westerly wind. By 9 o'clock the wind had freshened and Andrée made the momentous decision to start. At once the expedition sprang to life; the north wall of the house was removed and at 1.43 p.m. Andrée and his two companions, Nils Strindberg and Knut Fraenkel took their places in the car. The long awaited moment had come. Andrée cried 'Cut away everywhere!' and three minutes late the *Ornen* rose from its house into the wind. Those left behind saw the balloon skim so low over the harbour that the trail and ballast ropes left a broad wake in the water. At one moment it sank so low that the car dipped into the sea, but with a visible jerk it recovered. At this moment, one of the sailors of the *Virgo* shouted from the edge of the bay 'The drag-lines are lying here on the shore!' The three trail ropes had been laid down the shore ahead of the balloon, but in some way they must have become twisted with the effect that the connectors had unscrewed themselves. Thus at the very start Andrée had lost two-thirds of the length of his trail ropes amounting to a weight of 1,160 lb. Upon the effect of this loss the shore party could only speculate as they stood in silence, watching the great globe of the *Ornen* dwindle to a speck in the northern sky over Hollander Naze. It was never seen again.

On the 15th July the captain of the Norwegian sealer *Alken* shot a strange bird which had settled on the rigging of his ship. It fell in the sea, but when it was almost miraculously recovered some while after it proved to be a carrier pigeon. In the tiny cylinder attached to its leg was the following message:

From Andrée's Polar Expedition to
     Aftonbladet, Stockholm
  13th July
12.30 midday, Lat. 82° 2′ Long. 15° 5′ E. good speed
to E. 10° south. All well on board. This is the third
pigeon post.
                       Andrée.

This raised hopes of success, but nothing more was heard of Andrée and his companions until 14th May, 1899, when a buoy was discovered on the shore of Kollafjord, Iceland. It was found to contain a message written at 10.55 p.m. on the 11th July and signed by all three explorers. It reported that they were over the ice and that all was well. On the 27th August, 1900, by which time all hope for the expedition had been long abandoned, a woman beachcombing at Loggsletten on the coast of Norwegian Finnmark, found a buoy containing a similar message written at 10 p.m. on the same day. Thus Andrée's last message was the first to be picked up.

It was assumed that the fate of Andrée and his companions in the arctic wilderness would never be known, but history decreed otherwise. The date was 5th August, 1930, and the scene White Island off the extreme north-eastern tip of Spitzbergen, one of the most inhospitable tracts of land in the world. The island's only resident population is a colony of Ivory gulls and normally the only sound to be heard there, apart from the grinding roar of the glaciers that fall from the island's ice cap, is their desolate crying. For the island is usually surrounded by pack ice throughout the year, but on this day the ice cliffs echoed the thudding of a Bolinder engine as the small Norwegian sealer *Bratvaag* of Aaesund, Master Peder Eliassen, edged close in shore. An exceptional summer had not only cleared the pack ice but exposed a dark band of rocky and barren ground along a shore line usually ice covered. The *Bratvaag* was doing her normal work, but fortunately she also carried a small party of scientists headed by the geologist Gunnar Horn.

On the following day, 6th August, two young sealers, Olav Salen and Karl Tusvig, put ashore in a whale-boat to flay walrus. After working for an hour or so they went in search of fresh water to drink and were astonished to find an aluminium lid. Looking about them they saw a number of dark objects sticking up out of a snow drift further up the shore. They had found the Andrée expedition. Here were their sledges and their canvas boat, their stores, instruments and equipment including a Primus stove still filled with paraffin and in working order. More important still, here were all the records of the venture, the logs, the diaries and the canisters of exposed film. In a narrow cleft of rock the remains of Strindberg were found. He had died first, for his companions had covered his body with loose stones. All that the bears had left of Andrée and Fraenkel lay side by side in the sleeping bag where they had died together in their tent of balloon cloth. The remains were brought home and honoured by a state funeral, while a special expedition in the S.S. *Isbjorn* was sent to White Island to recover all traces of the expedition.

From the written records and photographs found it was possible, after thirty-three years, to discover what had happened after the departure from Danes Island. When the car dipped into the waters of Virgo Bay 450 lb of valuable sand ballast was discharged. This loss, combined with that of the greater part of the trail ropes caused the balloon to rise to a considerable altitude (700 metres maximum) and it was not until midnight on 11th July that the balloon descended and the planned low level flying, using trail ropes improvised from the ballast ropes, began. Andrée had never intended the *Ornen* to rise in this way and it resulted in a considerable loss of gas for there are repeated references to the sound of gas escaping from the safety valve. During the remaining part of the voyage, progress was erratic. Once the wind failed and the balloon remained motionless for a time. Once a trail-rope became fouled in the pack ice and held the balloon for some hours before a freshening wind broke it free. The wind shifted, carrying the balloon first to the east, then to the west and finally back to her original north-westerly course. What was far more serious, the car began to ground on the ice. Efforts to counter-act this by throwing overboard everything that could be spared were temporarily successful and on one occasion the *Ornen* rose to a height of 80 metres. But it must have been clear to Andrée and his companions that the end could not be long postponed. This end came at 7.22 a.m. on the morning of 14th July when the car of the *Ornen* came finally to rest on an ice-floe 216 miles from the nearest land. The explorers had been 65 hours in the car. In that time they had covered nearly 500 miles, but only 240 miles in straight line distance from Danes Island.

It is obvious that despite enlargement the *Ornen*, with its heavy envelope and mass of gear, lacked lift. This fatal defect was aggravated by the escape of precious gas during the high-level flight that followed the loss of the trail-ropes. Yet these factors only hastened an end that was inevitable, an end ordained by the one danger that Andrée had foreseen but could not guard against. He was not afraid of powder snow for he argued that the jerking effect of the trail ropes on the balloon would dislodge snow from the smooth surface of the calotte. But in a reported interview in 1896 he had said: 'Our chief danger will arise from snow or rain getting frozen on the balloon. . . . That would be a real danger, because it might overweight us and bring us to the ground.'[1] This is precisely what happened. At a temperature just below freezing point, the *Ornen* ran out of clear weather and into a dense Polar fog accompanied by a fine drizzle which deposited a thickening coating of ice on an already over heavy envelope.

The expedition had established emergency bases at Mossel Bay on Spitzbergen and at Cape Flora in Franz Josef Land. Taking their canvas boat with all their stores and gear loaded on the three sledges, the indomitable aeronauts began a hazardous, nightmare journey across drifting floes and pack ice in an attempt to reach Cape Flora before the winter set in. Travelling conditions were so appalling that they never managed more than three miles in a long day. Had they aimed for Mossel Bay in the first place they might have survived, but how were they to know that a westerly ice drift would defeat them? It was like struggling up a downward moving escalator. At the end of September they reached White Island were they made camp as best they could against the fast approaching Arctic winter. Under the date Sunday, 17th October, Strindberg's almanack contains the laconic entry 'Home 7.5 o'cl. a.m.' The rest is silence. What happened after that no one will ever know. The explorers had plenty of food and fuel, but in the opinion of the sealers their clothing was inadequate and they died of cold. Another theory is that infected bear meat may have hastened their deaths. So ended the Andrée Expedition; so perished also, along with these three very brave men, John Wise's dream of riding inter-continental air currents in giant balloons.

---

[1] Quoted in *Strand* Magazine No. 99, 1896.

CHAPTER EIGHT

Balloons at War

'I HOPE THESE new mechanic meteors will prove only play-things for the learned and the idle, and not be converted into new engines of destruction to the human race, as is so often the case of refinements or discoveries in science.' So wrote Horace Walpole in 1785, but his hope was vain for the military use of balloons had been recognized from the beginning. As we have seen, Joseph Montgolfier envisaged the capture of Gibraltar by means of balloons in 1782, while as he surveyed Paris from the gallery of Pilâtre de Rozier's captive Montgolfière in 1783, the first aerial passenger, Girond de Villette, immediately appreciated the value of the balloon for military reconnaissance. Benjamin Franklin, too, saw the value of the balloon for 'elevating an Engineer to take a view of an Enemy's Army, Works, &c; conveying Intelligence into, or out of, a besieged Town, giving Signals to Distant Places, or the like.'[1] Franklin also prophesied aerial invasion: 'Five thousand balloons', he wrote, 'capable of raising two men each, could not cost more than Five Ships of the Line; and where is the Prince who can afford so to cover his Country with Troops for its Defense, as that Ten Thousand Men descending from the Clouds might not in many places do an infinite deal of mischief before a Force could be brought together to repel them?'[2]

One of the first acts of 'The Committee of Public Safety', set up after the Revolution and execution of Louis XVI, was to appoint an advisory commission including some of the best brains of the Paris Academy. It was a member of this commission, Guyton de Morveau, who recommended the use of observation balloons to aid the armies of France. The revolutionary government accepted this proposal on condition that sulphuric acid was not used for gas generation because

[1] Letter to Sir Joseph Banks, 21st November, 1783.
[2] Letter to Jan Ingenhousz, 16th January, 1784.

all the available sulphur was required for making gunpowder. De Morveau consulted the great chemist Lavoisier who advised producing the hydrogen on the decomposition of water principle by passing steam over red hot iron. Two gifted scientists, Charles Coutelle and a young man named N. J. Conté, were engaged to carry out practical experiments on these lines and in this way a satisfactory apparatus was evolved.

When 18,000 cubic feet of gas had been successfully produced by this means, Coutelle was despatched to General Jourdain, commander of the Army of the North, who was holding Maubeuge against the Austrians. When he arrived, mud-spattered after a difficult journey, Coutelle was taken, not to Jourdain, but to a monster of the Terror named Duquesnez whose mission it was to 'see that the soldiers went into battle and to force the generals to conquer under menace of the guillotine'. This unpleasant character would not believe the balloon story and threatened to have Coutelle shot as a spy. Happily for the new enterprise, wiser counsels prevailed and he was able to explain to Jourdain the commission's proposal to bring a generator and a balloon to Maubeuge so that experiments could be continued in the field. Jourdain approved the idea in principle but considered that Maubeuge was too closely beset by the enemy and that on this account it would be wiser, for the time being, to pursue the experiments in the safety and secrecy of Paris.

Jourdain's advice was accepted and the Château and its gardens at Chalais-Meudon on the outskirts of Paris were made available to Coutelle and Conté. Here was made *L'Entreprenant* the world's first military observation balloon. The envelope and its net had to be made especially strong to withstand the buffeting of the wind and Coutelle himself declared that anyone accustomed to free balloons would find the car of *L'Entreprenant* in a wind very alarming. He insisted that such balloons should be manned by two persons when in action, one to manage the balloon and to signal to the ground crew controlling it so that the other could concentrate entirely on observation. The observer communicated with those below either by flag signals or by placing written messages in sand-bags fitted with rings which could be slid down the cables. The balloon was held captive at the equator by two cables, partly to obtain greater stability and partly because of the risk of a single cable being severed by enemy

Le Geant on display at the Crystal Palace, 1863

Wreck of Nadar's *Le Geant*, 1863

Giffard's giant captive balloon and its winch at the 1878 Paris Exhibition

The final landing on the Polar ice of Andrée's balloon *Ornen*, 1897

fire. It was supplied with sand ballast of a weight equal to that of the occupants of the car and as the balloon ascended this was discharged to compensate for the increasing weight of the suspended cables.

When all these details had been settled, Coutelle made a demonstration ascent at Meudon before the members of the Scientific Commission. He found that when he had risen to the limit of the cables (1,770 ft) he could clearly distinguish through his telescope the windings of the Seine as far as Meulan, eighteen miles away. The Commission was so impressed that on their recommendation the world's first 'air force', the Aerostatic Corps of the Artillery Service, was formed on the 29th March, 1794, a few days after the demonstration. It consisted of one Company; a second was formed on 23rd June. Coutelle was gazetted Brevet-Captain to lead the new corps in the field, while Conté was given the same rank and appointed director of the establishment at Meudon, which was to be at once a workshop and a training centre for new recruits.

This first corps commanded by Coutelle consisted of a lieutenant, a sub-lieutenant, a sergeant-major, four non-commissioned officers and twenty-six men including a drummer boy. They wore blue uniforms, braided red with black collar and facings their buttons being embossed with a balloon device and the word 'Aérostier'. They also had a plain blue working dress. Only commissioned ranks were allowed to ascend, the rest being ground crew. Without waiting for the balloon, they were at once despatched to join Jourdain's army at Maubeuge where the appearance of the new corps provoked much derision. With refugees from the Terror among them, including a priest, they were certainly a mixed bunch, but at Coutelle's instigation they were sent into action against the Austrians and fought with such gallantry that they won the respect of Jourdain's seasoned campaigners.

Meanwhile, back at Chalais-Meudon the generator was prepared for despatch to Maubeuge. The ingenious Conté also evolved a special balloon varnish which he claimed was completely impermeable by hydrogen.[1] In the course of his experiments he lost the sight

---

[1] The following is a contemporary British recipe for balloon varnish:
'To one gallon of linseed oil add 2 oz of litharge, 2 oz white vitriol and 2 oz of gumsanderick. Boil for an hour over a slow fire. When cool, strain off and mix with 1½ oz spirit of turpentine.' - From the Poynton Collection.

of one eye when a glass flask exploded. This was regarded as a war wound and led to his promotion to Brigadier. His new varnish was first tried out on the balloon constructed and used at Meudon for training recruits and was so successful that it is said that it would remain fully inflated for six months although the envelope was a perfectly normal one of single silk. The recipe for Conté's varnish, which was applied to all the Meudon war balloons, was subsequently lost, but if the reports of its gas-holding property are true it has never since been equalled let alone surpassed.

Delaunay, Coutelle's first lieutenant, was a master mason by trade. He needed to be, for when the seven iron retort tubes of the generator, which had been specially made at Creuzot Ironworks, arrived at Maubeuge with *L'Entreprenant* they had to be set in a brick furnace and this involved laying 12,000 bricks. It was therefore by no means a portable field generator; hence the importance of Conté's varnish. Moreover it took from 30 to 40 hours to inflate *L'Entreprenant*.

A few days after the generator had been completed in the College Court at Maubeuge, Coutelle rose in the balloon to the cheers of the troops and a deafening salute of cannon. He was able to report in detail the disposition of the Austrian and Dutch troops outside the town and this information gave a great boost to French morale whereas the effect of the balloon's appearance on the enemy was quite the opposite. The Austrian commander considered such surveillance a most unsporting breach of the gentlemanly rules of war and determined to shoot down the balloon. When *L'Entreprenant* appeared on its fifth ascent a seventeen pounder opened fire from a concealed hollow, one ball passing over the envelope and the next grazing the bottom of the car, whereupon the intrepid Coutelle saluted and shouted defiantly 'Vive la Republique'. At the same time, however, he prudently signalled his ground crew to pay out cable as quickly as possible so that he was soon out of range.

This episode made the Balloon Corps the heroes of the hour, particularly with the ladies of the town. Like the Battle of Britain pilots of World War II, the gallant aeronauts became the great glamour boys on whom favours were bestowed all too freely. Unfortunately for discipline there was more room in a balloon basket than in the cockpit of a Spitfire, nor did a captive balloon require the undivided attention of the pilot. When no danger threatened it became the highly irregular practice to take young women aloft. What went on in the balloon basket on these occasions is best left to the bawdy speculations of the ground crews. Suffice it that when Lieutenant Beauchamp was hauled back to earth in the *Hercule* after such a clandestine ascent at Stuttgart he appeared completely bemused and spoke of seeking immediate permission to marry the lady. He was speedily transferred to army headquarters at Dunavert. Writes de Fonvielle: 'The favour of the ladies followed the balloonists wherever they went, which was not an unmixed blessing, and seems in the end to have contributed to the suppression of the corps.'

From Maubeuge the balloon corps accompanied the army to Charleroi. With its gear stowed in the basket, *L'Entreprenant* was borne, fully inflated, across country for twenty-four miles in great heat by twenty sweating Aérostiers, stripped to the waist. Each man held a rope attached to the balloon at the equator, while Coutelle rode in the car and directed the operation. His men formed two files and their ropes were sufficiently long to enable cavalry to pass beneath the balloon car.

The day following the first ascent of the balloon from its new location, Charleroi capitulated and the greatest triumph of Coutelle and his *L'Entreprenant* soon followed. This was at the battle of Fleurus on the 26th June, 1794. Coutelle ascended with General Morlot as observer and remained aloft throughout the engagement, a period of ten hours. Written questions from those below were attached to a light cord and hauled up by Coutelle while Morlot sent his despatches by bag down the cable. In this way French tactics were entirely directed from the air and the result was a resounding victory. Fleurus was thus the first battle in history where mastery of the air played a decisive part. To the tactical advantage must be added the effect of the balloon on enemy morale. Very few of the Austrian troops had ever heard of a balloon, let alone seen one, before. They regarded it as a supernatural object, confirming the widely held belief that the French Republic had signed a treaty of alliance with the Evil One. For the French troops, on the other hand, the balloon gave an assurance of victory, its continuing presence contradicting any rumour of retreat.

The triumph at Fleurus opened the gates of Brussels, but the victory march of the Aérostiers into the city was somewhat marred when *L'Entreprenant* was accidentally ripped by a stake and deflated. However, it was soon repaired and was laid up at Liege for the winter.

The campaign of 1795 saw Coutelle's corps again in the field. In the previous year the Austrians had threatened to shoot as a spy any balloonist who fell into their hands, but during the siege of Mainz it became clear that the exploits of the Aérostiers had even won the admiration of the enemy. On one occasion during this siege Coutelle ascended in a wind so strong that it required sixty-four men manning thirty-two ropes to hold the balloon down and even so they were sometimes lifted off their feet. While they were struggling with the balloon a small party of Austrian officers was seen approaching from Mainz under a flag of truce. They had, they said, observed the extreme danger to which the brave aeronaut was exposed and offered to allow Coutelle to visit their fortress if only the French commander would order the balloon down. Coutelle politely declined this suggestion, but in return he offered as courteously to demonstrate his ballooning techniques to the Austrians. Such was the chivalry of war in 1795.

The success of Coutelle's pioneer corps led to great activity at Meudon both in balloon construction and in the training of recruits with the effect that three more balloons, the *Celeste*, *Hercule* and *Intrepide*, each with a corps and complete equipment, were fielded on different fronts in 1796. Equipment now included a special form of tent beneath which a balloon, minus its car, could be securely pegged down, ready for use, when not required.

In 1797 Conté persuaded Napoleon to allow the first corps of Aérostiers to accompany him on his Egyptian campaign, but they were not used to advantage and their equipment was destroyed by the British at the battle of Aboukir in the following year. On his return to France in 1799 Napoleon disbanded the Aérostiers and the balloon school at Meudon, which he had already starved of funds, was finally closed down. The old château there was demolished and the marble columns of its portico used in the construction of the Arc de Triomphe. Thus was a promising experiment brought to a premature end by one vain and short-sighted man. It has been said, probably with truth, that Napoleon spurned the tactical aid of the

new arm as unbecoming a man who, in his own opinion, was an
inspired military genius, while, as we have seen, after the episode of
the Garnerin balloon and the tomb of Nero, the emperor's dislike of
balloons became almost pathological.

In this, as in every other developing field of science and technology, the dead hand of the Corsican corporal cost France very dear.
Impracticable though it may have been, the French dream of an airborne invasion of Britain on the lines envisaged by Franklin faded
and no organized effort to use balloons for military purposes was
made in France for forty years. In France and in Austria the theory
that Montgolfières might be more suitable for military use became
popular for a time, but with little practical result. The brothers
Godard experimented with a Montgolfière during the Italian campaign of 1859 but achieved no success because its advantage – ease
and speed of inflation in the field – was nullified by its inability to
remain aloft for any useful length of time. Ten years before this,
during their siege of Venice in June 1849, the Austrians made 200
small Montgolfières, each carrying a 24/30 lb bomb to be released
by a time fuse. The idea was to direct these over the city when the
wind favoured, but this first attempt at aerial bombardment was a
failure. A fickle wind caused many of the bombs to fall upon their
senders and the few that found their target did negligible damage.
Curiously enough, the idea was revived by the Japanese in World
War II but without success. The flotilla of balloons sent to bombard
the western seaboard of the United States never reached its target.

It was during the Civil War in America that the next serious
attempt was made to use balloons for military observation when the
best known American aeronauts of the day, John La Mountain,
Samuel King, John Wise, the brothers James and Ezra Allen and
Thaddeus Lowe volunteered for service with the armies of the
Union. James Allen was the first to make an observation ascent,
closely followed by La Mountain and Wise. These first efforts were
mostly unsuccessful for they were not only hampered by a conserva-
tive military bureaucracy which gave them inadequate help on the
ground even when it did not actively discourage them, but they
attempted to operate under crippling practical difficulties. Initially
the aeronauts used their own balloons which were never designed to
stand the strain of captive use. Having no generators, the aeronauts

had to fill these balloons at the nearest gas works, in Washington or
Alexandria, and then transport them, inflated, into the field as
Coutelle had done so many years before. But since Coutelle's day the
progress of technology had created a new hazard to this operation in
the shape of telegraph poles and wires. Their avoidance created
extraordinary difficulties and balloons were frequently damaged.

Wise was the first to construct a special balloon to army order. Its
car was provided with an iron bottom as a protection against enemy
fire, and the aeronaut planned to carry percussion grenades and
bombs to be discharged if the balloon position was overrun. An
attempt to carry this balloon by night to the scene of the first battle
of Bull Run failed when it became entangled in trees and the party
had to return it to the Columbia Armoury in Washington for repair
after twenty-four hours of exhausting and quite fruitless effort. Later,
when Wise was ordered to move from Georgetown to Ball's Cross
Roads, a cross wind caught the balloon on the bridge over the
Potomac and drove it into telegraph wires. The balloon escaped the
carrying party and drifted away bearing with it all their rifles and
rations which they had loaded into the car. To prevent it falling into
Confederate hands, the balloon was shot down at Arlington. To
overcome such troubles as this, Wise designed a field generator on
the water decomposition principle used by Coutelle, but the firm of
Tasker & Co. of Philadelphia quoted $7,000 to make it and the
authorities refused to stomach the expense.

It was La Mountain who made the first successful aerial reconnaissance of the Civil War. Sent by sea from New York to assist General
Butler at Fortress Monroe, the aeronaut ascended from the Fort at the
end of July 1861 and spotted two concealed Confederate camps from
a height of 1,400 ft. Soon after this, on 3rd August, La Mountain enraged the Confederates by making a successful ascent to 2,000 ft from
the deck of the armed transport *Fanny* in the James River. Later, La
Mountain used the Union tug *Adriatic* for the same purpose so that
these two small craft became the world's first aircraft carriers.

La Mountain was also the only aeronaut to make free reconnaissance flights over enemy territory. He would drift eastwards across
the enemy lines when the wind near ground level favoured him,
then discharge ballast and rely upon the prevailing westerly air
stream at greater altitude to carry him back. It says much for La

Mountain's courage and for his acute weather sense that he repeated this feat successfully many times. His narrowest escape came when he was descending behind his own lines and was fired upon by Union troops who, seeing the balloon come from Confederate territory, somewhat naturally took him for an enemy. In these daring exploits La Mountain used his old ocean challenger *Atlantic* and his larger *Saratoga* until the latter broke from its moorings at Cloud's Mill and drifted away over the enemy lines. Unfortunately La Mountain's activities aroused the jealousy of his fellow aeronauts who denounced them as theatrical and in February 1862 he was dismissed the service as a result of a quarrel with Thaddeus Lowe, who had by this time built up an unassailable reputation with the Union commanders.

Lowe may have lacked La Mountain's individual brilliance and daring, but he excelled all his fellow aeronauts in his organizing ability and inventiveness. The fact that he was all too conscious of this and made no secret of his opinions did not endear him to his rivals. In his unpublished reminiscences he said of Wise and La Mountain that they had not 'the least idea of the requirements of military ballooning, nor the gift of invention which later made it possible for me to achieve success'. The fact that Lowe's words were true made them the less palatable; he did indeed make the first positive contributions to the art since the days of Coutelle and Conté.

Following his adventures in North Carolina with his *Enterprise* balloon, Lowe went to Washington where, with the help of his friend Professor Joseph Henry, he was able to enlist the sympathy and support of President Lincoln himself. This enabled him to cut through the inevitable barriers of red tape and led to his appointment as balloonist to General McClellan's Army of the Potomac. Fortunately, McClellan was an enlightened commander who fully appreciated the importance of the observation balloon.

Lowe's first captive ascents in his balloon were no more successful than those of his rivals, but after the defeat of the Union forces at the first battle of Manassas (Bull Run) he ascended free from Fort Corcoran to a height of three miles and his report that there was no sign of an enemy advance prevented panic in Washington. His first innovation was to install electric telegraph apparatus in the car of the *Enterprise*, the insulated wire being led down one of the cables. He made his first experimental ascent with this equipment from the grounds of the Columbia Armoury on the 18th June, 1861 and his first message was transmitted directly to President Lincoln. It read as follows:

> To the President of the United States
> Sir:
> This point of observation commands an area nearly 50 miles in diameter. The city, with its girdle of encampments, presents a superb scene. I have pleasure in sending you this first despatch ever telegraphed from an aerial station, and in acknowledging indebtedness for your encouragement for the opportunity of demonstrating the availability of the science of aeronautics in the military service of the country.
>
> T. S. C. Lowe.

The first new military balloon of Lowe's design was completed in August 1861 and named the *Union*. It was of 25,000 cubic feet capacity. Lowe introduced a second hoop below the main one to act as a spreader for the car lines so as to keep them well clear of the observer. On the 28th August the *Union* was inflated in Washington and towed to Fort Corcoran where, between 29th August and 1st October, Lowe made observation ascents on twenty-three days out of thirty-four. On 24th September, Lowe used his telegraph to direct artillery fire on the enemy at Falls Church, the first operation of its kind in military history.

Meanwhile, in Washington, fifty seamstresses were at work making balloon envelopes and by the end of the year six more balloons had taken to the air to make a total of seven under Lowe's direction. These new balloons were the *Intrepid, Constitution, United States, Washington, Eagle* and *Excelsior*. So far from being camouflaged, all were brilliantly decorated with appropriate devices such as the American eagle and a portrait of George Washington, the car coverings representing either the standard of the Union or the device of white stars on a blue ground. The balloons varied in size from the 32,000 cubic feet *Intrepid* to the 15,000 cubic feet *Eagle* and *Excelsior*. Each was equipped with enough manilla cable to raise the balloon 5,000 ft. Lowe specified not less than three cables and four in windy weather. They were controlled manually by ground crews using lignum vitae snatch blocks, Lowe, like his French forerunners, rightly judging that winches would be too slow in action. It was only in the process of ascent or hauling down that the balloon became an inviting target for enemy guns, so it was vital that these operations should be completed as speedily as possible. When hauling down, the crews 'ran out' the cables at the double so long as the balloon was within the critical field of fire.

Each balloon was furnished with five miles of insulated telegraph cable and alternative colour-coded signals. The latter consisted of small paper Montgolfières and the equivalent coloured flares for night use. In addition, Lowe provided each unit with a powerful oxy-hydrogen searchlight with an eighteen-inch reflector for use on night ascents. His first experiences with his *Enterprise* and the *Union* convinced Lowe that if they were to succeed each unit of his new air arm must be equipped with portable hydrogen generators, but, unlike Wise and the French engineers, he chose the 'wet' sulphuric acid/iron process. Mounted on four-wheeled horsedrawn carriages, Lowe's generators, twelve of which were built, were very heavy and cumbersome, but they were the first of their kind and a vast improvement on anything used before. They proved capable of inflating a balloon in $2\frac{1}{2}$ hours on an average consumption of 1,600 lb of acid and 3,300 lb of iron filings. The cost of inflation averaged from five to six dollars a day, for it was found that in reasonable weather an inflation would last for a fortnight.

Under Lowe's direction a coal barge was rebuilt with a special launching deck as a mobile balloon base. This vessel, the *G. W. Parke Custis*, entered service on the Potomac in November 1861 and was the first in the world to be specially designed as an aircraft carrier. On one occasion she towed one of Lowe's balloons for 13 miles at a 1,000 ft while the aeronaut made continuous observations.

The persistent but unsuccessful efforts made by the Confederates to destroy Lowe's balloons was the best tribute to their success. Twice Lowe's aerial observations saved the Union forces from heavy defeat at the battles of Four Oaks and Gaines's Mill. But the greatest value of the balloons was that they hampered the enemy seriously by enforcing concealment, including the blacking-out of camps after dark. The Confederates countered this unwelcome surveillance by

creating dummy encampments and gun emplacements, an activity
that absorbed valuable time and man-power. 'I have never understood', wrote the Confederate General Alexander after the war, 'why
the enemy abandoned the use of military balloons early in 1863.' The
reason was not technical but bureaucratic. Lowe was never commissioned and therefore possessed no rank; his mixed corps of civilians
and private soldiers had no military status and so far as the army
command went it was anybody's – or nobody's – baby. Consequently it fell a prey to bureaucratic muddle and confusion on a scale that
infuriated Lowe. The last straw came when Cyrus B. Comstock,
Chief Engineer of the Army of the Potomac, was made responsible
for the balloon corps. Comstock had no sympathy for, or interest in,
the corps and made no secret of the fact, so the exasperated Lowe
resigned. He was succeeded by the brothers Allen who had earlier
joined one of his units, but though they were capable pilots they
lacked Lowe's leadership and the corps rapidly disintegrated.

With their material supplies increasingly limited by the Union
naval blockade, the Confederates forces were never able to field an
air arm on the scale of Lowe's corps. A Confederate balloon was
sighted from Washington in the early days of the campaign, on 14th
June, 1861, but no details of it are known. It may possibly have been
the balloon used later by General Joseph Johnston in the Yorktown
Peninsula. For after the Confederate victory at Manassas, Johnston
moved his forces south in the spring of 1862 to resist the advance of
the Union troops under Generals Grant and Sherman following
their landing at Fortress Monroe. This balloon was a cotton Montgolfière manned by a zealous young staff captain named John Ran-
dolph Bryan. This was inflated with hot air from the flue of a stove
fired with pine cones liberally soaked in turpentine. Since it carried no
stove, the balloon could not remain aloft very long and Bryan's
observations were further hampered by the fact that, owing to its
very limited lifting power, only one control cable could be used.
That the balloon persistently rotated about the axis of this single
cable did not help matters.

Bryan's first ascent in this contraption attracted such a withering
fire from Union batteries that he was lucky to escape with his life.
Thereafter the balloon was hauled down through the danger zone
of fire by a team of six artillery horses driven at full gallop. Bryan's

last ascent was made in bright moonlight from the shelter of a wood near Yorktown. As the balloon was rising, a too inquisitive soldier contrived to get his ankle firmly caught in a loop of the control cable and cried out in panic when he found himself being irresistibly drawn towards the snatch block. A comrade promptly cut the cable, thus not only liberating the victim but the balloon also and Bryan found himself drifting over the enemy lines in the cooling Montgolfière. When the wind changed and brought him back his position was no more comfortable for, despite his shouts, Confederate troops opened fire believing him to be a 'Yankee' spy. Bryan next prepared to swim for his life as the balloon floated low over the York river, but it reached the shore and carried him behind his own lines where he contrived to swarm down the severed cable and tether the balloon to an apple tree where it quickly collapsed.

The Montgolfière was replaced by a gas balloon made in Savannah on the initiative, and at the expense, of Captain Langton Cheves. Its silk envelope was treated with a varnish made by dissolving rubber railway coach springs in naptha. The bolts of silk used were of different colours and patterns, this giving birth to the romantic legend that the ladies of the Confederacy had sacrificed their dresses to make it. For this reason it became known as 'the Silk Dress Balloon'. Manned by Major E. P. Alexander, this balloon was inflated at the Richmond gas-works and conveyed to the field of operations by tethering it to a locomotive on the adjoining York River Railroad. When the battle area moved too far from this railroad in the summer of 1862, the proximity of the James River to the gas-works suggested another method of transport and the balloon was transferred to the deck of the armed steam tug *Teaser*. Unfortunately, on the 4th July, 1862 *Teaser* ran aground on a bar at Turkey Bend in the James River where she presented a sitting target for the Union Ironclad *Monitor* and her armed escort *Maratanza* on river patrol. The *Teaser* was holed and abandoned and the balloon captured.

This loss was quickly replaced by a second 'Silk Dress' balloon built, like its predecessor, at Savannah, but this time at government expense. It was flown by the civilian aeronaut Charles Cevor in the Savannah-Charleston area, inflation being carried out at the Charleston gas-works. In July 1863 the balloon escaped without its pilot in a high wind and was blown over the Union lines where it was captured. It was never replaced, perhaps because by this time the Union forces had abandoned their balloons.

Although the Confederates captured three of Lowe's portable field generators they made no attempt to use them and a dependence on urban gas supplies necessarily restricted their use of balloons. According to contemporary reports, the two 'Silk Dress' balloons had a capacity of only 7,500 cubic feet, so bearing in mind that they used coal gas and not hydrogen their lifting power must have been very limited indeed. Thus among Civil War aeronauts the honours clearly go to Thaddeus Lowe whose achievement was not matched in any other field of war for many years.

The scene now shifts back to Europe where the Siege of Paris in 1870 brought about the most remarkable and extensive operation ever carried out with free balloons. During the early stages of the Franco-Prussian war somewhat half-hearted attempts to use observation balloons were made by both sides. In their preparations for the campaign the Germans ordered two balloons with all their equipment from Henry Coxwell and made him responsible for organizing two balloon detachments of twenty men each. Coxwell had long been known to the Germans as an advocate of the military use of balloons for as early as 1848–9 he had demonstrated aerial bombing at Berlin and Elberfeld. For this purpose he had used Gale's balloon with its double car, which he had acquired on Gale's death and named *Sylph*. The aeronaut dropped his 'aerial torpedos' from the lower car. Coxwell's two detachments were of practically no value to Moltke's army because they were not equipped with field generators. One of the balloons actually accompanied the army to Paris, but as there was no means of inflating it there it was sent back to Germany and the corps disbanded.

On the French side, the Minister of War, Leboeuf, refused to use balloons and it was not until the old régime of the Third Empire ended with the fall of Sedan that offers of help from French aeronauts were belatedly accepted. At the battle of Valenton on 17th September, 1870, four balloons were sent up and while the Prussians were investing Paris two old private balloons were flown captive from Montmartre and Montsouris. Visibility was so poor, however, that no worthwhile observations could be made.

It was when Paris had been completely surrounded and all surface communications cut that the aeronauts approached Rampont, the head of the Post Office, with the proposal that balloons should be used to maintain communications with the outside world in general and the provisional government at Tours in particular. The suggestion was accepted and at 11 a.m. on 23rd September the professional aeronaut Jules Duruof took off alone with 227 lb of mail from the Place St Pierre in Montmartre. Duruof made a sensational departure, discharging so much ballast that he shot into the air like a bullet from a gun. This was not exhibitionism; his balloon, *Le Neptune*, was old and leaking and he calculated that his only hope of clearing the Prussian lines was to 'fire himself off' on a bullet-like trajectory. This plan succeeded. Three hours and fifteen minutes later, Duruof landed safely well behind the enemy lines in the grounds of the Château de Craconville, six kilometres from Evreux. To show that their blockade was not complete, Duruof infuriated the enemy by dropping visiting cards on their positions as he soared high overhead, well out of range of their guns.

So far so good. Duruof had shown the way to get mail *out* of Paris, but how to get communications *in* was quite another matter. A solution to this was put forward by a Parisian pigeon-fancier named Van Roosebeke who suggested that the balloons should transport carrier pigeons supplied by him and his fellow 'colombophiles'. The suggestion was accepted and the next balloon to leave on 25th September, *La Ville de Florence*, carried three of Van Roosebeke's pigeons as well as 231 lb of mail. Later, as many as thirty-four pigeons would be carried in a single balloon.

Next, on 29th September, none other than Louis Godard took off successfully from the gas-works at La Villette in a most extraordinary device which he had named *Les Etats-Unis*. This consisted of Godard's two small exhibition balloons *Hirondelle* and *Napoleon* connected together vertically by a pole. The aeronaut occupied the car of the *Hirondelle* above and, in addition to mail and nine pigeons, he carried a single passenger named Courtin in the lower car. To land this contraption safely at Magnanville, near Mantes, must have been no mean feat.

It was obvious that the supply of 'private' balloons – and professional aeronauts – would very soon be exhausted; in fact the last of these, *Le Céleste* piloted by Gaston Tissandier flying alone, left on the last day of September. This end had been foreseen and by this time two of the great, silent railway terminals of Paris, the Gare du Nord and the Gare d'Orléans, presented a remarkable spectacle of intense activity. On the long platforms between the rusting rails balloons were being built in quantity with a speed unprecedented. Bolts of balloon cloth, washed to remove acidity, were hung out to dry, festooning the great iron-columned aisles like banners in a cathedral. Women cut out gores and stitched seams, some by hand, others, at the Gare du Nord, using sewing machines. Sailors made nets, spliced lines and constructed baskets. Completed envelopes were inflated with air to dry their varnish and to test for leakage. Those at the Orléans station were parti-coloured, but at the Gare du Nord they were all white and looked like gigantic button mushrooms. Both these temporary balloon factories were run by the postal department with Jules Godard in charge at the Gare d'Orléans and the great Paris balloon makers Yon and Dartois at the northern station. The balloons were large – they averaged a little over 70,000 cubic feet, but since they were not intended to last, cheapness and simplicity was the key-note and all the envelopes were made of calico.

As each balloon was completed it was inflated and despatched from one or other of these two stations, the great majority with sailors as pilots, these intrepid men setting off after only the most cursory briefing in balloon management. All balloons were named, many of them after famous people: *Victor Hugo, George-Sand, Daguerre, Newton, Volta, Montgolfier, Lavoisier, Denis Papin, Davey, Fulton, Jacquard, Vaucanson;* one after another they were launched into the Paris sky bound for unknown destinations.

The first of the new balloons, the *Armand Barbès*, left Paris on a most vital mission for it carried Léon Gambetta, the architect of the Second Republic whose energy recreated the French army after the disaster at Sedan. The pilot, Trichet, was a cousin of the Godards, but it would appear that he did not manage the balloon very cleverly. He did not succeed in keeping out of the enemy range and Gambetta was wounded in the hand by a Prussian bullet. Finally, Trichet brought the balloon down in a field at Epineuse which the Prussian troops had left only half an hour before and Gambetta narrowly escaped a capture that might have changed the course of European history. In fairness to the aeronaut, however, it must be said that he carried two passengers and that the *Armand Barbès* was smaller by 20,000 cubic feet than any of the balloons subsequently built. Paris breathed a sigh of relief when one of the sixteen pigeons carried on the balloon returned with the news that Gambetta was safe.

For the incoming pigeon post a photographic method by which from two to three hundred messages could be reduced to a single sheet of paper was at first used. These could be read by the aid of a powerful glass, but inequalities in the paper sometimes made them difficult to decipher. The Paris photographer Dagron then evolved a vastly improved microfilm process using tiny 'pellicules', as they were called, treated with collodion emulsion. Six of these minute films, representing five thousand letters, could be carried by one pigeon. They were usually attached to the central tail feathers. Before this new system could be introduced, Dagron had to be got out of Paris with his micro-photographic apparatus. With three companions, he left from the Orléans station on the morning of 12th November in the balloon *Niepce* piloted by a seaman named Pagano. The balloon came down at Châlons-sur-Marne perilously close to the enemy lines. It was with great difficulty that Dagron evaded capture and got clear away to Bordeaux with his precious equipment after it had lain concealed for eight days. His fate was not known in Paris until the end of the month when the first microfilms began to come in. They were taken to an office in the Rue de Grenelle where they were thrown onto a screen by a magic lantern fitted with a special electric arc magnifier devised by Dagron. Clerks transcribed the messages from the screen for onwards transmission.

The range and fire power of Prussian weapons was far superior to those used in the American Civil War and the French aeronauts considered they were not safe from unwelcome attention below 3,500 ft. In an attempt to check the Paris air-lift a special anti-aircraft gun mounted on a light four-wheeled carriage was supplied by Krupps of Essen to the troops investing Paris. This does not appear to have been particularly effective, but such exaggerated rumours about the new weapon were circulated in Paris, perhaps through enemy agents, that the authorities ruled that in future balloons must leave by night, the last to leave in daylight being the *Général Ulrich* on 18th November.

This night flying rule probably added more hazards than it obviated. Until daylight dawned, the amateur pilots generally had no idea of their whereabouts so, favoured by the more constant night temperature that reduced the gas loss, they tended to play safe and keep going with sensational and sometimes fatal results. The first balloon to leave by night, *L'Archimède*, which left the Orléans station at 1 a.m., landed at Castelze in Holland, while the second, *La Ville d'Orléans* made the most remarkable flight of all. Taking off from the Gare du Nord half-an-hour before midnight on the 24th November, the seaman Deschamps and his passenger Béziers crossed the Baltic to land near Kongsberg in Norway, 600 miles north of Christiania, after a flight of 3,132 kilometres accomplished in 14 hours 40 minutes. Pilot Vibert in the *Steenackers* made one of the fastest balloon flights on record. Leaving the Gare du Nord at 7 a.m. on 18th January, Vibert landed three hours later at Hynd, near the Zuyder Zee, 285 miles away, an average speed of 95 m.p.h. A number of balloons landed in Belgium; others less fortunate came down in enemy territory, while the luckless crew of the *Général Chanzy* flew right into the lion's mouth by landing at Munich where they were promptly imprisoned. Two balloons were lost without trace. The seaman Prince who took off alone in the *Jacquard* from the Gare d'Orléans on the night of 28th November was last sighted by Cornishmen near Land's End heading out into the Atlantic. One of his mail-bags was subsequently found among the rocks of the Lizard. The penultimate balloon to leave Paris, the *Richard Wallace* piloted by the sailor Emile Lacaze, met a similar fate. Spectators who saw the balloon pass very low over La Rochelle shouted to Lacaze to come down, but he discharged ballast and flew out to sea never to be seen again. The last balloon to leave Paris, the *Général Cambronne*, despatched on 28th January, 1871, carried orders to French shipping to proceed to Dieppe for the revictualling of the capital. For an armistice had been declared and the five balloons that were ready to sail at this time never did so.

Altogether, a total of 66 balloons left Paris during the siege of which 58 landed safely in friendly territory. They carried 102 passengers, over 400 pigeons, 5 dogs and 2,500,000 letters weighing about ten tons. They also carried propaganda leaflets which were broadcast over the enemy lines and copies of the first lightweight aerial newspaper *The Balloon Post*, produced by de Villemessant, the

Two of Lowe's portable field generators inflating a balloon at the battle of Fairoaks, 1861

The first aircraft carrier: The *G. W. Parke Custis* with the balloon *Washington* near Budd's Ferry, Maryland

Siege of Paris, 1870: Night departure of a balloon

enterprising editor of *Figaro*. The passengers included the astronomer Janssen who was given a balloon to himself so that he could observe an eclipse of the sun from Algiers. Seaman Chapelain with the balloon *Volta* brought the astronomer and his precious telescope safely to earth at Savenay, near Saint-Nazaire and he was able to see his eclipse. The five trained dogs were intended to find their way back to Paris with microfilm concealed in their special collars, but the experiment was a failure. The dogs never returned. Neither did Gaston Tissandier, the only aeronaut who boldly planned to fly a balloon back to Paris. He was frustrated by unfavourable winds. The pigeons were also hampered by the weather, notably bad visibility, while the Prussians took toll of them with shot guns and trained hawks. Consequently, out of the 300 pigeons that were sent back only fifty-seven actually returned to their lofts. The results of the pigeon post, however, were better than these figures would suggest, for some of the gallant fifty-seven made two, three and even four trips while one bird managed five journeys. Moreover, losses were anticipated by despatching a number of copies of each microfilm.

This, the world's first air-lift, was a truly astonishing achievement, but when peace returns the perils of war are soon forgotten. The courage of the French aeronauts might never have been acknowledged but for an adventure that befell Duruof, the man who had pioneered the great operation. After the war Duruof resumed his career as a professional aeronaut and advertised an ascent with his wife from the Place d'Armes at Calais in July, 1873. Because the wind threatened to sweep the balloon straight over the North Sea, the Mayor forbade the ascent, but the crowd, not knowing this, began to taunt Duruof with cowardice until the aeronaut became exasperated. 'Let us show them,' he said to his wife, 'that we are not afraid to die.' Whereupon the couple stepped into the car, cast away and, carried before a strong wind, disappeared rapidly into the gathering darkness over a stormy sea. They had been given up for lost when, after some days, news came of their dramatic rescue from the waters of the Skagerrak by the British fishing boat *Grand Charge* which had landed them in England. The publicity which this drama received called attention to the courageous part Duruof and his fellow aeronauts had played in the Siege of Paris. As a result, a special medal was struck by the Council of Paris and presented to each aeronaut.

12

From a military point of view, the balloons of Paris had provided an object lesson that no European power could afford to ignore. In France a 'Commission des communications aeriennes' was formed in 1874 with Captain Charles Renard as one of its members. On the strength of their report a military aeronautical establishment was set up in 1877 at Chalais-Meudon under the direction of Charles Renard and his brother Paul. Existing to this day, it occupies the site of the pioneer activities of Coutelle and Conté and is thus the oldest establishment of its kind in the world. It is therefore appropriate that a fine aeronautical museum should have been opened beside it.

In Germany, a Balloon Corps was organized in 1884 and Austria followed suit in 1893. In Russia, a school for aeronautical training on the lines of Chalais-Meudon was opened at Wolkowo Polje, near St Petersburg. In this manner the balloon paved the way for man's complete conquest of the air, for these establishments inevitably brought greater resources, more brains and more experience to bear upon the problems of powered flight.

In the American Civil War, a British officer, Captain F. Beaumont, R.E., had attached himself to Lowe's balloon corps and had been duly impressed. On his return to England, he and a brother officer, Captain G. E. Grover, R.E., made persistent but unsuccessful efforts from 1862 to 1873 to persuade the British Army to recognize the military value of balloons. As members of the Ordnance Select Committee they arranged the hire of a balloon and equipment from Henry Coxwell, using it for demonstration reconnaissance ascents at Woolwich and Aldershot in 1863, but this failed to disturb an entrenched military bureaucracy that used 'a time of profound peace' as a welcome pretext for doing nothing. It was not until the Franco-Prussian war that the subject of balloons was permitted to live again. However, an offer by Coxwell to supply for £2,000 two silk balloons for use on the Ashanti Expedition in 1873 was turned down as too costly and it was not until Captain J. L. B. Templer joined an experimental balloon team at Woolwich in 1878 that things really began to move.

Templer was an enthusiastic amateur aeronaut who brought with him to Woolwich his own balloon *Crusader* and to this was added in 1879 the small *Pioneer*, the first British military aircraft ever made. In the following year, military balloon training was begun at Aldershot and for the first time a balloon detachment took part in military manoeuvres there. As has always been the practice since the days of Coutelle, all potential balloon observers were trained in free flight so that they would know what to do if a captive balloon broke away. Many free flights were made by the detachment and in one of these Templer nearly lost his life.

In December 1881, Templer took off from Bath in the military balloon *Saladin* accompanied by Walter Powell, M.P. for Malmesbury, and Lieutenant Agg-Gardner with the intention of making meteorological observations. The weather deteriorated and as dusk was falling they lost sight of land under a blanket of low-flying cloud. Bringing the balloon down through the clouds, Templer picked up his bearings and realized that they were being driven rapidly towards the Somerset coast and must land immediately. After skimming the roof-tops of a village, Templer valved and the *Saladin* came down near the edge of a low cliff overlooking Bridport Bay. Finding that the grapnel would not hold, Templer jumped from the car, still clutching the valve line, and shouted to his companions to do likewise. Agg-Gardner obeyed, but Powell hesitated. Templer clung desperately to the valve line till his flesh was cut to the bone, but in vain. Like the unfortunate sailor, Prince, Powell was swept out to sea in the *Saladin* and was never seen again.

At this time the military balloons were made of varnished cambric, as used for the Siege of Paris balloons, and they were inflated with coal gas at the nearest gasworks to the scene of operations. Experiments were made at Woolwich with a hydrogen generator very similar to that used by Coutelle in 1793, but it was not considered satisfactory. Templer and his associates realized that success depended on the availability of gas in the field. Even the Lowe type of portable generator was rejected as too cumbersome and slow in action. In 1882 a suggestion first put forward in 1875 that hydrogen might be stored under compression in cylinders became the subject of much experiment. The greatest difficulty was to devise a truly gas-tight valve for the cylinder, but by 1884 the problems had been solved and the first cylinders came into use. This was Britain's great contribution to military ballooning and it was quickly adopted by other countries. Storage pressures were at first low, but the technique was developed so rapidly that by 1890 the French were using a pressure of 300 atmospheres and claimed that they could inflate a small observation balloon in 15 minutes.

With the introduction of hydrogen, Templer realized that some material lighter and at the same time more impervious than varnished cambric was needed for his balloon envelopes. In the East End of London he discovered the Alsatian family of Weinling who for some years had been making and selling toy balloons made from gold-beater's skins which they imported in barrels from the Continent. This had achieved the status of an ancient craft for not only small balloons but elaborate floating figures had been made in this way ever since the eighteenth century birth of the balloon. But gold-beater's skin had seldom, if ever, been used for large man-carrying balloons, possibly on the score of expense. However, Templer resolved to make the experiment. He persuaded the Weinlings to enter Government employ and set them up in a workshop at Chatham, the balloon establishment having been transferred there from Woolwich in 1882.

By the end of 1883, the Weinlings had produced their first balloon, the 10,000 cubic feet *Heron* which subsequently saw service in South Africa. Henry Coxwell waxed very scornful about the diminutive size of British military balloons, but they were capable of lifting one light observer to a useful height and it was Templer's aim to secure rapid inflation and to ensure maximum economy in the use of hydrogen in the field. It is a tribute to Templer that when the United States army reintroduced balloons in 1892 after a lapse of thirty years they adopted British methods including gold-beater's skin. Thus any debt that Britain owed to Lowe through Captain Beaumont's agency was repaid with interest.

Managing the Weinling family, seven in number, at Chatham was by no means easy. Their method of joining the skins was a jealously held family secret and for this reason attempts to introduce English labour to the work in order to speed up production were strongly resisted. Production of the first balloon was seriously delayed when one of the Weinlings was sent to prison for three months for assaulting the police. However, these troubles were overcome and members of the Weinling family continued in the employ of the Balloon Department for more than thirty years.

For transporting hydrogen cylinders in the field steam traction engines were used. The unit that set out from Chatham to take part in the Aldershot manoeuvres of 1889 consisted of a single traction engine drawing five trailers loaded with cylinders plus the inevitable water-cart. Preceded by a man on foot carrying a red flag as required by law, this caravan took three days to reach Guildford. On the return journey the engine proved unable to haul its heavy train up the steep High Street of Guildford. It had to be uncoupled and taken to the top of the hill where its winch rope was used to haul up the wagons one at a time. 'It was market day,' writes Brigadier Broke-Smith, 'and the combination of a dense crowd, a doubtful wire rope, and wagons filled with compressed hydrogen caused the officer in charge an anxious half-hour.'

Despite these incidental difficulties the performance of the unit on the manoeuvres so impressed the brass-hats that in 1890 it was transferred to a new and larger depot beside the Basingstoke Canal at Aldershot and was included for the first time in British Army establishments. Four Balloon Sections took part in the South African War and the expansion of activity at Aldershot was so great that early in 1903, Templer (now a full Colonel) recommended removal to a new site adjoining Farnborough Common. This move was made during the winter of 1905–6 and so the present Royal Aircraft Establishment at Farnborough was born.

The general acceptance of the balloon for military observation made the deficiencies of its traditional form the more obvious. For free flight its spherical or pear shape was logical and perfect, but when held captive such a shape was quite unsuitable except under very favourable conditions. Various attempts were made to improve matters by devising new methods of suspension such as the special 'bridle' developed by Templer, but it was considered undesirable to fly a spherical balloon captive when the wind speed exceeded 20 m.p.h. Experiments were made with sausage and cigar shaped balloons, but they showed no marked improvement so that it seemed that for military observation the balloon could never be more than a fair weather friend. The box kite developed by the Australian Lawrence Hargrave in 1893 appeared to offer an alternative to the observation balloon in windy weather and in the course of experiments in America in January 1897, Lieutenant Wise was lifted 50 ft into the air by four Hargrave kites.

Experiments with man-lifting kites were continued, but in the meantime the problem was solved in 1896 by two officers of the German army, Major von Parseval and Captain von Sigsfeld. They ingeniously combined their experience of dirigible balloons with the kite principle to produce the *Drachen* (Dragon) kite-balloon. The idea was not new, but theirs was the first successful design. Like a kite, the *Drachen* set itself in a diagonal attitude to the wind and proved perfectly stable at wind speeds of 66 ft per second. It was the forerunner of the observation balloons used in the first world war and the barrage balloons used in the second. It also revealed that growing mastery of the science of aerodynamics which in a few more years would complete man's conquest of the air.

CHAPTER NINE

Science in the Sky

AT THE TIME THE Montgolfier brothers carried out their first successful balloon experiments there was still living in St Petersburg, aged eighty and almost blind, the great Swiss mathematician Leonhard Euler. A few days before he died in September 1783, his friends found chalked upon a slate a calculation designed to determine the height to which a given balloon could ascend. Thus there was forged at the outset an enduring and fruitful link between scientists and the balloon. While the general public, influenced by the activities of the great showmen aeronauts, learned to regard the free balloon as a sensational but useless vehicle for stunt displays, while armies tethered it above their battle lines and eager technicians tried to transform it into a controllable aerial ship, men of science accepted it as it was, instantly recognizing its value as a research vehicle. James Glaisher, F.R.S., summed up the scientist's point of view in 1872 when he wrote:

'I have elsewhere expressed my opinion that the Balloon should be received only as the first principle of some aerial instrument which remains to be suggested. In its present form it is useless for commercial enterprise, and so little adapts itself to our necessities that it might drop into oblivion tomorrow, and we should miss nothing from the conveniences of life. But we can afford to wait, for already it has done for us that which no other power ever accomplished; it has gratified the desire natural to us all to view the earth in a new aspect, and to sustain ourselves in an element hitherto the exclusive domain of birds and insects. We have been enabled to ascend among the phenomena of the heavens, and to exchange conjecture for instrumental facts, recorded at elevations exceeding the highest mountains of the earth.'

Many of these 'instrumental facts' recorded in balloons proved somewhat negative in that they dispelled some long cherished illusions, but they were none the less valuable for that. Because Benjamin

Franklin had shown in his famous kite experiments how 'atmospheric
electricity' could be conducted to earth by a wire in the kite line, the
Abbé Bertholon and other French scientists believed that by means of
captive balloons such electricity might be usefully harnesssed. It was
also believed that by scientific balloon ascents straightforward laws
governing temperature and humidity would be established and that
these would make such meteorological phenomena as wind currents,
cloud formation and rainfall not merely readily explicable but accurately predictable. For example, it was hoped that balloon ascents
would confirm the mountaineer's theory that the temperature of the
atmosphere invariably fell by 1°F for every 300 ft of ascent.

Of this first fine scientific rapture evoked by the birth of the balloon, Camille Flammarion wrote: 'This marvellous world of air, so
mild and yet so strong, where tempests, whirlwinds, snow and hail
are elaborated, was henceforth opened to the inhabitants of the terrestrial soil. Its secrets would be disclosed, the movements of the
atmospheric world would be counted, measured, and determined
as scrupulously as astronomers can determine those of celestial bodies;
and man, once placed in possession of this terrestrial mechanism,
would be able to predict rains and storms, drought and heat, luxuri-
ant crops and famines, as surely as he can predict eclipses, and thus
ensure an ever-smiling and fertile soil! Such was the magnificent
dream. . . .' But the balloon soon taught man that meteorology was
by no means so simple a study as he had supposed and despite all our
modern aids the eighteenth century dream remains unfulfilled.

Another persistent illusion concerned the nature and origin of
meteorites. Scientists who went aloft in balloons for the express purpose of observing meteor showers were considered particularly venturesome, if not foolhardy, for it was widely believed that these
bodies whizzed about in the air only a few thousand feet above the
earth like some heavenly anti-aircraft barrage. 'He knows, too, or
should know', wrote Thomas Jolliffe of Somerset in 1826, 'that he is
in the region where the most subtle meteors are kindled, and that the
contact of one electric spark may set fire to his frail vehicle and
annihilate it like a stroke of thunder.'[1] As late as 1887, Henry Coxwell could write: 'I noticed a splendid meteor, which was below the
level of the car and apparently about six hundred feet distant – it was

[1] Description of a voyage with the aeronaut Corneillot in the Poynton Collection.

blue and yellow, moving rapidly in a north-easterly direction and became extinguished without noise or sparks. It is just possible that the apparent closeness of this meteor was illusory, and that the real distance was very many miles; its size was half that of the moon, and I could not but feel that if such another visitor were to cross my path, the end of the *Sylph* and its master would be at hand.'

It will be recalled that both Sheldon and Jeffries carried scientific instruments on their flights with Blanchard, but these ascents were not made expressly for the purpose of research and the aeronauts evidently treated their equipment with scant respect as so much expendable ballast. At the same early date (1784), Boulton and Watt carried out a simple but sensational experiment in Birmingham. They attached what was described as 'a sort of squib' two feet long to the neck of a small balloon of varnished paper which was filled with two parts hydrogen and one part common air. On a dark and calm summer night, a time fuse attached to the squib was lit and the balloon released. A large crowd waited expectantly until, after six minutes, the balloon exploded 'with a success that gave delight to all'. James Watt subsequently explained the object of this exercise in a letter to his friend Dr Lind of Windsor. 'Our intention', he wrote, 'was, if possible, to discover whether the reverberating sound of thunder was due to echoes or to successive explosions. The sound occasioned by the detonation of the hydrogen gas of the balloon in this experiment does not enable us to form a definite judgement; all that we can do is to refer to those who were near the balloon, and who affirm that the sound was like that of thunder.'

The first balloon ascent undertaken expressly for scientific purposes with the object of making observations at high altitude was made from Hamburg on 18th July, 1803 by Etienne Robertson accompanied by a teacher of music named Lloest. When Napoleon I disbanded the corps of Aérostiers, Robertson had bought at auction the *L'Entreprenant* balloon which had served at Fleurus. This was the balloon he used at Hamburg. Quite an elaborate research programme had been drawn up for him by the savants of the French Academy, but although Robertson claimed to have reached an altitude of 23,526 ft, a height far exceeding anything achieved before, no very positive results emerged. Many believe that Robertson was a charlatan. Certainly his design for a giant balloon, mentioned in an earlier

chapter, does not inspire confidence; nor does his report on the
Hamburg flight in which he claimed that reduced pressure at high
altitude caused their heads to swell so much that Lloest could no
longer wear his hat. This smacks of the tall tales of an ancient mariner
and provoked from Coxwell, in his account of his record ascent with
Glaisher, the dry comment: 'Mr Glaisher's head and mine were
covered with caps, but I did not notice any cerebral expansion, being
very intent upon the expansion of the gas; in short, we were always
sticking to more important business.'

Both Coxwell and Green cast serious doubt on what the latter
sarcastically called the 'miraculous ascents' made by Robertson and
other early aeronauts. This doubt was based on the small size of the
balloons used, even when due allowance was made for the fact that
they used pure hydrogen. As Coxwell pointed out, given the weight
of the observers, their car and equipment plus sufficient ballast to
ensure a safe descent, the maximum height that a balloon of a certain
capacity can attain may be calculated. If a very high altitude is aimed
at a correspondingly great expansion of the gas in the envelope must
be allowed for. This means using a large balloon only partially filled
with enough gas to provide the initial lift. For a balloon so small as
L'Entreprenant even to approach the height claimed by Robertson
would, Coxwell argued, involve the sacrifice of all ballast and the
loss of so great a volume of gas through the neck, that a safe descent
would be impossible.

Robertson made another scientific ascent on 30th June, 1804 from
St Petersburg accompanied by Professor Sakharoff of the Russian
Academy. A height of only 8,868 ft was estimated on this occasion,
while the Professor complained that he was unable to carry out his
projected experiments with the magnetic needle because the balloon
continually rotated. That such a motion of the balloon is caused by
unequal weight distribution in the car does not seem to have been
understood. The fact that other scientists besides Sakharoff made the
same complaint may have been due to the unbalanced weight of the
quite formidable array of instruments that some of them carried
aloft.

Robertson did at least stimulate others to do likewise, all the more
so because his report and its findings were held suspect. At the suggestion of Laplace, the Paris Academy acquired another of the

Meudon war balloons for scientific research. Two young scientists, J. B. Biot and Gay-Lussac agreed to make the experimental ascents and Conté offered to supervise the preparation of the balloon. The first ascent took place from the Conservatoire des Arts et Métiers in the Rue St Martin on 24th August, 1804, but the explorers were unable to exceed 13,000 ft according to their barometer. Nevertheless, the results of their electro-magnetic experiments disproved those claimed by Robertson. In an attempt to match the latter's alleged achievement it was agreed that Gay-Lussac should ascend alone. Because he had to manage the balloon, Gay-Lussac was unable to make detailed instrumental observations, but he claimed to have attained an altitude of 23,000 ft. From the experience gained by these ascents the scientists of the Academy came to the conclusion that the height achieved by Robertson could not have exceeded 21,400 ft.

It is important to remember that all estimates of altitude made at this time were based on the theory of Blaise Pascal, proved by Florin Perier on the Puy de Dôme in 1648, that the mercury column of a Torricelli barometer would record that the weight of the earth's atmosphere decreased with altitude. Hence the Torricelli barometer became a measure of altitude by comparing its readings at ground level and at maximum height. This method, however, could not allow for meteorological variations in atmospheric pressure at different altitudes. Moreover, the greater the altitude the greater the risk of human error in taking the reading. Due to the physical effects of lack of oxygen, even the most honest and conscientious observer was liable to make mistakes.

Though Robertson was probably a charlatan, Zambeccari's associate, Andreoli, and the Astronomer Royal of Naples, Carlo Brioschi, may have been genuinely mistaken when they recorded a minimum barometer reading of 8 inches on an ascent from Padua in a combination hydrogen/hot air balloon. Such a reading represents a height of at least 30,000 ft, which they certainly could not have attained, but it is probably fair to credit them with an all-time altitude record for a balloon carrying fire. Their balloon is said to have burst and parachuted them to earth, Brioschi receiving injuries from which he never recovered.

Between 1805 and 1810 the German Professor Jungins made a number of ascents from Berlin in the course of which he claimed a maximum of 21,000 ft. Thereafter no notable scientific ascents were made until the early autumn of 1838 when it was the turn of England to field a formidable entrant for the high altitude stakes – none other than our old friend Charles Green and his *Nassau* balloon. It is entirely typical of the England of that time that Green's undertaking was not sponsored by any scientific institution but was financed entirely by one private individual. This was George Rush, of Elsenham Hall, Essex, a wealthy amateur scientist and astronomer who wished to experiment with an improved aneroid barometer that he was developing. Green welcomed such a patron, for he had been sceptical of all the continental claims and was glad of an opportunity to prove what he and his famous balloon could achieve.

On their first ascent from Vauxhall on the 4th September, Green and Rush were accompanied by Edward Spencer. It will be recalled that Green and Spencer had had a previous experience of high altitudes when they had borne the unfortunate Cocking aloft a little over a year before. The *Nassau* reached its ceiling at just over 19,000 ft, far short of the height involuntarily attained on the Cocking flight, a result that evidently failed to satisfy Green and his patron. Careful plans and preparations were made for a second flight on 10th September. The large circular car of the *Nassau* was replaced by a small basket only just large enough to accommodate two aeronauts and their equipment, the result at the weighing off being as follows:

	Pounds
Balloon, netting and car	700
Ballast	1500
Mr. Rush	145
Mr. Green	145
Light grapnel and rope	52
Clocks, barometers, etc.	30
Total	2572

Green then adopted a very unusual course. A total of $14\frac{1}{2}$ cwt of ballast was added and the balloon was fully inflated. Gas was then released through the valve until equilibrium was achieved with $13\frac{1}{2}$ cwt of this additional ballast removed. This left ample room for gas expansion at high altitude but, as Coxwell pointed out, had the wealthy Rush not been the paymaster, the same result could have been achieved without such a prodigious waste of gas. However, maybe the proprietors of Vauxhall had something to do with it, for their patrons expected to see a nice rotund balloon. Coxwell also argued that if the amount of ballast carried had been reduced from 1,500 lb to 500 lb, precisely the same result could have been achieved with a lesser volume of gas, but he admits that the *Nassau* would then have presented 'a miserable aspect' as it left the ground.

At the moment before starting, Green discarded the remaining hundredweight of extra ballast. He evidently determined to give the *Nassau* far more than the normal ascending power with the idea of attaining an impetus that would cause the balloon to overshoot its ultimate equilibrium point by the greatest possible margin. The *Nassau* certainly did shoot into the sky, for in less that seven minutes from take off it was two miles high. Green continually threw out ballast to maintain this rate of ascent until he was left with a little under 70 lb which he regarded as the safe minimum for checking the descent. When the balloon attained its ceiling, the barometer had fallen from 30.5 at ground level to 11, readings that Green translated as a height of 27,146 ft or a little over five miles.[1] From this great height Green brought the *Nassau* down to a safe landing in a field at Southover, near Lewes. Apart from the head swellings, the continental explorers had described other dire physical symptoms such as bleeding from the eyes and ears. Rush admitted to an attack of nausea induced by the smell of the gas and both men acknowledged suffering acutely from cold feet and hands in the sub-zero temperature, but otherwise these two stalwarts declared that they experienced no physical effects whatever, contemptuously dismissing the earlier reports as so much moonshine. Nevertheless, they must have been a remarkably tough couple, for even if the height claimed was exaggerated, they had sailed pretty close to the limit that man can attain without the aid of oxygen.

The reply to this by the two Frenchmen Barral and Bixio in 1850 was something of a burlesque of Green's highly competent performance. This couple announced their intention of exceeding 30,000 ft and the ascent was made on 29th June from the grounds of the Paris

[1] The figures quoted are those given by Coxwell in his very detailed and circumstantial account of the flight. Coxwell was a rival, not a partisan of Green. Hodgson quotes 20,352 ft. Hildebrandt says Green claimed 29,000 ft but that Professor Assmann calculated that he could not have achieved more than 26,000 ft.

Observatory where a hydrogen generator had been installed by permission of the great astronomer Arago. Barral was a lecturer in
chemistry and Bixio the editor of an agricultural journal. Neither
had any previous experience of balloons, but unlike George Rush
they decided not to employ a competent professional aeronaut. They
evidently failed to realize how greatly the gas would expand at high
altitude, with a result that was comical but might have been tragic.
Not only was their balloon grossly over-inflated but the net was too
small and the car lines much too short. As the balloon rose its distended fabric gradually forced its way downwards through the hoop
until it completely overlaid the car and its two occupants. The balloon
would certainly have burst had it not been torn by one or other of
the amateur aeronauts in the course of a farcical and fruitless struggle
to find the valve line. Gas issued from the rent in such volume that
they then immediately passed out, but the balloon landed them
safely, if heavily, in a vineyard near Lagney. To give them their due,
Barral and Bixio were not discouraged by this experience. Having
learned their lesson, they tried again on 25th July and this time safely
achieved an ascent to an estimated 23,000 ft.

None of the ascents so far recorded yielded very positive or reliable
results and this was partly due to the inadequacy of the instruments
used. For example, the thermometers could not record air temperature accurately because they were not protected from the effect of
solar radiation. But at least the records made on the different flights
showed that temperatures in the upper air could fluctuate as widely
as those at ground level and exploded the simple 'one degree per
300 ft' theory.

John Welsh of Kew Observatory seems to have been the first
observer to seek more accurate results by shielding the bulb of the
thermometer and circulating air through the shield. Between 17th
August and 10th November, 1852, Welsh made four ascents in the
Nassau with Green, then at the end of his long career. The greatest
height recorded was 22,930 ft on the last flight. These ascents enjoyed
the support of the British Association, but this seems to have been
moral and not financial, for they were made from Vauxhall Gardens
where the cost could be covered by gate money from spectators. The
illness of John Welsh, followed by his early death in 1859, brought
this series of experiments to an end.

To the average frequenter of the gardens of Vauxhall or Cremorne it mattered not at all whether a balloon bore aloft a serious looking boffin with a lot of queer instruments, an over-bold acrobat, a lady in spangles, or a jaded masher in search of a new thrill. A balloon ascent was as well worth watching as the fireworks with the possibility of an accident to add a bit of spice to it. For so many years now the printed semblance of the balloon had headed the bills advertising popular places of amusement, that, like the red sails of Le Moulin Rouge, its familiar candy-striped shape had come to signify sex and sensation, two opiates that those of little wit have ever flown to as a refuge from the monotony and frustrations of urban life. The balloon meant the clink of glasses and randy laughter; it meant assignations in cigar-scented private rooms or sequestered pavilions where the ladies of the town plied a profitable trade; it meant the enticing twinkle of garters on plump thighs as a prancing chorus flounced their skirts and the audience roared the refrain:

> *Up in a balloon, up in a balloon,*
> *All among the little stars*
> *Sailing round the moon,*
> *It's something very jolly*
> *To be up in a balloon.*

Nor was this association between high flying and high living by any means confined to the lower orders. For had not one member of Brooks's successfully wagered another, in the frankest Anglo Saxon terms, that he would couple with a woman in a balloon?

That the inventors of the balloon were men of serious purpose, that it could still be used to increase the sum of knowledge and that it might foreshadow a complete conquest of the skies never occurred to the raffish frequenters of London's pleasure gardens and tavern yards. For them it had no more serious significance than a sky rocket. It would be unfair to lay the blame for this state of affairs on the great showmen aeronauts; they had their living to earn. Nor must it be forgotten that many a worthwhile project such as Green's great flight to Nassau was only made possible by the support of pleasure ground proprietors without which aeronautics might have languished for half a century. Nevertheless, one is bound to sympathize with the zeal of those men of science who felt that, like too many of the ladies who flaunted their charms at Cremorne or Vauxhall, the balloon had been debauched and was overdue for rescue and reformation. Foremost of these champions in Britain was James Glaisher, F.R.S. He was very concerned, as he himself expressed it, 'to make the Balloon a philosophical instrument, instead of an object of exhibition, or a vehicle for carrying into the higher regions of the air excursionists desirous of excitement, mere seekers after adventure'. His influential advocacy won from the British Association far more substantial support than had previously been accorded to Welsh. A combination of hard cash with the encouragement of such men as William Fairbairn and James Nasmyth, the two great elder statesmen of British engineering, enabled Glaisher to plan and carry out a programme of scientific ascents upon a scale never attempted before. By subsequent standards, Glaisher's apparatus and his methods may have left much to be desired, but in the light of history the immediate results are less important than the long term influence of Glaisher's experiments. Their very defects were a stimulus. His methodical mind set a course and an example for others, better equipped, to follow and in this way he can be said to have initiated a programme of research that has carried man to the limits of the earth's atmosphere and beyond.

As a young man, James Glaisher was engaged on the Trigonometrical survey of Ireland and it was his observations of cloud formations from the summits of the Irish mountains that first quickened his interest in meteorology. He subsequently worked, first in the observatory at Cambridge University and later at Greenwich where in 1838 he was appointed head of a new department of magnetics and meteorology, a post he held until 1874. On the occasion of Welsh's last and most successful ascent with Green the weather was so remarkably clear that Glaisher was able to follow the whole flight of the balloon through a telescope from the roof of the Royal Observatory at Greenwich. This was the experience that persuaded him to urge the British Association to sponsor a research programme, though he did not at first contemplate making the observations himself. Apart from his desire to dissociate the experiments from the London pleasure garden milieu, Glaisher argued that the ascents should be made from some location in the English Midlands in order to minimize the risk of the balloon being carried out to sea. This was agreed and the Wolverhampton Gas Works was chosen.

Construction of balloons at the Gare d'Orleans, Siege of Paris, 1870

Projection and transcription of micro-filmed letters, Siege of Paris, 1870

High Altitude: Ascent of
Coxwell and Glaisher from
Wolverhampton, 1862

High Altitude: The *Zenith*
disaster, 1875

At first things did not go at all well. Obviously a large balloon was needed and, not surprisingly, Glaisher's first thought was of Charles Green and the *Nassau*. Aged seventy-four, the great aeronaut had been living in retirement at Aerial Villa, Highgate, for some years and his famous balloon was stored in a shed in his garden, but he was persuaded to bring the *Nassau* to Wolverhampton in August 1859. Two young observers, well briefed by Glaisher, were to accompany Green. The old aeronaut shared Glaisher's views and welcomed the opportunity to end his career on a serious scientific mission, but he suffered a bitter disappointment. For the *Nassau*, like its master, had grown old. Twice it was torn by the wind during inflation, on the second occasion so seriously that the idea of using the *Nassau* had to be abandoned.[1]

After the failure of the *Nassau*, the British Association bespoke the services of its nearest rival, the 50,000 cubic feet *Royal Cremorne* and its pilot Thomas Lithgoe. Lithgoe was an inspector of the Metropolitan Gas Company who turned professional aeronaut, making many ascents, first from Cremorne and later from the Crystal Palace at Sydenham which became the chief metropolitan centre for balloon ascents after the eclipse of the old pleasure gardens. The fabric of the *Royal Cremorne* proved to be as full of small holes as a sieve. Lithgoe confessed that the balloon had been in use for thirty years and was worn out and he recommended Henry Coxwell and his balloon *Mars*. This was also found to be in a bad state and although several tailors were engaged to repair it, Coxwell said he could not guarantee a safe ascent.

It was obvious that after such a disastrous series of fiascoes the honour of the Association and that of British aeronauts demanded that something drastic be done to retrieve the situation and Coxwell's offer to build a new large balloon especially for the experiments was accepted. The envelope of this new balloon was made of American cloth and had a capacity of 90,000 cubic feet. It does not appear to have carried a name at the time the historic research flights were made, but Coxwell later christened it the *Mammoth* when he used it for exhibition ascents at the Crystal Palace.

---

[1] This was not the end of the famous balloon. On the death of Green it was acquired by Henry Coxwell who thoroughly overhauled it and ascended in it to a height of 10,000 ft from Hornsey.

Although he had never set foot in a balloon car before, James Glaisher decided that he would himself ascend with Coxwell when the historic series of flights from Wolverhampton was planned for the summer of 1862. He devoted great care and thought to his preparations. The research programme he drew up for himself and particulars of the instruments carried will be found in Appendix I at the end of this book. Proud, the manager of the Wolverhampton Gas Company, co-operated by producing gas of an unusually light quality and storing it in a gas holder specially reserved. 60,000 cubic feet of this was passed into the *Mammoth* for the first ascent on 17th July. On this occasion the balloon was carried eastwards and reached a ceiling of a little over 26,000 ft. Unfortunately, Coxwell's fear that they might be carried over the North Sea, loss of gas and the weight of water vapour which the balloon picked up in descending through the clouds, all combined to make a heavy landing in which many of Glaisher's instruments were broken. This landing took place in a field near Langham in Rutland.

The second ascent on 18th August was made in light airs and clear weather, giving the aeronauts a magnificent view of the earth far below. It was on this flight that Glaisher recorded a spectacle that has delighted many an aeronaut – the shadow of the balloon thrown upon a cumulus cloud and surrounded by a corona of brilliant rainbow colours. After exceeding 24,000 ft, the balloon came back to earth at Solihull.

The third and last ascent of the series took place on 5th September and was one of the most remarkable in the history of ballooning. It had been delayed by unfavourable weather and when Coxwell and Glaisher took off from Wolverhampton just after 1 p.m. the temperature was only 59°F and the sky heavily overcast. However, at a little over 11,000 ft the balloon 'surfaced' as it were, rising in brilliant sunshine above the rolling cloud plateau into a clear heaven of the deepest blue. The scene was set for an historic and heroic achievement. One hour and forty minutes after take-off the balloon was four miles high, but so rapidly was it now rising that a height of five miles was reached only ten minutes later. At this point Glaisher should be allowed to tell his own story of what followed. It has been quoted before, but no second-hand account could possibly match its dramatic quality. It is the sheer matter-of-factness of Glaisher's report which makes it so moving. As the balloon rose into the cold, midnight-blue loneliness of an upper air never penetrated by man before, this dedicated scientist continued coolly and objectively to record the readings of his instruments and to note his physical reactions, a concentration of intellect and will so intense that it armoured his mind invincibly against any fear of death. Perhaps it was precisely because of this that few men have ever deliberately engaged death so closely and lived to tell the tale.

'Up to this time', writes Glaisher, 'I had taken observations with comfort, and experienced no difficulty in breathing, whilst Mr. Coxwell, in consequence of the exertions he had to make, had breathed with difficulty for some time. Having discharged sand, we ascended still higher; the aspirator[1] became troublesome to work; and I also found a difficulty in seeing clearly. At 1h. 51m. the barometer read 10.8. About 1h. 52m. or later, I read the dry-bulb thermometer as minus 5°; after this I could not see the column of mercury in the wet-bulb thermometer, nor the hands of the watch, nor the fine divisions of any instruments. I asked Mr. Coxwell to help me read the instruments. In consequence, however, of the rotatory motion of the balloon, which had continued without ceasing since leaving the earth, the valve-line had become entangled, and he had to leave the car and mount into the ring to readjust it. I then looked at the barometer, and found its reading to be 9¾ in., still decreasing fast, implying a height exceeding 29,000 ft. Shortly after, I laid my arm upon the table, possessed of its full vigour, but on being desirous of using it I found it powerless – it must have lost its power momentarily; trying to move the other arm, I found it powerless also. Then I tried to shake myself, and succeeded, but I seemed to have no limbs. In looking at the barometer my head fell over my left shoulder; I struggled and shook my body again, but could not move my arms. Getting my head upright for an instant only, it fell on my right shoulder; then I fell backwards, my back resting against the side of the car and my head on its edge. In this position my eyes were directed to Mr. Coxwell in the ring. When I shook my body I seemed to have full power over the muscles of the back, and considerably so over those of the neck, but none over either my arms or my legs. As in the case of the arms, so all muscular power was lost in an instant from my back and neck. I dimly saw Mr. Coxwell, and endeavoured to speak, but could not. In an instant intense darkness overcame me, so that the optic nerve lost power suddenly, but I was still conscious, with as active a brain as at the present

[1] This was not a breathing apparatus. It was a bellows for circulating air past the bulbs of the thermometers to counteract the effect of solar radiation.

moment whilst writing this. I thought I had been seized with asphyxia, and believed I should experience nothing more, as death would come unless we speedily descended: other thoughts were entering my mind, when suddenly I became unconscious as on going to sleep. I cannot tell anything of the sense of hearing, as no sound reaches the air to break the perfect stillness and silence of the regions between six and seven miles above the earth. My last observation was made at 1h. 54m. above 29,000 feet. I suppose two or three minutes to have elapsed between my eyes becoming insensible to seeing fine divisions and 1h. 54m., and then two or three minutes more to have passed till I was insensible, which I think, therefore, took place about 1h. 56m. or 57m.

'Whilst powerless I heard the words "temperature" and "observation", and I knew Mr. Coxwell was in the car, speaking to me and endeavouring to rouse me, – therefore consciousness and hearing had returned. I then heard him speak more emphatically, but could not see, speak or move. I heard him again say, "Do try; now do." Then the instruments became dimly visible, then Mr. Coxwell, and very shortly I saw clearly. Next I arose in my seat and looked around as though waking from sleep, though not refreshed, and said to Mr. Coxwell, "I have been insensible." He said, "You have, and I too, very nearly." I then drew up my legs, which had been extended, and took a pencil in my hand to begin observations. Mr. Coxwell told me that he had lost the use of his hands, which were blacked, and I poured brandy over them.

'I resumed my observations at 2h. 7m., recording the barometer reading at 11.53 inches and the temperature minus 2°. It is probable that three or four minutes passed from the time of my hearing the words "temperature" and "observation", till I began to observe; if so, returning conciousness came at 2h. 4m. P.M., and this gives seven minutes for total insensibility.

I found the water in the vessel supplying the wet-bulb thermometer one solid mass of ice, though I had, by frequent disturbance, kept it from freezing. It did not all melt until we had been on the ground some time. Mr. Coxwell told me that while in the ring he felt it piercingly cold, that hoar frost was all round the neck of the balloon, and that on attempting to leave the ring he found his hands frozen. He had, therefore, to place his arms on the ring and drop down. . . . He wished to approach me but could not; and when he felt insensibility coming over him too, he became anxious to open the valve. But in consequence of having lost the use of his hands he could not do this; ultimately he succeeded by seizing the cord with his teeth, and dipping his head two or three times, until the balloon took a decided turn downwards.'

After a rapid descent, this historic flight ended at 2.50 p.m. when Coxwell landed the *Mammoth* safely in a large meadow at Cold Weston near the village of Clee St Margaret below the western slopes of the Brown Clee. So far from feeling exhausted after his experience, Glaisher tramped the seven and a half miles into Ludlow to commission a cart and assistance while Coxwell remained on guard.

How high did Coxwell and Glaisher actually climb? This question became the subject of much debate. The minimum thermometer registered minus 11°9 compared with Glaisher's last conscious reading of minus 5°. Coxwell believed that when he came down from the hoop the barometer reading was 7 inches. When Glaisher lost consciousness, the balloon was still ascending at the rate of 1,000 ft per minute but by the time he recovered it was falling, he alleged, at twice that velocity. Taking all these facts together, Glaisher estimated that the balloon had reached a height of 37,000 ft or 7 miles. This estimate has been disputed on two grounds; first, the unreliability of readings taken under such circumstances, and secondly that the balloon could not possibly have descended at such a rapid rate. Nevertheless, it would be fair to say that this intrepid pair certainly exceeded 30,000 ft, a height that no other man has ever attained without the aid of oxygen breathing apparatus or, in more recent times, a pressurized car. Their feat is the more remarkable when it is remembered that neither man was in the full vigour of youth at the time, Coxwell being forty-three and Glaisher ten years older.

Between 1862 and 1866 Glaisher went on to make many more research flights both by day and by night, using different starting points, the Crystal Palace, Windsor, Woolwich and Wolverton where a series of ascents were made from the London & North Western Railway works with the co-operation of that Company. For night ascents he used a Davey safety lamp to read his instruments. But he never scaled such a dizzy height again and, like every seasoned aeronaut, having touched the sublime he suffered at least one salutary encounter with the ridiculous. Most, but not all, of these flights were made with Coxwell and on the occasion of a night ascent from Woolwich Arsenal in October 1865 for the purpose of recording air temperatures over London, Glaisher was piloted by an aeronaut named Orton. The scientist obtained a magnificent view of London by night as an easterly breeze carried the balloon right over the city and then away into the darkness of the Buckinghamshire and Oxfordshire countryside. Unfortunately, Orton suddenly became convinced that the balloon was about to be blown out to sea. Glaisher, who knew perfectly well that they were nowhere near the sea, argued in vain against this extraordinary aberration. The aeronaut insisted upon making so rapid a descent that nearly all poor Glaisher's instruments were broken when the balloon landed heavily at Highmoor in Oxfordshire. On the conversation that then ensued, history is silent.

Glaisher was one of the founders of the (Royal) Aeronautical Society in 1866, becoming first the society's treasurer and later its chairman. He was responsible for the finest of nineteenth century books on ballooning, *Travels in the Air* with its superb illustrations and flight charts, its contributions by Flammarion, de Fonvielle and Gaston Tissandier and, above all, Glaisher's own graphic descriptions of his flights. He writes of the great sense of peace he felt in the intense silence of the upper air and of his delight in scenes 'so varied and so beautiful that we feel that we could remain forever to wander above these boundless plains'. Certainly Glaisher's balloon explorations did not shorten his life, for he lived into the twentieth century, dying in 1903 at the age of ninety-four. His companion, Henry Coxwell, is commemorated by a memorial in the parish church of Seaham in Sussex where he died in 1900, aged eighty. In early life he had practised as a dentist and began ballooning under the alias 'Henry Wells' for fear of parental disapproval. He claimed a thousand ascents in his long and adventurous career as an aeronaut, his last being at York in June 1885 during gala week, a festivity he had enlivened with his balloon for twenty-seven successive years without a single disappointment.

The first serious attempt to rival the performance of Glaisher and Coxwell ended in tragedy. It was made by Gaston Tissandier accompanied by two scientists named Sivel and Crocé-Spinelli in the balloon *Zénith*. They ascended from the La Villette gasworks near Paris in April, 1875 their main purpose being to try out an oxygen breathing apparatus which they had previously tested successfully in a decompression chamber. This consisted of mouthpieces connected by tubes to bladders filled with a mixture of air and oxygen and by its aid they hoped to surpass the British height record. The apparatus was first used when the balloon reached equilibrium at 22,800 ft and had such a restorative effect that it was resolved to throw out ballast and ascend. Soon after this Tissandier lost consciousness. When he came round he heard Crocé-Spinelli urging him to throw out ballast as the balloon was falling rapidly. Tissandier obeyed, but at the same moment Crocé-Spinelli most unwisely jettisoned a piece of scientific equipment weighing eighty pounds with the effect that the *Zénith* began a second fast upward run and Tissandier again lost consciousness. He recovered to find that the balloon was again descending very fast and that his two companions were lying prone in the bottom of the car. Their faces were black, blood had run from their mouths and noses and they were quite obviously dead. In this frightful situation Gaston Tissandier, great aeronaut that he was, did not lose his presence of mind and despite lack of ballast managed to bring the *Zénith* safely, if heavily, to earth. Regarded by the Parisians as martyrs to science, Tissandier's companions lie in the cemetery of Père Lachaise, near the grave of Madame Blanchard, beneath a tomb surmounted by their life-size prostrate effigies.

This disaster revealed the danger of depending on a 'hand to mouth' method of taking oxygen and so led eventually to the adoption of masks. It was also shown by subsequent experience that the amount of oxygen taken aloft was quite insufficient. Even so, why was it that the two men died when Coxwell and Glaisher attained a greater height without oxygen and suffered no ill effects? One theory advanced at the time was that the *Zénith* encountered much lower temperatures than did the *Mammoth*, but physical fitness and acclimatization doubtless had a lot to do with it. Their two previous high altitude flights had acclimatized Coxwell and Glaisher. Similarly, Tissandier's long aeronautical experience probably accounts for his survival whereas Sivel and Crocé-Spinelli wrongly assumed that a decompression chamber faithfully reproduced conditions at high altitude.

In 1893–4 a number of high altitude scientific ascents were made in Germany by Herr Berson and Professor Süring of the Prussian Meteorological Institute. On 4th December, 1894 Berson ascended alone from Strasburg in the 92,000 cubic feet *Phoenix*, using hydrogen, and achieved, 30,000 ft. As a result of these experiments the

300,000 cubic feet *Preussen* (Prussia) balloon was constructed with which, after a number of trial flights, Berson and Süring ascended together in 1901 to a height of 35,500 ft, a record which was not surpassed until 1931 when Professor Piccard began his famous series of high altitude flights using a pressurized gondola. In all the German ascents oxygen was carried in cylinders, but it was still inhaled through the dangerous hand-held mouthpiece and both Berson and Süring lost consciousness for a time on their record ascent when they achieved what was believed at the time to be 'the greatest height at which existence is possible'.

These German aeronauts were equipped with vastly improved instruments, specially developed for use in balloons by Berson, Süring, Professor Assmann and others and made by the Bosch Company. They included the Baro-thermo-hygrograph and Assmann's aspirator-psychrometer which made possible accurate recordings of air temperature unaffected by solar radiation. It was the French scientist Gustave Hermite and the aeronaut Georges Besancon who first questioned the need to hazard human life in high altitude meteorological research and pioneered in 1892 the use of unmanned instrument-carrying balloons, forerunners of the indispensable 'met' balloons of today. At first light balloons of silk, cambric or paper were used, their capacities varying from 1,000 to 17,500 cubic feet, but in 1901 Assmann and Berson introduced small rubber balloons. These were designed to expand on rising until, at a given altitude, they would burst, their instruments descending by parachute.

Following an international conference in Paris in September 1896, meteorological research using 'weather balloons' was organized upon a world scale. With this development the need for manned research flights in the upper levels of the earth's atmosphere disappeared and this explains why the height record established by Berson and Süring stood unbroken for so long.

By 1893, French sounding balloons, bearing light but very precise instruments constructed by Jules Richard, had approached an altitude of 50,000 ft. From a station which he established at his own expense at Trappes, near Versailles, the meteorologist Teisserenc de Bort succeeded in penetrating further than this with results which astonished the scientific world by contradicting accepted theories. In 1902 he announced his discovery of a zone between the 33,000 and 66,000 ft altitudes where the temperature ceased to fall and might even rise. It was this zone, which we now call the stratosphere, that a new generation of aeronauts would explore in their huge balloons with pressurized nacelles, thus paving the way for man's conquest of outer space.

CHAPTER TEN

The Navigable Balloon

WHENEVER GENIUS BLAZES a new trail an eager army of camp followers, schemers and dreamers, rogues and eccentrics, is bound to set out in hot pursuit. So every great invention produces a heavy crop of parasitic patents, some sensible, some impracticable but prophetic, too many pathetic in their absurdity. To this rule the balloon was no exception and it will not surprise the reader to learn that the proportion of absurdities was unusually high. There was, for instance, Mr Horace De Manara who in 1853 proposed to apply the balloon as a remedy for sea-sickness. The recipe? Mount a series of seats in gimbals on the deck of the vessel and then suspend each seat from a small balloon. Of the unsuccessful but prophetic species were the several inventors who proposed to use balloons for weight lifting, a principle now successfully applied in American and British Columbian lumber camps to lift logs from inaccessible locations. It was, however, the problem of making the balloon dirigible (i.e. controllable) instead of the sport of the winds that attracted an overwhelming majority of these aspiring inventors.

It was in connection with heavier-than-air flight that Sir George Cayley did his most brilliant work, but this greatest and most far-sighted of all the aeronautical pioneers realized that for the dirigible balloon, no less than for the aeroplane, success depended upon the development of an engine having – by the standards of his time – a very high power to weight ratio. Although he hoped that a suitably light steam engine might be evolved, he recognized the advantage of a form of power unit which would eliminate the need for a boiler. He experimented unsuccessfully with a hot-air engine and a piston engine using gunpowder and he prophetically forecast the coming of an internal combustion engine using 'inflammable gas, oil or tar, or other inflammable matters'. But Cayley's was a voice crying in the wilderness. The lack of suitable motive power in no way inhibited the enthusiastic inventors of dirigible balloons. Screws or paddle wheels worked manually, by clockwork, or even by horses were proposed. Propulsion by the expansion of hot air or by jets of steam was also considered. The notion of harnessing birds to the balloon was seriously canvassed. Eagles were the most popular choice though the pigeon had its advocates. Sometimes the whole envelope of the balloon might take the form of a huge screw. Unholy marriages were consummated – most of them only on paper, fortunately – between the balloon, the kite, the ornithopter and the helicopter.

The notion of a balloon/glider was a recurring one, cropping up on both sides of the Atlantic in different forms, the idea being that on each down run the balloon would make a controlled glide by means of plane surfaces adjustable by the pilot. The most eccentric variant on this theme was the cubiform Montgolfière proposed by Georg Rebenstein of Nuremburg in 1835. His idea was that on reaching the desired ceiling this box-shaped balloon would collapse as completely as an opera hat, leaving a single plane surface consisting of a series of slats, like a venetian blind, controllable by the aeronaut. Yet even such dreams as this make sober sense compared with some of the ideas quite seriously put forward. For example, the specification of the English Patent taken out in 1856 by an individual named Jean Baptiste Justin Lassie begins as follows:

'This invention consists in an improved aerial ship or carriage, constructed with an outer and inner cylinder on an axis, so that the crew or passengers, by walking inside the inner cylinder supported by gas, cause it to rotate, and with it the outer cylinder, furnished with a screw, and thus propel the vessel in the air.

'It is proposed that the outer cylinder be ninety feet diameter and nine hundred feet long, and that a crew of three hundred men be employed to work the apparatus, one hundred and fifty in action at a time. . . .'

Such nightmare visions as this gigantic aerial treadmill are best left to the psychologists, so at this point it becomes appropriate to leave the realm of high lunacy and to consider those more soberly concerned in the development of the dirigible balloon.

The first hydrogen balloon made by Charles and the brothers Robert was the magnified equivalent of Cavallo's hydrogen filled soap bubbles. Its form was logical and definitive. A free balloon of

any shape other than that of the orange or the pear would be as wildly
illogical as a square wheel. But a complete surrender to its element
was implicit in that shape; as soon as man rejected that surrender and
attempted to drive the balloon through the air its unsuitability for
such a purpose became obvious. Blanchard, defying the wind by
rowing with his 'wings' or twirling his moulinet while tethered to a
great globular bag of gas, was like a man trying to run with an iron
ball chained to his ankle. Clearly what was needed for a dirigible
balloon was a shape of envelope less resistant to wind and some less
flexible form of connection between the car that supplied the horizontal driving force and the envelope that suspended it. The answer
was to elongate the envelope into a streamlined form, elliptical,
cylindrical or cigar-shaped, a step which also met the second require-
ment by making possible the triangulation of the car lines. But this
use of an elongated envelope at once raised problems of stability
which did not exist in the case of the spherical balloon. No loss of gas
could cause the latter to lose its symmetry and balance; even if it
became completely deflated it could still act as a parachute. Not so
the elongated dirigible; loss of gas would deform the whole frail
structure, set up unequal stresses in the car lines and eventually lead to
'jack-knifing' of the envelope with dire results. Moreover, such a
dirigible would need to be trimmed like a boat; unequal distribution
of weight in the car, or a sudden shift of weight, could be as disastrous as loss of gas. Thus, in addition to the quest for a suitable form
of motive power, the protagonists of the dirigible had to face entirely
new difficulties and dangers. Complexity was the price that had to be
paid for the complete mastery of the air.

Although his design was never executed, the father of the dirigible
balloon was undoubtedly Lieutenant (later General) Jean Baptiste
Marie Meusnier (1754–93) who has been justly described as one of
the most remarkable Frenchmen of his day. A fine soldier equally
distinguished as an engineer and scientist, there is no telling what he
might have achieved had he not been killed in action against the
Prussians at Mayence. On the 3rd December, 1783, Meusnier presented to the French Academy an historic Paper: *Mémoire sur
l'équilibre des Machines Aérostatiques*, in which he published his idea of
the ballonnet.

The ballonnet is an auxiliary reservoir within the main envelope of a balloon which may be filled with air from the car of the balloon – by a hand bellows in Meusnier's example, but later by a powered compressor. It can consist of the annular space between the two layers of a double envelope, an arrangement Meusnier proposed for a spherical balloon, or it can take the form of an air bag within the main envelope. Meusnier conceived the ballonnet as a means of conserving gas and ballast and regulating height; he did not originally appreciate its value as a means of preserving the form of an elongated envelope, but this soon became apparent. If the balloon and its ballonnet were both fitted with safety valves, the latter set to lift at a slightly lower pressure than the former, then no gas would be lost from the balloon through expansion until that expansion had driven all the air out of the ballonnet. Conversely, contraction or loss of gas could be compensated by inflating the ballonnet and the form of an elongated envelope thus preserved under constant pressure.

Early in the present century it became customary to classify dirigibles in three groups: non-rigids, where the car is suspended from the envelope as in a free balloon; semi-rigids, where some form of rigid boom or framework is interposed between envelope and car, and the rigid, where the envelope itself becomes an inflexible structure, containing the gas either directly or in a series of gas bags. In practice, however, the line between the first two groups is sometimes very difficult to draw and since both rely upon Meusnier's ballonnet to maintain their form it is simpler to classify dirigibles as pressure airships and rigid airships, the latter only appearing in practicable form right at the end of this history.

In 1784, when his Paper was published, Meusnier produced a classic design for a dirigible balloon. The sixteen water-colour drawings of this design are preserved in the Musée de l'Air at Chalais-Meudon and they were also reproduced and published as an *Atlas des dessins relatifs à un Projet de Machine Aérostatique*. Here the road that others would follow is surely mapped by a masterly hand. The drawings depict an envelope in the form of an ellipsoid, 260 ft long with a capacity of 60,000 cubic feet. This has a strong 'belly-band' of fabric to which the car lines, properly triangulated, are attached. Between these car lines, flexible pipes can be seen connecting the bellows on the car with the ballonnets. The car is a long, slim, boat-like hull. It was indeed a boat, being designed to float in the event of a landing on water. There is a rudder aft and also a rudimentary form of elevator plane. Mounted coaxially in a framework between car and balloon are three large diameter propellers designed to be manually driven from the car by rope and pulley. Although for lack of adequate motive power this arrangement could have had little effect, and although Blanchard with his little moulinet was the first to use a propeller in the air, this is the first fully developed design for a propeller-driven aircraft. A contemporary of Meusnier's named Vallet is generally credited with the earliest use of an airscrew – on a river boat – in 1784, but whether there was any interchange of ideas is not known.

Although he was cut off in his prime, Meusnier's aeronautical ideas were not without influence in his lifetime. At his suggestion a ballonnet was used in the first elongated balloon ever to take the air. This venture was promoted by the Duc de Chartres in 1784 and the balloon, 52 ft long, 32 ft deep and 30,000 cubic feet capacity, was built by Charles and the brothers Robert. It was intended to be dirigible, proudly bearing a large sail-like rudder aft, but the method of propulsion was so completely ineffective that it scarcely merits the term. This consisted of two parasols mounted at the bow of the car and designed to reciprocate in such a manner that they moved backward when open and forwards, in the direction of flight, when furled. This machine took off from St Cloud on the 15th July before a distinguished assembly with the Duke in charge and the brothers Robert hopefully manning the parasols. Most unfortunately, the ballonnet was so arranged – or disarranged – that it blocked the neck of the balloon and as there was no valve to relieve the situation a most alarming distention took place at high altitude. With commendable presence of mind, the Duke pierced the bloated envelope with a flag-stick (some say with his sword) and the balloon came down to a safe and appropriate landing near Chalais Meudon. For this remedial action, but for which the balloon would undoubtedly have burst and plunged them to death, the Duke was most unjustly accused of cowardice.

The brothers Robert went on to make a second elongated balloon, this time of an almost cylindrical form. It was no more dirigible than its predecessor, but they had evidently mastered the principle of the ballonnet, for it was in this balloon that Cadet Robert made the celebrated long distance flight from Paris to Béthune described in Chapter 3.

Had Meusnier lived he would inevitably have been frustrated, as a designer of dirigibles, by the lack of suitable motive power. For this reason it is possible to move forward sixty years without omitting any important landmark in the history of the navigable balloon. During this long period so many men, Monck Mason among them, tried their hands at designing dirigibles that a lengthy catalogue of curiosities could be compiled from their work, but it would not be particularly edifying. None surpassed Meusnier and few reached the stage of actual construction. Of those that did, only two merit a passing mention.

Two expatriate Swiss, John Pauly, an engineer, and Durs Egg, a gunmaker, made the first serious attempt to construct a dirigible in England in 1816–17. The envelope, made of goldbeater's skin, was in the shape of a dolphin with an almost flat belly and had a spherical ballonnet, 21 ft in diameter, within. Known as 'Egg's Folly', it became the subject of unkind cartoons and much ridicule. While it was under construction, Pauly died and the project was abandoned. The only part of the balloon to fly was the ballonnet which was acquired by the great American showman P. T. Barnum who converted it into a small balloon in which his famous Dwarf, Tom Thumb, made an ascent from the Surrey Gardens. Designed to be propelled by 'oars', 'Egg's Folly' was rightly named, but it deserves to be remembered where other follies are forgotten for one reason. Its design included a weight, moveable longitudinally, so that the balloon could be trimmed and its nose elevated or depressed when it was desired to climb or to descend. This consisted of a box filled with sand which could be moved along a cable extending from the tail of the 'dolphin' to the stern of the car, the latter being suspended well forward. This was the first application of a principle that became accepted practice.

In 1834 a highly speculative, not to say shady, company called the 'European Aeronautical Society' was promoted for the purpose of establishing a regular service of airships between London and Paris. The hope of this organization was yet another 'rowing balloon' named *Eagle* which was constructed in Paris by an odd character name the Comte de Lennox, a French colonel of Scottish descent. It is said that a French representative of the Company came over to London and installed himself in the world's first airline office in Golden Square, Soho, to await the coming of the *Eagle*. Needless to say, it never arrived. In August, when the *Eagle* was inflated before a large crowd in the Champ de Mars, the balloon escaped from its net, shot into the air and burst. The mob then moved in and completed the work of destruction in the customary manner. Undeterred, Lennox next proceeded to build a second airship inside a wooden enclosure in York Road, Kensington, which was euphemistically called the Company's 'Dockyard'. This was completed and exhibited at Vauxhall, but it never flew. Not surprisingly, certain pecuniary difficulties overtook the Company and the balloon was seized for debt. It was borne away in wagons by the Sheriff of Middlesex and was seen no more.

The serious story of the navigable balloon really begins in 1850 when a French clockmaker, Pierre Jullien of Villejuif built a superb model airship which he demonstrated in flight at the Paris Hippodrome. With its long, slender, beautifully streamlined shape, its rudder and elevators and its gondola mounted close under the forward part of the envelope, Jullien's little model more closely resembled the large rigid airships of the twentieth century than any of the navigable balloons that followed it. It was propelled by a clockwork motor driving two airscrews set one upon each side of the centre line. The form of the envelope was maintained by a light wire frame stiffened longitudinally by a truss. It is said that Jullien built a full-sized dirigible in 1852, but it never flew and how he proposed to propel it is not known.

Among those who had helped Lennox with his first *Eagle* balloon in 1836 was Henri Giffard, but this abortive project did not arouse his enthusiasm for aeronautics and after experimenting with Le Berrien on a model steam balloon in 1844 this brilliant engineer returned to his steam engineering. It was, as Giffard himself admitted, the work of Pierre Jullien that revived his interest and inspired him to build a steam-propelled balloon. In order to familiarize himself with a new element, Giffard made his maiden flight in a free balloon with Eugene Godard in 1851 and from this moment his long and fruitful association with the balloon began.

The envelope of Giffard's first balloon was 144 ft long, sharply

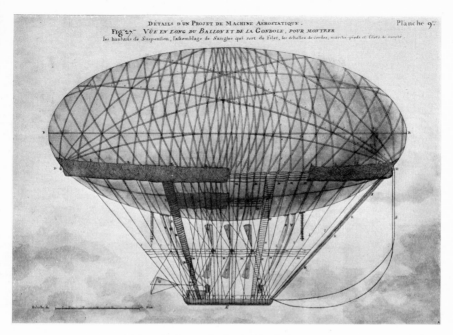

Meusnier's prophetic airship design, 1785

The first powered flight: Giffard's steam airship, 1852

The Tissandier brothers' electric airship, 1883

Renard and Kreb's electric airship *La France* at Chalais-Meudon, 1884

pointed at both ends and completely symmetrical in longitudinal section, its midship diameter being 40 ft. Its capacity was 88,000 cubic feet. A net covered the envelope and from this a single wooden pole, 66 ft long was suspended by many closely spaced lines. At the rear of the pole was a rudder in the form of a triangular sail. The car containing the aeronaut and his machinery was hung from the pole by the usual triangulated car lines. This intermediate pole in no way contributed to the rigidity of the balloon. Giffard's concern was to minimize the fire risk by placing the car as far below the envelope as possible, over 40 ft in fact. Giffard had no desire to share the fate of Zambeccari and his countryman Olivari in their combination balloons and was much more alive to this danger than some later experimenters.

The engine and boiler designed and built by Giffard for this craft weighed 100 lb and 250 lb respectively. The engine indicated 3 h.p. and drove a single three-bladed propeller, 11 ft in diameter, at 110 r.p.m. Giffard calculated that this should give the balloon a maximum speed of 6 m.p.h. in still air. Most unfortunately no technical details of this historic power unit appear to have survived. The fire-hole door of the boiler was protected by a wire safety gauze, so there was no risk from this source except when firing was actually taking place. Finally, the chimney was projected downwards from the side of the car. With Giffard on board, the weight of the balloon was $1\frac{1}{2}$ tons, a figure that made it possible for him to carry 5 cwt of coke[1] and water.

Very properly, though somewhat incongruously, clad in a top hat and frock coat, Giffard rose in his steam balloon from the Paris Hippodrome on the 24th September, 1852 and, to the amazement of a large crowd, flew slowly out of sight, trailing in the still air a triumphal white pennant of exhaust steam. This first powered flight ever made by man ended safely at Trappe, seventeen miles away. On another occasion Giffard was able to prove that the balloon was under control by describing a circle in the air. These were very remarkable achievements and an inspiration to future aeronauts, but they represented only a small and tentative beginning and not a real conquest of the air as Giffard would have been the first to acknowledge.

---

[1] 'Coal' has been mentioned as Giffard's fuel, but for obvious reasons he would have favoured coke as both safer and lighter.

14

His balloon had achieved its estimated speed of 6 m.p.h. but, as he must have realized before he ever flew it, such demonstrations of controlled flight would only be possible under the comparatively rare conditions of perfect calm. Under average weather conditions his little aerial ship would have been almost as helpless as a free balloon.

It was the old problem; Giffard knew that he needed much more power without extra weight, but this was beyond the compass of his art to achieve. As it was he judged the power plant too heavy for the balloon and he therefore installed it beneath a second, larger envelope of 113,000 cubic feet capacity. This was of the same form as its predecessor but slimmer in order to reduce wind resistance, being 230 ft long but only 33 ft diameter. The pole was dispensed with, the car being attached directly to the net. It is strange that Giffard, so brilliant, so far-sighted in most respects, used neither Meusnier's ballonnet nor the trimming weight introduced by Pauly and Egg. This brought disaster. On a trial trip with Yon, the Paris balloon maker, deformation of the balloon occurred due to loss of gas; the nose tilted right up throwing an unequal strain on the car lines, some of which tore away. The balloon then escaped from the net and burst. Fortunately Giffard and his companion were only slightly injured, but the balloon was a complete wreck.

Giffard then planned a third balloon of truly heroic proportions: 1,970 ft long, 98 ft in diameter at the middle section and a capacity of 7,800,000 cubic feet. For this monster he designed a steam plant weighing 30 tons which, he estimated, would give the ship a speed of 45 m.p.h. in still air. As he was unable to improve the power to weight ratio of his steam machinery, Giffard saw that the only answer was to increase the size of the envelope. It will be recalled that engineers had earlier doubted whether a steamship could possibly carry enough coal for an ocean voyage until Brunel pointed out that whereas the area of a hull represents the square of its dimensions, its capacity increases as the cube of those dimensions. Brunel's three great ships proved his point, but although Giffard realized that precisely the same argument applied to the envelope of a balloon, his huge aerial ship was never built on the score of its immense cost. Perhaps this was just as well. The tragic drama of Brunel and his *Great Eastern* might have had an exactly contemporary parallel. As it was,

Giffard thereafter confined himself happily to his injectors and his large captive balloons.

With Giffard out of the running, no significant progress was made until after the Franco-Prussian war. During that war, the French Government had commissioned a marine engineer named Dupuy de Lôme to build a dirigible and this made its one and only flight on 2nd February, 1872. Using a ballonnet, Dupuy de Lôme made a very workmanlike job of his egg-shaped balloon, but he made no attempt to solve the crucial motive power problem. The large four-bladed propeller was driven by gearing and hand-cranks in such a way that eight men could be harnessed to it. As more men were needed to work the air pump for the ballonnet, the total weight of this 'power plant' must have substantially exceeded that of Giffard's steam machinery. By a most prodigious effort, the eight aerial galley slaves, generously lubricated with rum by their captain, succeeded in equalling Giffard's speed in still air.

Six years later, Charles F. Ritchel of Corry, Pennsylvania constructed a tiny man-powered dirigible which could be called the first powered air-craft to fly in the new world. This was really a flying bicycle. A cylindrical envelope 25 ft long suspended a light metal framework wherein sat the aeronaut, actuating a small four-bladed bow propeller by means of pedals. This propeller could be angled for directional control. Ritchel was a bulky individual, so he had to find a suitably scaled-down man to fly his invention. Pedalling frantically through the skies of Hartford, Connecticut, this unnamed hero succeeded in making a circular flight in still air at a speed of about $3\frac{1}{2}$ m.p.h. Throughout his life, Ritchel stubbornly insisted that mechanical power could never be successfully applied in the air. Yet his flying bicycle, like Dupuy de Lôme's 'man-engined' dirigible, belonged to the past; developments in technology were now taking place which would soon make the impossible possible.

The first portent of things to come appeared in December 1872 in the shape of Paul Haenlein's airship, the first in the world to use an internal combustion engine. The Frenchman, Etienne Lenoir, had patented his gas engine in 1860. It did not operate on the four-stroke cycle – that was yet to come – and it looked very much like a steam engine. Like most steam engines, it was double acting, that is to say a mixture of gas and air was admitted to each end of the cylinder alternately by means of an eccentric driven slide valve. The charge was fired by an electric spark, a very advanced feature, but because that charge was not compressed in the cylinder the engine was very inefficient. In fact, the Lenoir engine produced less power than a steam engine of the same size and weight, but it dispensed with the need for a boiler and Haenlein was the first man to attempt to exploit this advantage in the air.

As early as April 1865 Haenlein took out a Provisional Patent in England (No. 930 of 1.4.65) for 'Improvements in Navigable Balloons' in which he specified propulsion by a gas engine, driving two helical propellers with axes at right angles to provide both lift and horizontal motion. Presumably the war delayed the inventor's plans, for it was not until 1872 that he was able to build a balloon to his design in Vienna. The envelope was 164 ft long with a maximum diameter of 30 ft and a capacity of 85,000 cubic feet. It was of a curious shape, resembling that of two ships hulls placed deck to deck, but it was one which would thereafter become very popular with French designers. For the sake of rigidity, the skeleton car was slung close to the belly of the envelope. There was a large ballonnet.

In the car was mounted a gas engine having four horizontally opposed cylinders driving a single tractor propeller at 40 r.p.m., this being the earliest use of an airscrew to pull rather than to push. Evidently Haenlein had abandoned his idea of using a second screw as a helicopter rotor. Unfortunately, technical details of this historic engine are lacking, but if they followed Haenlien's patent specification the valves were driven by eccentrics on the crankshaft and the 'principal working parts' were 'constructed hollow' to save weight. Six horse-power was developed on a consumption of 250 cubic feet of coal gas per hour drawn from the balloon. As Haenlien explained in his Patent, this loss would be compensated by inflating the ballonnet and discharging ballast; nevertheless it was a somewhat self-destructive principle reminiscent of a man sawing off the branch he is sitting on.

Unfortunately, despite Haenlein's efforts to save weight, the engine was too heavy and, bearing in mind that coal-gas was used and not pure hydrogen, the balloon lacked lift. It was never flown freely. Trials at Brunn in Moravia on 13th and 14th December, 1872 were carried out at low level, the balloon being restrained by ropes held by soldiers. Nevertheless a speed of 9 m.p.h. in still air was claimed and more might have come of this bold pioneer project had it not been halted by lack of money. Paul Haenlein died in 1896.

Meanwhile another new power was beginning to attract the attention of the aeronauts. At the Electrical Exhibition in Paris in 1881, the brothers Gaston and Albert Tissandier showed a model electric dirigible which attracted so much interest that they were encouraged to build a full-sized version. The 37,500 cubic feet envelope of this electric balloon resembled Giffard's though somewhat more corpulent, being 30 ft in diameter at the midpoint but only 92 ft long. From it was suspended a skeleton car resembling a bamboo bird-cage which contained the batteries and a Siemens motor. The motor produced $1\frac{1}{2}$ h.p. at 180 r.p.m. and drove a large two-bladed pusher propeller through reduction gearing. The speed achieved in still air was barely 3 m.p.h., which is hardly surprising because, from the point of view of power to weight, an electric motor and its batteries was no improvement upon Giffard's steam engine and boiler. Each of the 24 bichromate cells used by the Tissandier brothers weighed 17 lb. Nevertheless, while they were experimenting in 1883–4 a much larger electric balloon was under construction.

Two officers in the French army Corps of Engineers, Charles Renard and Arthur Krebs, had been scheming to build a navigable balloon since 1878. Through the influence of their commanding officer, Colonel Laussedat, they hoped to persuade the Minister of War to finance the project, but following the Dupuy de Lôme affair the Government had decided to spend no more money on such schemes. Finally, however, Gambetta, who had not forgotten that he owed his escape from Paris to a balloon, agreed to finance construction personally to the tune of £8,000.

Messrs Renard and Krebs had evidently had a close look at Paul Haenlein's design, for the envelope of their dirigible *La France* was of the same curious form. Its length was 165 ft, maximum diameter 27 ft and capacity 66,000 cubic feet. Beneath it was suspended a very long and slender car, 108 ft long, $4\frac{1}{2}$ ft wide and 6 ft deep, consisting of a silk-covered bamboo framework lined with canvas. This housed the lightweight pile batteries developed by Renard and a Krebs multi-polar motor constructed by Renard which produced $7\frac{1}{2}$ h.p. This was subsequently replaced by one of Théophile Gramme's series-wound motors which gave one horse-power more. This represented a weight of 210 lb per horse-power for batteries and motor, a formidable figure by our standards but a vast improvement on the figure of 400 lb for the Tissandier installation. The motor drove a four-bladed wooden tractor propeller. This was 23 ft in diameter but was designed so that its axis could be inclined upwards to avoid damage to the blades on landing. Renard provided a very efficient rudder and elevator plane aft, ballonnets, a sliding weight to compensate for any shifting of the centre of gravity, and a heavy guide-rope to facilitate landing. Such were the ingredients of success meticulously prepared by the brilliant Renard.

Most appropriately, *La France* was constructed at Chalais-Meudon and for two months Renard and Krebs waited there with such patience as they could muster for calm conditions in which to try out their brain child. At last, on 9th August, 1884, the weather favoured them and at 4 p.m. the two aeronauts stepped into the slender car and rose gently into the air. As soon as they were clear of the trees, Renard switched on the motor, the big propeller began to revolve and in a few moments they could feel a perceptible breeze in their faces as *La France* headed south; moreover experiment proved that the little ship was answering to her rudder. They turned to the west after they had crossed over the road from Choisy to Versailles. A light breeze was blowing from the north and they had never counted upon returning to Chalais, but the behaviour of the balloon gave them such confidence that they presently made a successful turn in a radius of 160 yards and headed homewards. Arrived back over Chalais at an altitude of 1,000 ft, the aeronauts valved gas and, by manoeuvring with motor and rudder, were able to bring *La France* lightly down to the parade ground from which they had started twenty-three minutes before. They had made a flight of less than five miles, but it was the first of which it could truly be said that the aircraft was under the full control of its pilot throughout.

During 1884–5 *La France* made seven flights, the last two over the city of Paris, and on five of these she was able to return to her starting point. On the other two occasions the wind was too strong for her. She has been called the world's first practical dirigible, but this is a claim of limited truth. Her motor gave her a speed of $14\frac{1}{2}$ m.p.h. so that she was only fully dirigible in light airs. Moreover, the limited capacity of her batteries severely restricted her flying range. Nevertheless, *La France* most convincingly demonstrated that controlled flight was perfectly practicable provided the engineers could supply a sufficiently powerful lightweight motor.

In the 1880s two concurrent but quite independent technical developments took place which would together solve the aeronauts' long-felt need for a light power unit. In 1885 Gottlieb Daimler took out his historic patent for a 'benzine motor' or petrol engine which he had developed from Otto's improved four-stroke gas engine. In 1886 the Frenchman P. L. T. Heroult and C. M. Hall of America independently invented the electrolytic process which made the large scale production of aluminium commercially practicable. Here, at one stroke, was a new self-contained source of power and a new light but strong metal with which to construct it. Both inventions would need development, but together they made man's complete conquest of the air certain.

The first man to use the new power in the air was the German Doctor Karl Woelfert, the most undeservedly neglected of all the great pioneers. Aeronautical history contains no coherent account of his experiments; only their tragic end attracted attention. Born in Thuringia in 1852, Woelfert was ordained and became a protestant minister in Leipzig. After losing much money in an ill-advised property speculation, he started a bookselling business in that city, but this was not so profitable as he had hoped, nor did it satisfy his adventurous disposition. He therefore turned professional aeronaut, making public ascents at fairs and pleasure gardens with a curious elongated balloon which became popularly known as 'The Cucumber'. He also used a second balloon of more orthodox form named the *New World*. Because of these activities Woelfert seems to have been regarded by his countrymen, quite unjustly, as a mountebank whose activities did not merit serious consideration.

In 1882, Woelfert became associated with a verderer of the royal forests of Saxony named Baumgarten who had earlier begun to experiment with navigable balloons. The partners were two of the first members of the Berlin Aeronautical Society. Baumgarten had constructed in 1879 a small airship employing a manual helicopter screw for lift and adjustable glider planes for forward flight. At Woelfert's suggestion the glider plane idea was abandoned and the two men constructed a larger airship with three small cars set one behind the other along the centre line, each equipped with a manually rotated propeller for forward propulsion. That this craft proved extremely unstable is not surprising. Its first flight ended disastrously in the manner of Giffard's second airship when the envelope tilted to an almost vertical position and the whole contraption crashed to the ground, fortunately without causing serious injury to the aeronauts.

The Berlin Aeronautical Society subscribed 50 marks towards further experiments, but these ended in a second and much more violent crash at the Charlottenberg Gardens on 5th March, 1882 in which Baumgarten was injured and the airship completely destroyed. This second disastrous failure broke Baumgarten's heart and he died in the following year, but the indomitable Woelfert soldiered on alone. Notwithstanding the fact that his efforts were ridiculed and that he could obtain no financial help, he continued to devote all his limited resources to aeronautics. He constructed a small elongated balloon with a closely attached skeleton car fitted with two manual propellers, one on a horizontal axis for forward propulsion and the other on a vertical axis below the floor of the car for lift. The latter was protected from damage on landing by a simple framework. A large sail-like rudder was attached to the rear of the car.

It was at this point in his experiments that Woelfert began to make history. In October 1887, the *Leipziger Illustrierte Zeitung* published an account of some test flights he had made with his small balloon and this was read by Gottlieb Daimler. Daimler's first small experimental horizontal petrol engine had run for the first time in November 1883 and in 1885–6 he had developed an enclosed vertical single-cylinder engine of improved design and power output. Already this revolutionary new power unit had been tried out in a boat and in both road and rail vehicles; why should it not conquer the air also? So Daimler wrote to Woelfert inviting him to visit him at Cannstadt. Woelfert accepted and from that moment became a passionate believer in the future of the petrol engine in the air.

De Fonvielle, who knew Woelfert, said of him that while he would discuss aeronautical matters generally in excellent French, he was very secretive about the petrol engine and his experiments therewith. This probably accounts for the lack of reliable information about

Woelfert's work in aeronautical literature. Such information as we have comes from the Daimler side.

Woelfert brought his small balloon to the Daimler works where a Daimler single-cylinder vertical engine of 2 h.p. was mounted in the car. According to the Daimler records this engine was fitted with a type of transmission whereby either of the two propellers could be engaged at will. From a contemporary photograph of the car it would seem that the engine was directly coupled to the screw for horizontal propulsion only, but a form of transfer gearbox may have been fitted at some later stage in the tests.

The first test flight of the world's first petrol-engined aircraft was made in calm weather from the Daimler factory site at Seelberg on Sunday, 12th August, 1888. It would appear that the intrepid pilot on this occasion was a young Daimler mechanic named Michaël, the capacity of the little balloon, (8,750 cubic feet) being insufficient to lift Woelfert's weight in addition to that of the engine. Like all Daimler units built before 1900, the ignition system of the engine consisted of a platinum tube maintained at high temperature by an exposed bunsen-type burner fed with vaporized petrol from a small pressure tank. This constituted a terrible fire hazard made all the greater by the fact that the car was directly attached to the envelope instead of being suspended far below it after the method used by the prudent Giffard. Several times during this first flight the air stream from the propeller blew out the burner. It was promptly re-lit by Michaël, using a lighted candle which he kept screened from the wind for this purpose! A more perilous exploit would be difficult to conceive, but fortune favoured the brave and Michaël landed the balloon safely at Kornwestheim, two-and-a-half miles from the starting point.

It is obvious that with so small an engine the balloon could not have been navigable except in the lightest airs, but it was a promising beginning. Apart from the difficulty of keeping the burner alight, the engine had run well, fulfilling all Daimler's expectations and the little ship had answered her rudder. Both Daimler and Woelfert were delighted. The former set to work to improve the power-to-weight ratio of his engine while the latter was eager to continue his experiments.

It is said that further test flights were made from Cannstadt in

September and from Ulm in November 1888, but details are lacking and after this a curtain of obscurity falls over Woelfert's activities for several years. It is likely, however, that his experiments were frequently frustrated and brought to a standstill by lack of money. Evidently Gottlieb Daimler was too preoccupied with the more immediately promising application of his engine to road vehicles to subsidise Woelfert and it was money furnished by an unnamed patron that finally enabled Woelfert to build the new and larger balloon which he exhibited to the public at the Berlin Trade Fair in August 1896. This was fitted with a Daimler twin cylinder Phoenix engine of 6 h.p. and the Daimler records have it that Woelfert flew the machine successfully during the Exhibition. According to a French account,[1] however, the balloon never ascended because it lacked the necessary lift; it was merely exhibited in an enclosure to which the public were admitted by turnstile at a charge of half a mark. The same account states that this failure discouraged Woelfert's backer who lost patience with him and withdrew his support.

Undaunted by yet another setback, the indefatigable Woelfert found another supporter in Herr von Tucholka who helped him to form a Company to develop and exploit the navigable balloon. This venture won the patronage of no less a person than the Emperor Wilhelm II. Woelfert's efforts had at last won the recognition they deserved. Not only were funds now available to modify and develop the balloon, but the Emperor's interest ensured the co-operation of the Prussian Balloon Corps in carrying out full-scale trials on the Tempelhofer Field, Berlin, in June 1897.

As presented for trial in 1897, Woelfert's balloon had a cigar-shaped envelope approximately 100 ft long and 36 ft maximum diameter.[2] To this a large skeleton car of bamboo was directly attached by longitudinal steel rods carried in pockets in the fabric, the weight being distributed by a network of cords carried round the circumference of the envelope. Woelfert had abandoned his lifting propeller. The Daimler engine, mounted on wooden bearers on the floor of the car, drove a single aluminium tractor propeller over 7 ft in diameter. A large rectangular rudder of stiffened fabric was

[1] *L'Aeronaute*, July, 1897.

[2] These figures are estimated from contemporary photographs, using a human figure beside the balloon as the scale, since quoted figures vary widely from 252½ ft long down to 36 ft, the latter perhaps applying to the balloon of 1888.

attached to the central upright at the rear of the car. The engine, of course, still employed the hot tube ignition system, but with an incredible disregard for the danger involved Woelfert persisted in retaining the close connection between car and envelope, his argument being that the result was more rigid and offered less wind resistance. No ballonnet was fitted and, as the French aeronauts pointed out, the connection was so close that if the envelope lost gas and began to sag it would descend upon the heads of those in the car. Another important point to be borne in mind is this: in Woelfert's first small motorized balloon the lifting power of the gas had been negligible for he had planned to use the helicopter screw for lift, maintaining the balloon as nearly as possible in equilibrium. Since the screw cannot have been very effective the first flights must have been made at so low an altitude that expansion and consequent loss of gas from the envelope was minimal. That these test flights were accomplished without accident, thus giving Woelfert a fatal false confidence, can only be attributed to this fact. Now, however, he had abandoned the screw for lift so that, like any free balloon, the height his airship would attain depended entirely on the adjustment of weight to lifting power.

The balloon was inflated with hydrogen by the Balloon Corps in their own hangar and drawn out onto the field on the evening of Saturday, 12th June. The weather was calm and perfect and a number of foreign ambassadors and military attachés had been invited to witness the ascent. Woelfert announced his intention of flying to Findorf and returning to the Field in order to demonstrate convincingly the dirigibility of his balloon. He was to be accompanied on the flight by his mechanic, Robert Knabe and by Major Rieber of the Balloon Corps, but after two breakages had been discovered in the network that distributed the weight of the car it was agreed that Rieber should stand down. It was lucky for him that he did so.

At 7 p.m. Woelfert and Knabe climbed into the car and the engine was started. Many of those who were standing by were alarmed by the jet of flame from the tube heating burner and some tried to dissuade Woelfert from making the ascent. He appeared quite unconcerned, however, and, having assured them that he would see them again very soon, he gave the order 'Let go all'. The balloon ascended rapidly, so rapidly that it is doubtful whether sufficient ballast had been added following the decision to leave Major Rieber behind. As it climbed the balloon began to move in the direction of the Tempelhof station but on a very erratic course and it appeared to the anxious watchers that the rudder had been damaged, a portion of fabric being seen trailing behind the car. The balloon had crossed the perimeter of the field and was directly above the station approach road at a height of 3,000 ft when the inevitable happened. Those who were watching the balloon from the gardens of their houses said afterwards that they saw leap from the engine two flames, small when first seen but growing so rapidly that within seconds they were taller than the balloon. The next instant there was a loud explosion – the petrol tank, no doubt – followed by a single despairing cry for help as the airship became a mass of flame, plunging down to earth. It is obvious that the ignition burner set fire to the hydrogen which would have been released by expansion from the balloon at this height. The flaming wreckage plunged into a timber yard, situated between a school and a private house on the station approach, setting the timber store alight. For poor Woelfert and his companion there was, of course, no hope. They suffered the same terrible fate as the world's first aeronaut, Pilâtre de Rozier and his companion. Woelfert was only forty-five and, like Pilâtre, he was engaged to be married. The design of the petrol engine was by this time improving so rapidly that had he not stubbornly clung to his particular airship design with such complete disregard for the fire hazard, Woelfert's persistence might well have been crowned with complete success. As it was, the disaster discouraged further development, particularly in France where the use of the petrol engine in balloons was condemned as far too risky.

The introduction of aluminium had made possible the rigid airship. The term 'airship' is the only correct one to use in this context. For whereas the pressure airship was so clearly a navigable balloon and was almost invariably referred to as such at this time and for many years after, the use of a rigid envelope represented a radical breakaway from the simple concept of the free balloon. Although both share a common principle, the successful development of the rigid airship involved the solution of many novel technical problems both structural and aerodynamic. With each solution the rigid airship moved further away from its venerable parent. The story of this development is a fascinating and tragic one, but in a book about balloons only its beginning – the chrysalis stage, as it were – is relevant.

In 1843, Jean-Francois Dupuis-Delcourt[1] built with the financial assistance of his contemporary Marey-Monge a rigid spherical balloon. This extraordinary feat of craftsmanship was constructed entirely of copper, using sheets only ·02 in thick. Thirty feet in diameter and weighing less than 800 lb, in theory it could have flown but the problem of filling it with gas was not satisfactorily solved before Dupuis-Delcourt had to scrap his copper balloon for the lack of further financial support. In order to fill the interior of a rigid balloon with gas the air must first be expelled. There are several methods by which – in theory at least – this can be done. The balloon could be submerged and filled under water, or it could be filled with steam, and the gas passed in as the steam condensed. Alternatively, filling could be done by introducing a fabric ballonnet of a volume equal to that of the rigid balloon. Either the ballonnet could be filled with air which the entry of gas would expel, or the ballonnet could be filled with gas and then ripped. In both cases the ballonnet might then be withdrawn.

Although the copper balloon was a failure the notion of the rigid envelope lived on, though only in the minds of eccentrics like Prosper Meller who, in 1851, produced a design for a huge rigid airship made of sheet iron. It was not until aluminium became available commercially that the idea entered the realm of practicability.

The first to design an aluminium rigid airship was an Austrian engineer named David Schwartz. His conception dates from 1895. Construction was begun in Berlin and was not completed until 1897 by which time Schwartz had died, leaving his widow in charge of the project. In most illustrations the envelope of the Schwartz airship appears truly cylindrical, but in fact it was elliptical in cross section being 46 ft deep and 39 ft wide. It had a conical nose like a rocket and a slightly concave stern, the overall length being 156 ft, giving a capacity of 130,000 cubic feet. It consisted of a tubular aluminium framework covered with aluminium sheeting only ·008 in thick. The car – or gondola as it would be called in rigid airship parlance –

---

[1] Dupuis-Delcourt was a great aeronautical enthusiast and propagandist. In 1852 he founded the first aeronautical society in the world, the Société Aérostatique et Météorologique de France.

was attached by aluminium struts. There were two aluminium tractor propellers mounted abreast on either side the bow of the gondola
and a third pusher propeller above the stern which was moveable
upon its axis for control purposes. All three were belt driven at
480 r.p.m. from a single twin cylinder Daimler petrol engine[1] of
12 h.p.

The filling of the airship was carried out on the Tempelhofer
Field during the first two days of November 1897 by Captain von
Sigsfeld of the Balloon Corps, one of the two pioneers of the
'Drachen' kite balloon, using the expendable air ballonnet method.
When inflation had been completed, many spectators were aston-
ished to see that the ship was straining at her mooring ropes. They
had refused to believe that a metal ship could possibly float in air.
More than a century earlier their predecessors had believed that an
iron hull could never float in water until John Wilkinson proved
them wrong.

Most unfortunately, a single man undertook the first trial of
Schwartz's little silver ship. According to one account he was Herr
Jaegels, Schwartz's chief engineer, according to another he was a
young mechanic named Platz, while a third states that he was a soldier
of the Balloon Corps. Whoever he was he had no aeronautical experience and even if he had it is doubtful if he could have controlled
single-handed for the first time so novel and complicated a machine
even under ideal conditions. The conditions were not ideal, for there
was a 15 m.p.h. breeze blowing. So foolhardy an ascent can only be
explained by over-eagerness and it led to the inevitable result. When
released the ship shot up to a height of 82 ft and began to drift away
on the wind. As a result of the pilot's frantic effort to gain control,
the belt driving the propellers came off its pulley. At this point the
amateur pilot panicked and opened the valve. There was no means of
checking the ship's fall so it landed heavily, but at the last moment
the pilot jumped out and escaped injury. Not so the ship. The fruits
of three years' effort and the expenditure of £10,000 lay a crumpled
wreck like some tin toy that has been trodden underfoot by a

---

[1] E. Seton Valentine and F. I. Tomlinson state that there were four propellers, but I have
accepted A. Hildebrandt's account as the more reliable - and logical. According to the
Daimler records this was the second engine supplied to Schwartz, the first having been
delivered in 1892.

thoughtless child.[1] But Schwartz had not laboured altogether in vain, for he had proved that a metal ship could fly, and there was one man in Germany, Count Zeppelin, who would presently turn this demonstration to great account.

In 1884, a German inventor named Hermann Ganswindt had published a book in which he proposed a giant airship 500 ft long, pointing out that the cross-section and the air-resistance of an elongated airship does not increase in proportion to its volume. Hence the large airship has a great advantage in lifting power. This, of course, was repeating the doctrine of Brunel and Giffard and it is very likely that through the agency of Ganswindt it was transmitted to Count Zeppelin, true father of the rigid airship as the twentieth century would know it. Zeppelin saw the difficulty – indeed the absurdity – of using a rigid structure as a gas-tight envelope. For his first airship, 420 ft long and 38 ft in diameter, he used an aluminium framework like Schwartz, but he covered it in fabric and divided it into seventeen compartments each containing a lined gas bag holding a total of nearly 400,000 cubic feet of hydrogen. Daimler engines producing 32 h.p. were used for propulsion. Zeppelin had followed with interest the Daimler/Woelfert experiments in 1888 and as early as 1892 the Count had begun a thorough series of ground tests with engines and propellers, first at Cannstadt and later at Lake Constance. Zeppelin's airship emerged from its shed and moved out over the waters of Lake Constance in July 1900 and it is at this point that the stories of the balloon and the rigid airship diverge. The Count did not at first achieve success. First to build a practical aerial ship were the French engineers who followed the course mapped by Charles Renard.

In view of the promise shown by Renard's *La France* it is surprising that for the next fourteen years nothing was done to advance the dirigible in France. It is surprising, too, that the French engineers who exploited Daimler's invention so speedily and so successfully in road vehicles should have ignored for so long its potential in the air. The Woelfert disaster undoubtedly acted as a deterrent. It was a young Brazilian, Alberto Santos-Dumont, who generated a fresh wave of

[1] According to Moedebeck the airship sustained little damage on landing but was destroyed subsequently by a combination of wind pressure and vandalism. A photograph reproduced by Hildebrandt, however, clearly shows disastrous crash damage.

aeronautical enthusiasm in France by effecting a successful marriage between the internal combustion engine and the balloon. Santos-Dumont, a slim dandified little figure, arrived in Paris in 1897. The city captivated and dazzled him and no wonder, for this was the Paris of *La Belle Epoque*, a city that demonstrated the falsity of all puritanical theory in the way it combined a civilized but uninhibited pursuit of pleasure with a scintillating brilliance in the worlds of art and literature, science and engineering. A man like Santos, young, wealthy, unattached, personable, a sociable man who enjoyed good food and good wine, might easily have disappeared into the Paris so vividly portrayed by Toulouse-Lautrec, leaving no trace on the pages of history. Santos never eschewed that world; indeed the strange little figure in the inordinately high collars he always affected became very familiar in café society, but the alluring temptations that could debauch the weak-willed left him scathless for he became a dedicated man – dedicated to the air.

Santos-Dumont wrote a book[1] in which he describes very fully his aeronautical exploits. He is also the subject of an excellent recent biography.[1] Hence it would be superfluous to trace his career in detail and sufficient here to assess his contribution to the story of the navigable balloon. Taken aloft for the first time by the French aeronaut Alexis Macheron, Santos-Dumont at once became an enthusiastic balloonist with free balloons of his own in which he made a number of adventurous flights. He also entered the world of the motoring pioneers with equal zest and soon bought himself a De Dion tricycle. These two interests quickly fused into the idea of making a navigable balloon, using the De Dion engine. This was the most advanced small power unit then available, and its electrical ignition system made it a much safer unit in the air. The result was Santos-Dumont's 'Number One' and from then on there was no holding him. Altogether he built no less than fifteen dirigibles, though some of these were rebuilds of earlier models. He carried out all the design work and much of the construction himself, aided by his own team of devoted mechanics.

In his own book, Santos-Dumont refers briefly to Giffard as 'a courageous innovator' and makes a passing reference to the Tissandier brothers, but otherwise he ignores completely the work of his

[1] See Bibliography.

Schwartz aluminium rigid airship at Tempelhofer Field, 1897

Car of Wolfert's first balloon with Daimler engine, 1888

Success: Santos Dumont's "No. 6" rounds the Eiffel Tower to win the Deutsch Prize, 1901

Disaster: Wolfert's second airship explodes over Tempelhofer Field, 1897

predecessors. Hence an unsuspecting reader, knowing nothing of the historic background, might be led to believe that the author, almost alone and unaided, had transformed the free balloon into a successful airship. In fact, Santos-Dumont's airships show scarcely any advance upon Renard's *La France*, but they had the advantage of the new motive power that Renard had lacked. In other words, Santos-Dumont was not an inventive genius, but there is a great deal to be said on the credit side.

Previous attempts to build navigable balloons had all been frustrated to some extent by that bugbear of every inventor – lack of money. Whereas the inventor knows that even the most promising design needs 'development work' – in other words a lot of time and patience – before it can be brought to practical success, the non-technical patron, be he a representative of government or a private individual, expects quick results. Moreover, in the case of the airship it was not only the machine but the man that needed 'development'. The pilot had to learn to handle it. The sad end of the Schwartz airship had shown how a promising machine could be ruined by incompetent handling. With Santos-Dumont these problems did not exist. With the wealth he derived from his family coffee estate in Brazil, with his skill as a designer, mechanic and pilot, Santos was able to carry through what we would now call an intensive development programme entirely on his own. To call him a man in a million would be an understatement, so rarely do such advantages and attributes exist in combination.

Santos survived so many accidents when flying his airships that he was judged phenomenally lucky. There was certainly an element of luck, but judgement played a far greater part. He was a superb test pilot. He was absolutely fearless but never foolhardy; he never lost his presence of mind in an emergency and his reactions were lightning quick. He may have contributed little to the design of the dirigible, but what he did do was immensely important; he developed the art of flying the dirigible and demonstrated that art to the world in a most convincing and instructive manner. Two examples of this will suffice.

His first attempt to ascend in his No. 1 airship was made on 18th September, 1898 from a clear space ringed by trees in the Jardin d'Acclimatation, the new Paris Zoological Gardens. His instinct told him to take off into the wind with his motor running so that he could use, as he expressed it, 'the fulcrum of the air' to lift him over the treetops. The experienced aeronauts of the free balloon who had come to watch his ascent insisted that such a proceeding was unprecedented and suicidal; a balloon must take off with the wind. For the first and last time Santos yielded to the judgement of others. The balloon was moved to the opposite end of the enclosure and he took off down wind. A few moments later the balloon had become entangled in the upper branches of a tree and that was that. Two days afterwards, on 20th September, Santos ascended from the same place under similar weather conditions with perfect success. Like every other pilot of a powered aircraft from that day to this, Santos had taken off into the wind.

Encouraged by this success and by the performance of 'No. 1', Santos made a second mistake. He ascended to 1,300 ft, a very modest height in free balloon terms, but enough to lose him a substantial volume of gas as he discovered when he began to descend. The air pump supplying the ballonnet could not deliver a sufficient volume of air to compensate for this loss and the balloon envelope 'jack-knifed'. Looking like a toothpaste tube that has been trodden upon, No. 1 fell rapidly towards a field where several boys were flying kites. Santos shouted to them to catch the end of his trail rope and run with it into the wind. In this way 'the fulcrum of the air' saved a bad crash and Santos escaped with a shaking. His doctrine that flights in pressure airships should be made at low altitude was born of this experience; there was no need, he insisted, to fly high.

One of Santos-Dumont's most celebrated achievements was to win the Deutsch prize of 100,000 francs. In 1900, Henry Deutsch de la Meurthe, one of the first petroleum magnates and a member of the Paris Aero Club, offered this award to the first aeronaut who would take off from the Aero Club's ground at St Cloud, fly round the Eiffel tower, and return to his starting point in not more than thirty minutes. This was a course of 7 miles, and allowing for taking off, turning, and landing, Santos estimated that he would have to average $15\frac{1}{2}$ m.p.h. to win the award. After several attempts he finally succeeded – very narrowly – in doing so with his 'Number Six' on 19th October, 1901.

This flight created a tremendous sensation in Paris and in the aeronautical world generally, but it was his tiny 'Number Nine' that probably did more than any other balloon to 'sell' the idea of aerial navigation. With this miniature motorized balloon of only 7,770 cubic feet capacity, Santos would 'motor' from his base at Neuilly St James (the world's first airship station, he called it) to St Cloud and back or, in the early hours of a summer morning, fly along the deserted avenues of Paris using his trail rope. On one occasion, returning from St Cloud on a fine evening, he landed at one of his favourite cafés, 'The Cascade'; on another, he glided along the Bois de Boulogne in the early morning, passed the Arc de Triomphe obediently on the right having resisted a temptation to fly through it, and landed precisely at his own front door at the corner of the Champs Elysées and the Rue Washington. As he looked down at his parked airship from a first floor bay window while he sipped his morning coffee he reflected how easy it would be to extend that window into an ornamental landing balcony.

Such demonstrations and, above all, such burning enthusiasm inspired others to follow where Santos led, but his skill and judgement had made the art of aerial navigation appear too simple. These others had not learned the lessons that he had mastered by hard experience. On 12th May, 1902 a fellow Brazilian, Augusto Severo, and his French mechanic Sachet, took off from Vaugirard for a maiden flight in the airship *Pax* of Severo's design. The balloon shot into the air with such rapidity that the aeronauts seem to have lost their heads for, instead of taking steps to check the ascent, Sachet was seen to throw out a whole bag of ballast, causing the *Pax* to climb even faster and higher. A few moments later the ship exploded and burst into flames over the city, crashing to earth in the Avenue de Maine.

Santos-Dumont's explanation of this disaster in which two aeronauts met such a terrible death was probably correct. The pressure envelope of the *Pax* had been fitted with two safety valves, but just before the fatal ascent Severo had stopped up one of them with wax, declaring it to be unnecessary. The single valve could not sufficiently relieve the pressure created by such a rapid ascent and the balloon burst, a spark from the engine igniting the escaping hydrogen.

On 13th October of the same year Ottokar de Bradsky and his mechanic Morin left the same shed at Vaugirard in Bradsky's new dirigible intending to steer for the drill ground at Issy-les-Moulineaux, but the wind proved too strong for them. Fighting for control, the aeronauts were blown across Paris, over L'Opéra, over the heights of Montmartre, over the church of Sacré-Coeur, the balloon all the while slowly rotating on its axis. At a spot called Globe de Stains on the road to Gonesse, where terrified villagers had destroyed the first hydrogen balloon so many years before, a master-carpenter, walking to work, was startled to hear someone hailing him from the air. The aeronauts asked him where they were and as soon as he had told them the carpenter rushed back to his home where he had a pair of binoculars. Focussing them on the airship, he was horrified to see it suddenly tilt upwards by the nose. In their efforts to make a landing Bradsky and his companion had evidently upset its centre of gravity. The car broke away, first at the front, then at the back. As the balloon shot into the sky and disappeared the car crashed down beside the railway between Stains and Dugny, killing its occupants instantly.

It was on 22nd September, 1902 that Stanley Spencer, direct descendant of Green's friend, became the first English aeronaut to fly a powered balloon. Readers may have wondered why there has been practically no mention of England in this chapter. The sad truth is that until this date there had been no progress worthy of report. In this, as in other fields of technical endeavour, Britain sank into self-satisfied torpor during the second half of the nineteenth century and the tremendous drive that marked the preceding 100 years spent itself.

The envelope of Spencer's little airship was 75 ft long and 20 ft diameter, capacity 20,000 cubic feet. Beneath it was a triangulated 'girder' of bamboo, 42 ft long, to which the 4 ft square car and the engine were attached by wires. This engine was a water-cooled Simms unit, producing $3\frac{1}{2}$ h.p. at the remarkably high speed of 2,500 r.p.m. It drove a 10 ft diameter propeller through reduction gearing at 250 r.p.m. There was a gauze flame-trap on the carburettor and the petrol tank held two gallons, sufficient for two hours flying. The propeller, which had been designed by Hiram Maxim, was of pine wood, fabric covered and varnished. Spencer took off in this little ship from the Crystal Palace at 4.15 p.m. and landed at Eastcote at 5.55 p.m. This was a straight-line of sixteen miles, but Spencer estimated that he actually covered thirty miles, for he followed a circuitous route over East Dulwich, Battersea, Victoria Bridge, Earls Court, Gunnersbury, Ealing, Acton and Greenford. Spencer insisted that he had perfect control of his machine throughout, but the curious gyrations he was seen to execute en route led spectators to the conclusion that he was not entirely the master of the light southerly breeze that was blowing at the time. It seems certain that he could not have returned to his starting point. Nevertheless, this was a very courageous first flight for, as Santos-Dumont frankly admitted, he much preferred open fields to roof-tops when trying out his airships.

Spencer later used this little dirigible for aerial advertising and built a second, larger machine. On one occasion this second craft 'jack-knifed' immediately after a take-off at Ranelagh Gardens, damaging the propeller, but in order not to disappoint the spectators the resourceful aeronaut removed the engine and propeller and ascended as a free balloon.

In France, the Severo and Bradsky disasters did not cool the enthusiasm for aeronautics that Santos-Dumont had generated. In 1899 the proprietors of a large sugar refinery, Paul and Pierre Lebaudy, commissioned their chief plant engineer, Henri Julliot, to build them an airship. Julliot took great pains over his design for it was two years before construction commenced and it was not until 13th November, 1902, exactly a month after Bradsky's fatal crash, that 'Lebaudy I' took the air for the first time. Julliot followed Haenlein and Renard in adopting the former's curious ship's hull design for the envelope of bright yellow calico. This was 187 ft long with a maximum diameter of 32 ft giving a capacity of 80,000 cubic feet. The belly of the envelope was secured to a rigid flooring, elliptical in plan and trussed with steel tubes, 70 ft long and 20 ft wide. At the stern of this structure, and clear of the envelope, the rudder and elevator planes were mounted. The Lebaudy was thus a true semi-rigid airship though it was still referred to at the time as a balloon. The platform, it was argued, would have some parachute effect in the event of trouble, it would protect the envelope and also check rolling or pitching tendencies. Suspended by steel rods 19 ft below the platform was a boat-shaped car 16 ft long and 5½ ft wide. This housed a 40 h.p. Daimler water-cooled engine driving two 9 ft diameter airscrews mounted on either side of the car. Including 15 cwt of petrol, water and ballast, the Lebaudy weighed 2½ tons.

The Daimler engine gave the Lebaudy a speed of about 25 m.p.h.

and made it the world's first really practical airship, capable of flying under any conditions provided wind speed did not exceed 36 k.p.h. Between November 1902 and July 1903 the Lebaudy made twenty-nine flights from its hangar at Moisson near Mantes and failed on only one occasion to return to its base. On one of these flights on 8th May it set up a dirigible distance record with a flight of 37 kilometres in 1 hr 36 m, but shattered this on 24th June by covering 98 kilometres in 2 hr 46 m. On 12th November, 1903, pilot Juchmés and his mechanic, Rey, flew the Lebaudy from Moisson to Paris, covering the 62 kilometres in 1 hr 41 m and landing their ship, most appropriately, in the historic Champ de Mars where Charles had released his first hydrogen balloon one hundred and twenty years before. It was placed on display in the huge Gallerie des Machines nearby where this first true conqueror of the skies attracted as much attention from wondering crowds as Charles' balloon.

The successful prototype of all pressure airships, the Lebaudy was the culmination of years of endeavour. But it is not only the performance of the Lebaudy that makes the year 1903 a great milestone in the history of aeronautics and an obvious terminal date for this history. In France, the aeronauts, Santos-Dumont among them, were devoting increasing attention to powered heavier-than-air flight. The internal combustion engine had opened this door also and it was felt that complete success was almost in sight. Like Britain, America had played so small a part in the development of the navigable balloon, that serious competition from that quarter was never suspected in Europe. Yet all unknown to the aeronauts of the old world, on 17th December, 1903 the brothers Orville and Wilbur Wright had made the first powered, sustained and controlled aeroplane flight in history at Kitty Hawk, North Carolina. No longer would the balloon be sole mistress of the skies.

CHAPTER ELEVEN

Balloons at Play

FOR EVERY ADVANCE in science and technology a price has to be paid. Those who accept the natural world find freedom whereas those who seek to conquer it invariably, sooner or later, find themselves the slaves of their own weapons. The price of man's conquest of the air was exceptionally high and the history of the balloon illustrates an apparent paradox particularly well. The pilot of a free balloon must go where the wind drives him; in riding the aerial currents he may exercise great skill and judgement but he is ever their partner rather than their master. Some would say that he is nature's slave, yet every aeronaut affirms that the reward of flight in a free balloon is a sense of perfect freedom and an exaltation so great that it can amount to a mystical experience.

Contrast with this the lot of the first conquerors of the aerial currents in their navigable balloons. Crawling close above the earth, their only pleasure was in their new mastery and that would soon pall. To gain that mastery they had exchanged stillness and silence for the fume and din of an internal combustion engine in close companionship, had been forced to accept an ever present threat of fire and to transform the simple, stable free balloon into a precarious form of aerial ship that mechanical failure, human error or sudden storm could speedily and fatally crumple into ruin.

To appreciate this contrast is to understand why it was that, so far from banishing the free balloon from the skies, the coming of the internal combustion engine coincided with a renaissance of ballooning so remarkable that the period 1895–1914 might be called the golden age. By 1895 the day of the old professional showman-aeronaut was almost done. The old pleasure gardens were losing money; some had already closed down. Balloon ascents with fireworks, acrobatics or other stunts were no longer a profitable show business; as a popular attraction the balloon had been played out and there was a demand for some new and novel form of sensational entertainment which the cinema would soon supply, substituting a shadow world of celluloid for the flesh-and-blood feats of the old showmen. As we have seen, this decline was offset to some extent by a growing interest in military and scientific ballooning but, during the 1890s, another and, from the point of view of the professional aeronauts and balloon makers, more important trend gathered momentum. This was the growing interest of a wealthy minority in free ballooning as a sport and pastime. It originated in France but quickly spread across the English Channel and to other European countries. In the light of what has been said, a list of the members of this international sporting set is significant because it includes so many of those who, at the same time, were pioneering with equal enthusiasm the use of the internal combustion engine on the roads and in the air.

Today, when motoring on traffic-choked roads has ceased to be a pleasure and inter-continental air travel has become a mere interval of boredom to be alleviated by film shows and over-eating, we envy the pioneers their open roads and open skies. It is salutary to recall, therefore, that so many of these pioneers should have realized, if only subconsciously, that mastery of a new power had its debit side; that it imposed a new discipline from which they turned to find their purest pleasure in a vehicle of classic simplicity, powerless, unguidable, free from every mechanical complexity.

For the new sport of ballooning the halcyon years before the first world war were uniquely propitious. It was an expensive pastime, but at no time before or since has a fortunate and leisured minority commanded a greater purchasing power. Like the wind that drove it, the free balloon was no respecter of national frontiers; all over Europe the lights were on and, for that happy few, frontiers were no more than lines upon a map. After so long a peace it seemed that, as Yeats put it:

> *All teeth were drawn, all ancient tricks unlearned*
> *And a great army but a showy thing.*

The progress of technology had reached a stage that wholly favoured the sport of ballooning without in any way impeding it. Gas was readily available even in the smallest towns; an efficient and – for the first-class passenger – uniquely civilized network of steam transport by rail and sea could be depended upon to bring the enterprising aeronaut and his stowed balloon punctually back to base from the remotest corners of Europe. When flying he must avoid these railways and the telegraph and telephone wires that were his lines of communication, but this was a small price to pay for the advantages they brought. Other than these, man-made hazards were non-existent; there was no cat's-cradle of high voltage power lines to ensnare him; no airfields sterilising great tracts of country and even larger areas of sky; empty roads held no dangers from fast-moving traffic while urbanization and the population explosion had not yet created built-up areas so vast in extent that it would be risky to traverse them in a free balloon. Even in England an aeronaut could trail-rope his way across miles of open country with no more concern than to avoid damaging the occasional barn or hay-rick.

In this favourable climate the sport burgeoned. The last generation of showmen-aeronauts found new and lucrative employment instructing wealthy amateurs in the gentle art of aerostation. Balloon makers flourished as never before; in France, Henri Lachambre and his successor Juchmès at Vaugirard, Gabriel Yon and Louis Godard with workshops at Champ de Mars; in England, the Spencer brothers at Highbury and the brothers Short in Queen's Circus, Battersea Park; in Germany, Riedinger of Augsburg, to mention only the best known firms. In 1898 the Aéro Club de France was formed to organize the sport and similar national clubs were soon founded in Austria, Belgium, Germany, Great Britain, Italy, Spain, Sweden, Switzerland and the United States. Soon the need for some form of international regulation and government became apparent and on 14th October, 1905 the International Aeronautical Federation (F.A.I.) was formed in Paris.

The Aero Club of the United Kingdom, soon to be called the Royal Aero Club, was founded by Frank Hedges Butler on 4th September, 1901 and this, in his own words, is how it came about:[1]

'In September, 1901, my daughter and I decided to make a balloon ascent. A large number of friends came to see us off from the grounds of the Crystal Palace, and the aerial party consisted of my daughter, Miss Vera Butler, the Hon. C. S. Rolls, the late Mr. Stanley Spencer (in his professional capacity as aeronaut in charge), and myself.

[1] Delacombe, *The Boys' Book of Airships*, pp. 45, 46.

'It was a very calm day, and the *City of York* balloon, 42,000 cubic feet capacity rose almost straight in the air and remained over the Palace at a height of about 5,000 feet for nearly two hours. After discussing all the surroundings we thought out the idea of an Aero Club, and decided to set about its formation as soon as possible.

'A few days later the name of the Aero Club of the United Kingdom was registered at Somerset House, through the secretary of the Automobile Club, the committee of which institution looked to our Aero Club to control the science and sport of balloons, airships and aeroplanes in Great Britain.'

Frank Butler was a pioneer motorist and so, of course, was Rolls. Practically every motoring enthusiast in Britain hastened to join the new Aero Club, the early members including Charles Cordingley, Colonel R. E. Crompton, S. F. Edge, Charles Jarrott, E. M. D. Instone, L. A. Legros, Mark Mayhew, the Hon. J. Montagu, Montague Napier, Sir David Salomons, F. R. Simms and Henry Sturmey. In the Aero Club de France the situation was much the same with such well-known names as Santos-Dumont, Ernest Archdeacon and the Comte de Dion to the fore. Nor was the sport of ballooning by any means a male preserve. In France, Madame Du Gast, the intrepid woman racing driver, and Mesdames Omer-Decugis and Surcouf formed the feminine advance guard. Madame Surcouf, wife of the celebrated balloon designer Edouard Surcouf, made her first balloon ascent at midnight and was the first woman to be granted an Aeronaut's Licence by the Aero Club. So many followed the lead of this trio that the Stella Club for women aeronauts was formed in Paris in 1909. In England the three most dedicated women balloonists were Miss Vera Butler (Mrs Ilted Nicholl), Mrs Griffith Brewer and the Hon Mrs Assheton Harbord.

Aeronauts' Certificates were not lightly given. In the case of the British Club, aspirants were required to submit to the Secretary a record of twelve day ascents, one night ascent and certificates of two further ascents signed by competent observers. On the strength of this evidence the Secretary could, at his discretion, authorize the applicant to make a solo ascent under observation. If the certificate for this flight was approved by a two-thirds majority of the Club Committee, an Aeronaut's Certificate would then be granted.

The Club employed professional aeronauts and owned balloons

for the use of its members which were normally housed and maintained by Short Bros., 'Official Aeronautical Engineers' to the Club, at their Battersea Works. An arrangement was made with the Hurlingham Club by which Aero Club members could use the grounds for private balloon ascents between 6 a.m. and 6 p.m., seven days a week. For this purpose a special twelve-inch gas main capable of delivering 100,000 cubic feet of gas per hour was laid to Hurlingham.

The average cost of hiring a Club balloon was nine guineas. This covered the Club Aeronaut's fee for superintending inflation, gas, labour and ballast. In addition, members paid two and non-members three guineas for a place in the car, while if the balloon was away for more than three days it was charged at the rate of a guinea per extra day. If no member of the party was a qualified pilot the services of a professional aeronaut would have to be paid for additionally, and finally there was the cost of return transport which could be considerable.

At this time there was no need to join the Aero Club in order to go ballooning. Anyone could go to a firm such as the Spencer Brothers to hire a balloon and the services of a professional aeronaut. The cost of a ten days balloon holiday for four was budgeted in much the same way as an enterprising travel agent today budgets an 'all in' continental trip and it is interesting to compare the figures with the Club fees mentioned above:

Hire of balloon for 10 days	25	0	0
Aeronaut's wages	7	2	0
10 inflations of balloon at av. cost of £5.12.6	56	5	0
Beds for 5 men for 9 nights at 2s each per night	4	10	0
Meals for ditto for 10 days at 6s each per day	15	0	0
Carting balloon to a gas main ten times at 5s per time	2	10	0
Tips to voluntary assistants at ascents and landings	2	10	0

Total   £112 17 0

The one thing wrong with this estimate is that it evidently assumes that the end of the ten days would see the holiday-makers back at their starting point, a highly improbable assumption.

These figures underline the fact that, bearing in mind the then value of money, ballooning was a very expensive pastime indeed even for those who shirked the cost of buying and maintaining a balloon of their own. Remember, too, that they do not include the cost of making good any damage to the balloon, a strong probability in view of the fact that the landing of a free balloon and a spectacular and protracted accident can often be indistinguishable. 'Aeronauts', pleaded the Aero Club Rule Book, 'are earnestly requested to exercise the greatest care in the deflation, packing and transport of the balloon, and not to use the ripping cord except when necessary.'

Aeronauts also risked a claim for damage done to property, not only in landing, but in the use of the trail rope. The type of trail rope used by this date was so heavy that once it had been lowered it could not be hauled back. It tapered to a thick trailing end quite substantial enough to demolish a chimney stack or overset a hayrick. Its unheralded approach could cause considerable alarm as on the occasion when a trail rope burst through a hedge, rudely sundering a pair of rustic lovers who were sporting in its shade on the further side. The committee of the Aero Club was moved to warn members against the dangers of indiscreet trailing: 'In view of certain representations which have been made to the Committee of the Club respecting trailing, they deem it advisable to draw attention of Members to the fact that trailing, unless very carefully conducted, is likely to do considerable damage to property and thereby bring ballooning into discredit. The Committee, therefore, hope that all Members in charge of balloons will take particular care only to trail in suitable country, and to at once rise when there is any likelihood of a rope doing any damage. The Committee also hope that any Member in charge will at once take steps to make compensation for any damage done by trailing, and to report to the Club.'

The two major trophies competed for by members of the British Aero Club stressed individual performance. They were the Northcliffe Challenge Cup for the longest flight made during the year and the Hedges Butler Challenge Cup for the longest flight made within the confines of Great Britain. Professional aeronauts were not eligible to compete for these trophies but, here as in other countries, military balloonists could take part in club events and did so with great success. Competition proved a great stimulus to aerial expertise and the new generation of wealthy amateur aeronauts were soon performing feats that rivalled anything their professional predecessors had accomplished. In England the first outstanding amateur balloon pilots were Frank Butler, the Hon C. S. Rolls, Griffith Brewer, C. F. Pollock and John Dunville. In November 1902, Frank Butler made a remarkable solo flight of 115 miles from the Crystal Palace to Corby in Northamptonshire during which he saw neither earth nor sky, being enveloped throughout in a dense fog bank extending to 4,000 ft. This was blind flying with a vengeance, for even at night the aeronaut can usually get some clues to his direction and elevation from stars above or lights below. But Frank Butler seems to have taken things very calmly. According to his own account, as there was nothing to see he spent most of the flight sitting in the bottom of the basket munching his sandwiches, drinking sherry and reading a motoring journal. 'Sang froid, toujours sang froid.'

Crossing the English Channel became a commonplace. C. F. Pollock made his first crossing solo in a small balloon from Devonshire Park, Eastbourne in October 1897 and by 1910 he had crossed eleven times. Accompanied by Percival Spencer and Frank Butler, Mrs Griffith Brewer became the first woman to cross the channel in a balloon, while in the course of 150 ascents made before 1910, the Hon Mrs Assheton Harbord crossed the channel five times. Mrs Harbord owned her own balloon, the *Valkyrie* and was accompanied on at least one adventurous crossing by C. F. Pollock.

On flights of many hours duration undertaken in male company and in the extremely close quarters of a balloon basket, the relief of nature must have been something of a problem for these adventurous but decorous Edwardian ladies. That it was discreetly solved may be inferred from an account[1] by the Contessa Grace di Campello Della Spina of her adventurous honeymoon flight by moonlight over the Apennines from Rome to San Severino on which she was accompanied by her husband and a professional aeronaut named Demetrio Helbig. Her list of recommended equipment for female aeronauts includes: 'a small *nécessaire*,[2] a "first aid", a change of underwear, a light volume of a favourite author, a map and a guidebook.'

The Contessa Grace was a member of the Societa Aeronautica

[1] *The Century Magazine*, Vol. LXXIV, May, 1907.
[2] From the days of Blanchard onwards, aeronauts have sometimes equipped themselves with bladders. This was due neither to modesty nor to a tender concern for those below, but simply because they regarded urine as ballast to be conserved and released only when it became necessary to lighten the balloon.

Italiana and a great enthusiast. 'Sport of the Gods!', she writes, 'Who else flies over a sleeping world, through space, and knows the joy of motion without movement, without sound, without effort? . . . The strange sense of being disembodied, of flight without movement, of rapid travel, of motionless suspension in mid-heaven, of solemn silence, without oppression, makes a new environment for the heart of man.' The redoubtable Madame Surcouf agreed with the Contessa and refused to travel in airships, declaring roundly that she hated the noise, the smell and the wind.

Schooled by the professionals Alexis Macheron and Maurice Mallet, the Aéro Club de France could field a brilliant group of amateur aeronauts: Comte Henri de la Vaulx, Comte Georges de Castillion de Saint-Victor, Jacques Faure, Jacques Balsan and, of course, Alberto Santos-Dumont who did not abandon free balloons despite his preoccupation with airships. From 1899 onwards the Club became famous for its long distance races from Paris. The balloon that travelled furthest was the winner, but there was usually a duration award for the aeronaut who remained longest in the air. With the aid of instruments the pioneers had never known, the recording barograph and the altimeter (then known as a 'statoscope'), the 'star' performers in these events achieved extraordinary feats of balloon management, playing the aerial currents with superb judgement and handling their sand ballast literally by the tea-spoonful to maintain the balloon in equilibrium as nearly as was humanly possible.

In winning the first 1899 event, the Comte de la Vaulx, flying with Maurice Mallet, set new records for time and distance, but in the following year he eclipsed this performance. Flying his 59,000 cubic feet balloon *Centauri* and accompanied by the Comte Castillion de Saint-Victor, de la Vaulx landed at Korosticheff, near Kiev, a straight line distance from the starting point at Vincennes of 1,925 kilometres (1,193 miles), after spending 35 hours 45 minutes in the air. Before starting on this record flight the *Centauri* was filled with 50,000 cubic feet of hydrogen and a little over 7,000 cubic feet of coal gas. Presumably by this admixture de la Vaulx hoped to reduce expansion losses, though so small a proportion of coal gas is unlikely to have had much effect. Oxygen breathing apparatus was carried on the *Centauri*, and the maximum altitude achieved on the flight was 18,810 ft.

Maximum speed was 33⅓ miles an hour. Of the 1,500 lb of ballast carried 2½ sacks were left at the time of descent.

In strange contrast to this impressive display of skill, it is worth recording that one of de la Vaulx's rivals in this 1900 race, a M. Vernauchet in the balloon *Urania*, came to the start equipped with a rudder and a pair of umbrella type of 'oars' of the kind used by the brothers Robert in 1784. Old fallacies died hard.

Apart from the official records set up in competitions of this kind, an incautious aeronaut could be caught in a storm and quite involuntarily become an unofficial record-breaker as a result. The palm for this kind of achievement, if such it can be called, probably goes to the Belgian aeronaut Goossens, for if contemporary accounts are to be believed it is doubtful whether anyone has ever travelled so far so fast in a free balloon. Accompanied by an unnamed German nobleman, Goossens took off from Berlin in a 70,000 cubic feet balloon at 2 p.m. on 13th September, 1903. The balloon entered Holland where, over the Hague, it was caught in a violent cyclonic disturbance which whirled Goossens and his companion away on a terrifying circular tour of Europe. Though there was not, of course, any sense of motion, it was evident from their instruments and from the way the landscape reeled away beneath them that the wind was of hurricane force. So swiftly did it sweep them across Belgium and Northern France, veering the while from north-east to east, that at 6 p.m. they were in sight of the French coast at Sables d'Olonne. Fearing they were about to be swept out into the Atlantic, Goossens made a desperate attempt to land on the Isle of Oleron, off La Rochelle, but realizing that this meant certain death, he discharged ballast and the big balloon rose again. The gale now blew from the south whirling them northwards through the gathering darkness until they reached a position near the island of Jersey. By now the storm had practically boxed the compass and began to blow them up the English Channel. It was at this time that the gale attained its greatest violence and Goossens estimated from his instruments that the balloon achieved a maximum speed of 125 m.p.h. That they would be blown into the North Sea seemed certain and when the sight of Calais lighthouse gave him his bearings, Goossens determined to make a second desperate attempt to land. It was their last chance. By a miracle, he succeeded in bringing the balloon to earth near the coast at Fretham.

Both men were injured in their frantic jump from the car; to attempt
to restrain the balloon was out of the question and it was instantly
swept away with all their instruments and equipment. This landing
was made at 6 a.m., and in the 16 hours that had elapsed since their
ascent from Berlin, Goossens estimated that they had covered some
1,400 miles, an average speed of nearly 90 miles per hour.

Another remarkable flight of this kind was made in 1899 by
Captain von Sigsfeld with two passengers. Taking off from Berlin,
they passed over Breslau two hours later, an average of 92 miles an
hour, and eventually landed safely on deep snow in a remote part of
the Carpathians where a party of wood-cutters fled from them in
terror.

Where long distance balloon races were concerned the British
Aero Club was uniquely handicapped. To be successful, such an event
requires a land mass of continental proportions and although the
English Channel was no longer a formidable barrier, the prevailing
south-westerlies meant that from any starting point in Britain such a
race would usually end prematurely on the east coast. Consequently
the British Club devised competitions of a different kind for its
members. One of these was the point-to-point race in which the
victor was the aeronaut who landed his balloon nearest to a pre-
determined destination point. Such events were contested with great
enthusiasm and guile. A competitor landing near the target would
hurriedly deflate his balloon and conceal it, hoping that his rivals,
believing they had the field to themselves and were 'near enough',
would land short.

A variant of this type of race was the 'hare and hounds' contest in
which one balloon acted as the hare and the winner was the aeronaut
who landed his balloon nearest to the hare. Then there was the
'stability test' in which the prize went to the aeronaut who maintained
the most uniform altitude as recorded by barographs carried on the
balloons. There was also a trophy known as the Llangattock Plate to
be awarded annually to the aeronaut who, ascending from London,
landed nearest to the Rolls family home, the Hendre, Monmouth.
To be eligible for the plate, the contestant had to land within a
twenty mile radius of the Hendre.

Although it lies just outside the period covered by this history,
this chapter would be arbitrarily incomplete if it failed to mention

British Pioneer: the Spencer Airship ascending at Hurlingham

The first successful airship: the Lebaudy lands on the Champs de Mars, Paris, 1903

Scenes before the start of a balloon race from Hurlingham. Balloons filling up from the gas main and (below) "walking up" to the starting mat

that grand épreuve of the balloon racing world – the annual Gordon Bennett contest. James Gordon Bennett of the *New York Herald* had presented a motor racing trophy to be competed for annually by teams representing the national motoring clubs. This was first contested in 1902 and the interest aroused encouraged Gordon Bennett to put up a second trophy with an annual prize of 12,500 francs for a competition between the national Aero Clubs to be organized by the F.A.I. As in the case of the earlier motoring trophy, the first event would start from Paris, but the contest would thereafter be organized annually in whichever country had won the previous year's race. In presenting the trophy to the senior Club, the Aéro Club de France, Gordon Bennett proposed that the competition should be 'open in principle, in accordance with the progress of aeronautics and according to the judgement of the International Aeronautic Federation, to all kinds of apparatus for aerial locomotion, and especially on its first offering to motor aerostats'.

It is clear from this that Gordon Bennett's intention was that the competition should stimulate the development of powered flying machines, but the F.A.I., in their wisdom, decided to restrict the contest to free balloons and to make it a long distance race as earlier organized by the Aéro Club de France. So it would remain. The first race for the new trophy was started on 30th September, 1906 when sixteen balloons representing seven countries rose from the Tuileries gardens in Paris. All the star aeronauts were there: the Comte de la Vaulx, the Hon C. S. Rolls, Santos-Dumont and Frank Butler, but they were discomfited. The trophy went back across the Atlantic, for the winner was America's Frank P. Lahm who landed his balloon *United States* at Fylingdales, Yorkshire, 647 kilometres from Paris. Second place went to *L'Elfe* of Italy piloted by Alfred Vanwiller which came down at New Holland, near Hull, and the third man was the Hon. C. S. Rolls who brought his *Britannia* down near Sandringham. Only these three aeronauts succeeded in crossing the English Channel; all the rest landed near the north coast of France.

Rolls's *Britannia* was typical of the large racing balloons of this period. Of 78,500 cubic feet capacity, it was built for him by Short Bros and its car was specially designed to float with two passengers aboard in the event of a landing on the sea. All ballast was carried outside the car which was equipped with electric lighting installed by

16

the Portable Electric Light Company. The trail rope of coconut fibre was also designed to float. 'We found this useful on the sea,' said Rolls after the race, 'for when crossing the Channel we could not have made the English coast except by keeping very low with the end of the trail rope on the surface of the sea.'

With the exception of the war years and the great depression year of 1931, the Gordon Bennett balloon race was held annually thereafter until 1938 inclusive. Thus despite – or perhaps because of – the restriction to free balloons it had a far longer life than the motoring trophy. Because they never seem to have been assembled between one pair of covers and were often scarcely noticed even by the aeronautical press of the day, the results of these annual contests have been tabulated – as well as may be from different, and often indifferent, sources – at the end of this book.

The reason why the Gordon Bennett contests fell into comparative obscurity where the press was concerned is obvious. The aeroplane, and to a lesser extent the airship, made news; the free balloon did not. To the public of the changed world that emerged from the shadows of the first world war a balloon seemed no more than a useless and comical anachronism. There was thunder in the air and man had become obsessed by the space-shrinking feats of the internal combustion engine. The Gordon Bennett performed a valuable service by perpetuating a great tradition and a great skill throughout what might be called the years of indifference. For, as we now know, or should know, the balloon is not an anachronism nor is it likely to become one. The Edwardian gentlemen-aeronauts have gone the way of the Victorian showmen and the balloon has taken the course that Glaisher charted. Using materials and techniques that the pioneers never dreamed on, the scientists have made of the balloon an invaluable research vehicle. They have made it man's stepping stone to outer space and the modern balloon's contributions to meteorology and astronomy are of incalculable value.

Happily, however, the scientists have not monopolized the balloon. Despite the cost, despite man-made hazards and restrictions unknown in the golden age before 1914, 'the Sport of the Gods', as the Contessa Grace called it, is enjoying something of a revival both in Europe and in America. Whereas the Edwardians raced balloons as large as their incomes, this new generation of aeronauts necessarily fly balloons of much more modest proportions, small hydrogen or coal-gas balloons; even small Montgolfières kept aloft by propane gas-burners, but the skill and the pleasure is the same. This revival is in every way desirable and salutary in our supersonic age.

Just as only those who have voyaged under sail alone can claim to know the ways of the sea, so no man can know the air who has never ridden its currents in a powerless craft. The pioneers knew this. Santos-Dumont insisted that no man should attempt to design, still less to fly, a powered aircraft until he had become the master of a free balloon. Would he have added the glider to the balloon if the modern glider had existed in his day? Perhaps, for it could be fairly argued that the analogy between the glider and the sailing ship was the closer of the two. Yet this is not simply a question of gaining practical experience in a skilled craft, of serving an aerial apprenticeship. In the range of human experience there are many mansions and we may be sure that the aeronauts would claim that the balloon could unlock doors which remain closed even to the glider pilot. For there is a realm of incommunicable experience and knowledge only to be gained in the serenity of total surrender. Only the balloon, a frail bladder of gas, unguidable, beautiful, comical, tragically ephemeral, a spherical microcosm of the great globe itself, affords man an aerial platform upon which he may stand, staring down in silence upon the mystery of his turning world.

APPENDIX I

Chronology

1766 Henry Cavendish discovers hydrogen.

1776 Joseph Priestley's *Experiments on Different Kinds of Air* published in France.

1782 Joseph Montgolfier makes his first experimental hot-air balloon.

1783 5th June. First public balloon ascent at Annonay (Montgolfier).
27th Aug. First public ascent, Paris (Charles).
19th Sept. Versailles ascent with sheep, etc. (Montgolfier).
20th Nov. Man's first flight, de Rozier & d'Arlandes, Paris (Montgolfier).
1st Dec. First manned hydrogen balloon ascent (Charles).

1784 10th Jan. Ascent of first giant balloon, *Le Flesselle* (Montgolfier).
25th Feb. First ascent in Italy, Andreani (Montgolfier).
20th May. First free ascent by a woman; Mme Thible, Lyons (Montgolfier).
25th Aug. First ascent in Britain; Tytler, Edinburgh (Montgolfier).
15th Sept. First ascent in England; Lunardi, London (hydrogen).
Meusnier's prophetic airship design published.
4th Oct. First ascent by an Englishman; Sadler, Oxford (Montgolfier).

1785 7th Jan. First Channel crossing by air, Blanchard & Jeffries.
15th June. First aerial disaster, deaths of de Rozier and Romain.
First ascents in Germany, Holland & Belgium, Blanchard.

1793 9th Jan. First ascent in United States, Blanchard, Philadelphia.

1794 29th March. First Air Force 'Corps of Aérostiers' founded, Paris.
26th June. Battle of Fleurus; tactics first directed from balloon.

1797 22nd Oct. First parachute descent from balloon by Garnerin, Paris.

1802 21st Sept. First parachute descent in England by Garnerin, London.

1817 22nd July. First crossing of the Irish Sea, Windham Sadler.

1819 7th July. Death of Madame Blanchard, Tivoli Gardens, Paris.

1821 19th July. Coal gas first used in balloon by Charles Green, London.

1836   7–8th Nov. First long-distance flight, London-Nassau by Green.

1837   24th July. Cocking parachute disaster.

1838   8th Oct. First parachute descent by Englishman, Hampton, Cheltenham.

1839   27th April. Ripping panel first used by John Wise, United States.

1849   June. First aerial bombardment by Austrians of Venice.

1852   First Aeronautical Society founded in France.
       24th Sept. First flight by mechanical power (steam); Giffard, Paris.

1861–3 Observation balloons extensively used in American Civil War with first successful portable hydrogen generator by Lowe.

1862   5th Sept. Scientific ascent by Coxwell & Glaisher to over 30,000 ft.

1863   19th Oct. Crash of the *Géant* balloon.

1866   The (Royal) Aeronautical Society of Great Britain founded.

1868   First aeronautical exhibition in England at Crystal Palace.
1870–1 Siege of Paris air lift.

1872   13th Dec. First ascent by i.c. engined balloon, Lenoir gas engine, Haenlein, Brunn, Moravia.

1875   April. *Zénith* balloon high altitude ascent ends in tragedy, Paris.

1878   First experimental British military balloon section formed at Woolwich under Captain Templer.

1884   First compressed hydrogen cylinders introduced at Woolwich.
       9th Aug. First 'out and home' flight by powered aircraft, Renard & Krebs electric airship *La France*.

1888   12th Aug. First flight by petrol-engined aircraft, Woelfert airship with Daimler engine, Seelberg to Kornwestheim, Germany.

1890   British Army Balloon Corps a separate establishment at Aldershot.

1892   First 'met' sounding balloons used, Hermite & Besançon, France.

1896   First successful kite-balloon, *Drachen*, Parseval & Sigsfeld, Germany.

1897   12th June. Woelfert's second Daimler engined airship crashed in flames at Tempelhofer Field, Berlin.

1897   11th July. Andrée polar balloon *Ornen* leaves Danes Island.

1897   2nd Nov. First rigid airship (Schwartz) crashes after first ascent at Tempelhofer field.

1898 Aéro Club de France founded.
      20th Sept. Santos-Dumont's first successful flight with No. 1 airship.

1900 July. First Zeppelin trial, Lake Constance.

1901 19th Oct. Santos-Dumont wins Deutsch Prize by flying his airship No. 6 round Eiffel tower from St Cloud.

1901 Balloon ascent to 35,500 ft, Berson & Süring, Germany, with oxygen.

1901 (Royal) Aero Club of the United Kingdom founded.

1902 Stratosphere discovered by Teisserenc de Bort using sounding balloons.

1902 22nd Sept. First flight by powered airship in Britain, Spencer, London, Crystal Palace to Eastcote.
      13th Nov. First practical airship Lebaudy makes first flight.

1903 12th Dec. First powered, sustained and controlled flight by powered aeroplane; the Wright brothers, Kitty Hawk, N. Carolina.

Scientific Ascents by James Glaisher, F.R.S. 1862

Terms of Reference

1. To determine the temperature of the dew point by Daniell's dew-point hygrometer, by Regnault's condensing hygrometer, and by dry and wet bulb thermometers as ordinarily used, as well as when under the influence of the aspirator (so that considerable volumes of air were made to pass over both their bulbs) at different elevations, as high as possible, but particularly up to those heights where man may be resident, or where troops may be located (as in the high lands and plains of India), with the view of ascertaining what confidence may be placed in the use of dry and wet bulb thermometers at those elevations, by comparison with the results found from them, and with those found directly by Daniell's and Regnault's hygrometers; also to compare the results as found from the two hygrometers.

2. To compare the readings of an aneroid barometer with those of a mercurial barometer up to five miles.

3. To examine the electrical condition of the air at different heights.

4. To determine the oxygenic condition of the atmosphere by means of ozone papers.

5. To determine whether the horizontal intensity of the earth's magnetism was less or greater with elevation, by the time of vibration of a magnet.

6. To determine whether the solar spectrum, when viewed from the earth, and from far above it, exhibited any difference, and whether there were a greater or less number of dark lines crossing it, particularly near sunset.

7. To collect air at different elevations.

8. To note the height and kind of clouds and their density and thickness.

9. To determine the rate and direction of different currents in the atmosphere.

10. To make observations on sound.

11. To make observations on solar radiation at different heights.

12. To determine the actinic effects of the sun at different elevations by means of Herschel's actinometer.

13. To note atmospherical phenomena in general, and to make general observations.

Equipment

1. Dry and wet bulb thermometers.

2. Daniell's hygrometer.

3. Mercurial barometer.

4. Blackened bulb thermometer, its bulb fully exposed to the sun's rays.

5. Two thermometers, dry and wet bulb, in connection with the aspirator.

6. A blackened bulb thermometer, placed in an hermetically sealed vacuum tube, projecting outwards, as in No. 4, so that the bulb was in the full rays of the sun.

7. An aneroid barometer.

8. An excessively delicate thermometer, with its bulb in form of a gridiron. This arrangement was adopted for the purpose of increasing the sensibility of the instrument.

9. Regnault's hygrometer, with india-rubber tube in connection with the aspirator.

10. Two silver conical shields, one within the other with a space between, for protecting the dry thermometer from the sun's rays. These rested on a silver shoulder affixed to the thermometer tube, just above the bulb of each thermometer. The wet bulb thermometer was protected in a similar way.

11. A compass.

12. A watch or chronometer.

13. A lens to read the instruments.

14. The aspirator (bellows) arranged to be worked with the foot.

15. A magnet, for the purpose of giving vibrations to the compass needle.

16. A minimum thermometer.

17. An opera glass.

All these instruments, writes Glaisher, were attached to the table with strings, which could be cut immediately, or they merely rested on stands which were screwed to the table. This table was fixed across the car, and tied there with strong cord. On approaching the earth, all the instruments were rapidly removed and placed, anyhow, in a basket furnished with a number of soft cushions to cover them in layers, so that they were not broken by the shock on coming in contact with the earth.

Of Glaisher's work with this equipment, Hildebrandt wrote: 'It has been shown that on a journey made on July 21st, 1863, Glaisher must have made in a space of 60 seconds seven readings of the aneroid, accurate to the hundredth of an inch, and 12 readings of the thermometer, accurate to the tenth of a degree. On June 26th, 1863, he carried out the following observations in 1 hour 26 minutes, viz: 107 readings of the mercury barometer, a similar number of the thermometer attached to the barometer, 63 readings of the aneroid, 94 of the dry, 86 of the wet bulb thermometer, 62 of the gridiron, 13 of the dry and 12 of the wet bulb thermometer fitted with aspirator, besides several observations with the hydrometer, and noting the time on 165 different occasions. Each observation must therefore have taken on an average 9·6 seconds, including such necessary attention as was given to the adjusting of the various instruments and apparatus.'

The Gordon Bennett Balloon Race

1906 Paris, Tuileries.
1. Lahm (U.S.) *United States*, to Fylingdales, Yorks, 647 km.
2. Vanwiller (It.) *L'Elfe*, to New Holland, Hull.
3. Rolls (G.B.) *Britannia*, to Sandringham.

1907 St Louis, Missouri.
1. Erbsloh (Germany), 1,367 km, 650 m.
2. Leblanc (France), 1,366 km, 44 hrs, world duration record.
3. Von Abercron (Germany).

1908 Berlin.
1. Schaeck (Switz.) *Helvetia*, 1,212 km, 73 hrs 41 m world duration record.
2. Dunville (G.B.), 428 km.
3. Geerts (Belgium), 413 km.

1909 Zurich.
1. Misc (U.S.), *America II*, to Ostrolenka, Poland, 950 km.
2. Leblanc (Fr.) *Ile de France*, to Zargriva, Hungary, 832 km.
3. Messner (Switz.), *Azurea*, to Thule, Silesia, 828 km.

1910 St Louis, Missouri.
1. Hawley (U.S.) *America*, to near Quebec, 1,820 km.
2. Gericke (Ger.) *Dusseldoy*, to near Quebec, 1,769 km.
3. Von Abercron (Ger.) *Germania*, to near Quebec, 1,763 km.

1911 Kansas City.
1. Gericke (Ger.), to Holcombe, Wisconsin, 753½ km.
2. Lahm (U.S.), to La Cross, Wisconsin, 653 km.
3. Vogt (Ger.), to Austin, 560 km.

1912 Stuttgart.
1. Bienaimé (Fr.) *Picardi*, to Ryasan, nr Moscow, 2,191 km.
2. Leblanc (Fr.) *Ile de France*, to Kaluga, Russia, 2,001 km.
3. Honeywell (U.S.) *Uncle Sam*, to Sapadnaja, Russia, 1,800 km.

1913 Paris, Tuileries.
1. Upson (U.S.) *Goodyear*, to Bampton, nr Bridlington, 618 km.

   2. Honeywell (U.S.) *Uncle Sam*, to Finisterre, 483 km.
   3. Pastine (It.) *Roma*, to Finisterre, 447 km.

1914–1919 No contest.

1920 Birmingham, Alabama.
   1. Demuyter (Belg.) *Belgica*, to L. Champlain, 1,760 km.
   2. Honeywell (U.S.) *Kansas City II*, to Mt Tongue, 1,600 km.
      (48 hrs 26 m, American duration record).
   3. del Valle (It.) *L'Audiens*.

1921 Brussels.
   1. Armbruster (Switz.), to Lambay Island, Ireland, 750 km.
   2. Spencer (G.B.), to Fishguard, 675 km.   ⎫
   3. Upson (U.S.), to N. Cardigan Bay, 675 km. ⎬ Tie
                                                 ⎭

1922 Geneva.
   1. Demuyter (Belg.) *Belgica*, to Ocnitza, Roumania, 1,372 km.
   2. Honeywell (U.S.), to Hungary, 1,061 km.
   3. Bienaimé (Fr.) *Picardi*, to Hungary, 923 km.

1923 Brussels. This year competitors encountered a severe storm. Three
balloons crashed in flames with the loss of five lives. Two more of
the fifteen starters also crashed.
   1. Demuyter (Belg.) *Belgica*, to Skeelerota, Sweden, 1,600 km.
   2. Veenstra (Belg.) *Prince Leopold*, 1,000 km.
   3. Armbruster (Switz.) *Helvetia*, 550 km.

1924 Brussels.
   1. Demuyter (Belg.) *Belgica*, to St Abbs Head, Berwick, 750 km.
   2. Laporte (Fr.) *Ville de Bordeaux*, to Brighton, 395 km.
   3. Honeywell (U.S.) *Uncle Sam*, to Rouen, 320 km.

1925 Brussels.
   1. Veenstra (Belg.) *Prince Leopold*, 1,354 km.
   2. Demuyter (Belg.) *Belgica*, 661½ km.
   3. Valle (It.) *Ciampino V*, 596 km.
   (the *Elsie* of Capts. Johnson and Dougal (U.S.) was run down by a
   train near Etaples, while Van Orman (U.S.) achieved the remarkable
   feat of landing his *Goodyear III* on the bridge of a ship at sea. He was
   unplaced.)

1926 Antwerp.
   1. Van Orman (U.S.) *Goodyear III*, to Sodderborg, 843 km.
   2. ———(U.S.) *Army S.16*, to Krakau, 595 km.
   3. Demuyter (Belg.) *Belgica*, to near Hamburg, 336 km.

1927 Detroit.
    1. Hill (U.S.) *Detroit*, to Baxley, Georgia, 1160, km.
    2. Van Orman (U.S.)
    3. Vahe (Ger.) and Blanchet (Fr.) Tied.

1928 Detroit.
    1. Kepner (U.S.) *U.S. Army*, to Kenbridge, Va., 740 km.
    2. Kaulen (Ger.) *Barmen*, to Kenbridge, Va., 739 km.
    3. Dollfus (Fr.) *Blanchard*, to Walnut Cove, N.C., 720 km.

1929 St Louis, Missouri.
    1. Van Orman (U.S.), to Troy, Ohio, 545 km.
    2. Kepner (U.S.), to Neptune, Ohio, 541 km.
    3. Settle (U.S.), to Eaton, Ohio, 486 km.

1930 Cleveland, Ohio.
    1. Van Orman (U.S.), to North Canton, Norfolk, Co. Mass, 867 km.
    2. Demuyter (Belg.) *Belgica*, to North Canton, Norfolk, Co. Mass, 717 km.
    3. Hill (U.S.).

1931 No Contest.

1932 (New series), Basle.
    1. Settle (U.S.) *U.S. Navy*, to Vilna, 1,536 km.
    2. Van Orman (U.S.) *Goodyear VIII*, to Kovno, Lithuania, 1,383 km,
    3. Ravaine-Speiss (Fr.) *Petit Mousse*, to Tokary, Poland, 1,233 km.

1933 Chicago.
    1. Burzynski (Pol.), to Quebec, 1,361 km.
    2. Settle (U.S.) *U.S. Navy*, to Grove, Long Island, 1,248 km.
    3. Van Orman (U.S.) *Goodyear VIII*, to Sudbury, Ontario, 792 km.

1934 Warsaw.
    1. Hynek (Pol.), to Kosciuszko, Finland, 1,331 km.
    2. Burzynski (Pol.) *Warszawa*, to Finland, 1,304 km.
    3. Demuyter (Belg.) *Belgica*, 1,162 km.
    (The Polish balloon *Polonia* was actually second on distance but came down in a lake at Savonhanna, Finland and was disqualified. The two aeronauts had to swim for their lives.)

1935 Warsaw.
    1. Burzynski (Pol.) *Polonia II*, to Tiszkino, Russia, 1,650 km.
    2. Janusz (Pol.) *Warszawa II*, to Russia, 1,563 km.

3. Demuyter (Belg.) *Belgica*, to Russia, 1,455 km.
(Tiszkino is a desolate region, 63 km from Stalingrad, from which the competitors were rescued after a fortnight.)

1936 Warsaw.
1. Demuyter (Belg.) *Belgica*, to near Archangel, Russia, 1,800 km.
2. Goetze (Ger.), 1,600 km.
3. Burzynski (Pol.) *Polonia II*, 1,580 km.

1937 Brussels.
1. Demuyter (Belg.) *Belgica*, to Tukumo, Lithuania, 1,430 km.
2. Janusz (Pol.) *Warszawa II*, to Anec, Lithuania, 1,400 km.
3. ?

1938 Liége.
1. Janusz (Pol.) *L.O.P.P.*, to Trojan, Bulgaria, 1,630 km.
2. Krzyszkowski (Pol.) *Warszawa II*, to Catuselle, Roumania, 1,470 km.
3. Thonar (Belg.) *SII*, to Vidin, Bulgaria, 1,451 km.

Note. The distance record set up by Bienaimé of 2,191 km in the 1912 Gordon Bennett was broken by another French aeronaut, Rumpelmayer, flying his balloon *Stella* in the 1913 Coupe Lahm on 19th–21st March. Rumpelmayer reached Kharkhov, Russia, a distance of 2,420 km in 41 hours.

Bibliography

Andrée Diaries, The, translated from the Swedish Ed. by Adams-Ray, Edward, London: John Lane, 1931.

Annals of Mercedes-Benz Motor Vehicles and Engines (Trans. St John C. Nixon). Stuttgart-Unterturkheim: Daimler-Benz A.G. 2nd Ed. 1961.

BREWER, GRIFFITH, *Ballooning and its Application to Kite Balloons* (11th Ed. revised), London: The Air League of the British Empire. 1940.

BROKE-SMITH, Brig. P. W. L. The History of Early British Military Aeronautics, London: *Royal Engineers Journal,* 1952.

CAVALLO, TIBERIUS, *The History and Practice of Aerostation,* London: Cavallo, 1785.

CORNISH, JOSEPH JENKINS, III, *The Air Arm of the Confederacy,* Richmond, Virginia: Richmond Civil War Centennial Committee, 1963.

COXWELL, HENRY, *My Life and Balloon Experiences,* 2 vols., London: W. H. Allen, 1887–9.

DE FONVIELLE, WILFRID, *Adventures in the Air* (Trans. Keltie, J. S.) London: Edward Stanford, 1877.

DELACOMBE, HARRY, *The Boys' Book of Airships,* London: Grant Richards, 1910.

DOLLFUS, C, and BOUCHÉ, H. *Histoire de l'Aéronautique* (Rev. ed.) Paris: L'Illustration, 1942.

DOLLFUS, C. *Balloons* (Trans. Mason, C.) London: Prentice-Hall International, 1961.

EASTERBY, J. H. Captain Langton Cheves, Jr. and the Confederate Silk Dress Balloon, *South Carolina Historical and Genealogical Magazine,* Vol. XLV, 1944.

FAROUX, C. and BONNET, C. (Eds.) *Aéro-Manuel,* Paris: Dinot & Pinat, 1914.

GIBBS-SMITH, CHARLES, *A History of Flying,* London: Batsford, 1953.

GLAISHER, JAMES, with FLAMMARION, C., DE FONVIELLE, W. and TISSANDIER, G., *Travels in the Air,* London: Richard Bentley, 1871.

HAYDON, F. STANSBURY, *Aeronautics in the Union and Confederate Armies*, Baltimore: John Hopkins Press, 1941.

HILDEBRANDT, A., *Airships Past and Present* (Trans. Story, W. H.) London: Constable, 1908.

HODGSON, J. E. *The History of Aeronautics in Great Britain*, Oxford: The University Press, 1924.

LAUTIER, FERDINAND, 'L'Incendie du ballon dirigeable de Woelfert', Paris; *L'Aéronaute* No. 7, July 1897.

LUNARDI, V. *Account of the First Aerial Voyage in England*, London: 1784. *Manual of Military Ballooning*, London: H.M.S.O., 1896.

MARION, F. *Wonderful Balloon Ascents* (Trans.) London: Cassell, 1870.

MARSH, W. LOCKWOOD, *Aeronautical Prints and Drawings*, London: Halton & Truscott Smith, 1924.

MASON, MONCK, *Aeronautica*, London: Westley, 1838.

MILBANK, JEREMIAH, JR, *The First Century of Flight in America*, Princeton: The University Press, 1943.

MOEDEBECK, HERMANN W. L. (Trans. Varley, W. M.) *Pocket Book of Aeronautics*, London: Whittaker, 1907.

SADLER, JAMES, *An Authentic Account of the Aerial Voyage of Messrs Sadler & Clayfield*, Bristol: A. Brown, 1810.

SADLER, JAMES, *Authentic Narrative of Mr. Sadler Across the Irish Channel*, Dublin: Tyrell, 1812.

SANTOS-DUMONT, ALBERTO, *My Airships*, London: Grant Richards, 1904.

SQUIRES, J. DUANE, Aeronautics in the Civil War, New York: *The American Historical Review*, Vol. XLII, 1937.

TISSANDIER, G., *Histoire des Ballons et des Aéronautes Célèbres*, 1783–1890, 2 Vols., Paris: 1887–90.

TURNOR, HATTON, *Astra Castra*, London: Chapman & Hall, 1865.

VALENTINE, E. SETON and TOMLINSON, F. L. *Travels in Space*, London: Hurst & Blackett, 1912.

WOODCROFT, B. *Abridgements of Specifications Relating to Aeronautics 1815–66* London: Eyre & Spottiswoode, 1869.

WOODHOUSE, HENRY, *Textbook of Military Aeronautics*, London: Werner Laurie, 1919.

WYKEHAM, PETER, *Santos-Dumont, a Study in Obsession*, London: Putnam, 1962.

In addition to the above, the following were also studied:

The Cuthbert Collection
The Poynton Collection
The Norman Collection

The Cuthbert and Poynton Collections are in the Library of the Royal Aeronautical Society and the Norman Collection is in the Patent Office. They consist of press cuttings, prints, advertising bills, original letters, pamphlets, etc., all relating to the early history of aeronautics.

Index of Names